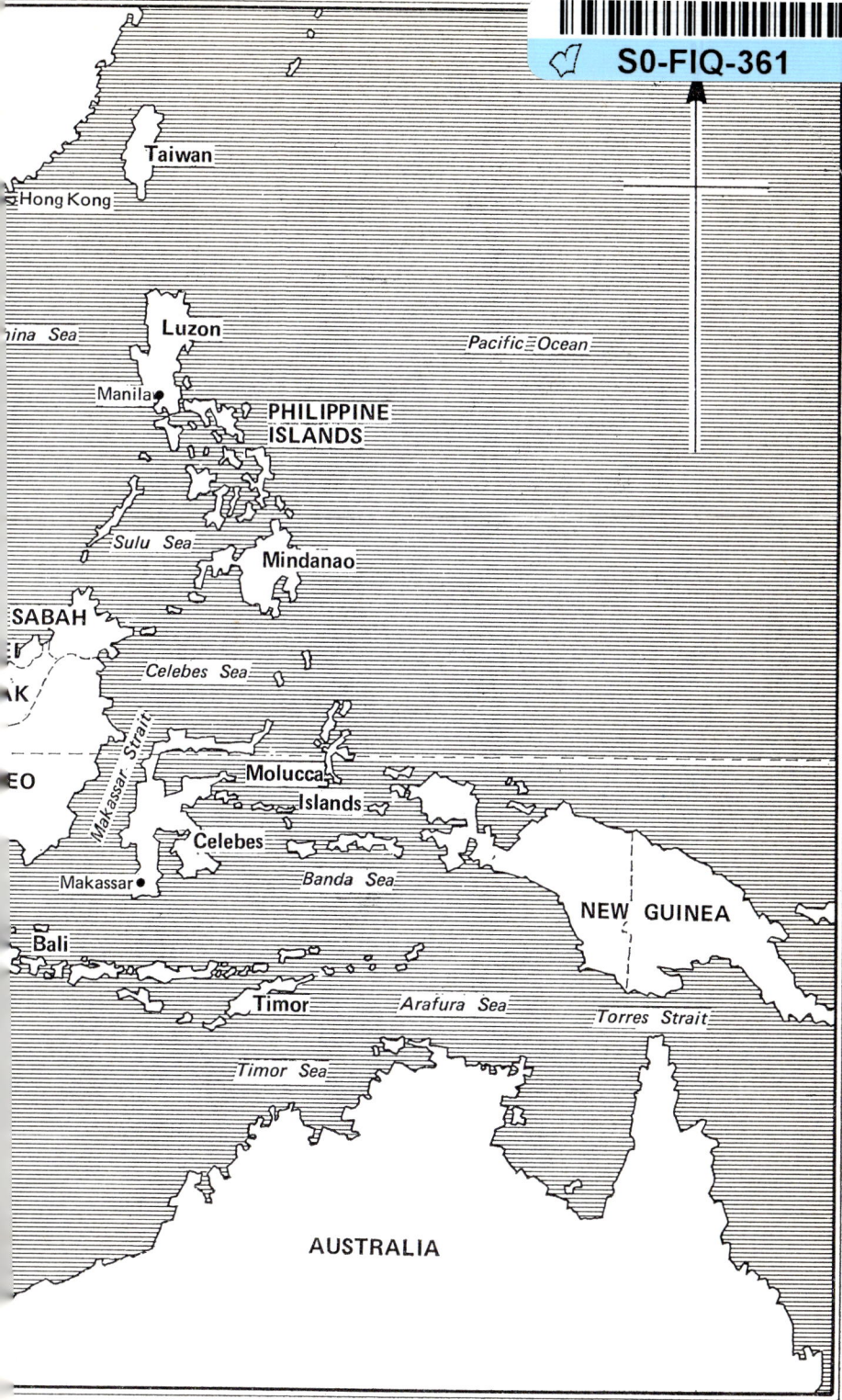

Taiwan

Hong Kong

Luzon

Pacific Ocean

...ina Sea

Manila

PHILIPPINE
ISLANDS

Sulu Sea

Mindanao

SABAH

K

Celebes Sea

EO

Makassar Strait

Molucca
Islands

Celebes

Makassar

Banda Sea

NEW GUINEA

Bali

Timor

Arafura Sea

Torres Strait

Timor Sea

AUSTRALIA

Lee Kuan Yew's
Singapore

WITHDRAWN

T. J. S. George

Thayil Jacob Sony

Lee Kuan Yew's Singapore

ANDRE DEUTSCH

First published 1973 by
André Deutsch Limited
105 Great Russell Street, London WCI

Copyright © by T. J. S. George
All rights reserved

Printed in Great Britain
by Ebenezer Baylis and Son Ltd
The Trinity Press, Worcester and London

Hardback edition ISBN 0 233 96456 8
Paperback edition ISBN 0 233 96517 3

Contents

FOR
My Fathers and Mothers
AT
Nediuzham and Anithottam

CHAPTER ONE

The Making of a City State

The Victorian splendour of Singapore's City Hall – balustrades etched against lavender sky – is deliberate. From every step and pillar and veranda and colonnade, it exudes power. One of the more enduring features of imperial Britain was the lavishness with which it ensconced viceregal authority in three-dimensional solemnity, calculated to leave the passing native with no doubt about the fount of all power, all benevolence and all reprisal.

Ironically, Singapore is ruled today from a second-floor office of City Hall by a man unmoved by majesty, untouched by awe. Outside, the colonnades have lost none of their imperial grandeur, but his office holds no trappings of power. Lee Kuan Yew started as a shirtsleeve prime minister and remains so today.

How did he get there and what has he come to represent? What is the historical significance of Lee Kuan Yew? The publicity surrounding him and Singapore is such that answers to such questions tend to be simplistic: Lee got there and stays there through a system meticulously modelled on Westminster; he represents an Asian version of pragmatism and a set of socio-political values adapted to suit the special conditions of a developing country; his place in history is solidly based on his achievements which have made Singapore's level of prosperity second only to that of Japan.

By all accounts, Lee Kuan Yew is Southeast Asia's best-known political leader today. In many circles he is also the most admired. Lee owes this image to the West, always the anchor of his reputation. But it is useful to remember that when Lee was on the make, the West often denounced him; those were the days when he worked hand in glove with the communists, called himself comrade and made the mailed fist a symbol of his socialist fervour. Denunciation turned to admiration as Lee settled down in power; by then he had become a most effective instrument for the elimination of communists on the one hand and, on the other, for the promotion of Western investments and business expansion in Southeast Asia.

Any suggestion that Western approval of Lee stemmed solely from selfish interests would of course be unjustifiable. Lee's emergence as a charismatic personality is also due to the fact that he genuinely compels attention. The West could look up to him as it could look up to Gandhi and Jawaharlal Nehru. In the 1960s Lee stood out as the only Asian leader with not only panache and style but also an indisputable record of achievement.

Lee had worked miracles in his country. He was not dependent on populist appeal and was thus free from any need to play to the gallery. He knew how to make more than slogans out of order and efficiency. True, there was a streak of arrogance in him. But he had plenty to be arrogant about. Lee was an outstanding leader by any yardstick and his Singapore had swiftly become a remarkable example of material progress.

What is equally remarkable is that Lee's reputation in the West appears to differ radically from his reputation in most Asian countries. If the West sees him as the most admired Asian leader, Asia sees him as the most controversial. There are other countries in Asia which have achieved economic progress no less impressive – South Korea, Taiwan, and of course Japan. None of them has produced among other Asian leaders the degree of resentment Singapore has generated. The Japanese miracle has struck many Asian governments as possibly foreboding a military threat, yet no one grudges Japan's achievements. Singapore poses no conceivable military threat to anybody, yet there is a widespread impression that its achievements are at the expense of other Asian countries. Above all, there are many who are deeply disturbed about the social and political basis of Singapore's economic prosperity.

The prime minister who presides over the running of a self-consciously prosperous city-state is not quite the barrister who started his public career as a hero of student idealists and a crusader against injustices. The question which arises is whether the changes which apparently have occurred in Lee's attitudes and methods are fully appreciated. Is what is known and cherished about him in the West seen in the perspective of present conditions in Singapore and of the geopolitical realities of Southeast Asia as a whole? Are Lee's obvious achievements their own complete justification or are there features in them which raise doubts about their ultimate worth? Is the political philosophy on which Lee has built Singapore tenable? What are the ultimate values he holds up for his people and what are their long-term implications? What indeed is the total Lee Kuan Yew?

That office in City Hall tells something about the man. It is spacious but spartan: no panelling, no historical regalia, no priceless paintings on the walls, no seal of office – and no ashtrays. Its only luxury is air-conditioning. The large table at which the premier labours is polished, shining.

From his office window Lee can derive satisfaction from the view: it reflects not only his own personality and the hopes he has cherished for his country, but the Englishness so dear to his heart. It is the cleanest part of a clean city whose dwindling band of litterbugs faces heavy penalties such as a maximum fine of S $500 for throwing a cigarette butt on the street. While indigenous zeal has erased colonial street names in other Asian cities, Lee Kuan Yew still can look out over St Andrew's Road and, across a stretch of green, to Connaught Drive and Queen Elizabeth Walk.

That stretch of green is probably the most English green east of Suez. It is maintained with one careful eye on beauty and the other, in the best of British tradition, on cricket. Strewn around the *padang*, as this city green is called, is a string of cricket clubs. Lee Kuan Yew prefers golf, the common occupational disease of Southeast Asia's political leaders. But he looks benignly on cricket, which apparently agrees with his vision of Singapore.

Beyond the *padang* and Queen Elizabeth Walk, the harbour from which Singapore has drawn its historical prosperity glistens as if in prideful contemplation of its own worth. It now acts as dispersal point not only for the entrepôt trade which the British conjured up but for the burgeoning manufacturing industries nourished by the Lee government, and ranks fourth among the world's ports. There was a time when a private yacht at anchor would inspire the alert government to send emissaries to the wealthy visitor, to ask politely whether he would like to invest in Singapore.

Down the road from City Hall and across the Singapore river, the converging point for Singaporeans is Raffles Place, a square named after the man who started it all. Thomas Stamford Raffles was just another young English explorer-trader when he set forth for the East. Stumbling upon Singapore, he quickly realized he was on to something good. Calling Singapore 'a child of my own' and announcing his intention to 'make this my principal residence and to devote the remaining years of my stay in the east to the advancement of a colony which . . . bids fair to be one of the most important which we possess', he settled down to convert a tropical swamp into a profitable island in the sun.

That was in 1819. The Malay Annals which recorded the legendary origins of Singapore are somewhat less specific about the feelings of Sri Tri Buana, the discoverer who preceded Raffles, the colonial master. King Sri Tri Buana was rock-climbing off Sumatra in what is now Indonesia when he spied an island with sand so white that it 'looked like cloth'. This was Temasek, the sea town, which was to humble him before he could set foot on it. As his fleet approached Temasek a violent storm struck. 'When all else was thrown overboard to no avail, Sri Tri Buana cast his crown into the sea,' the Annals record. 'Thereupon the storm abated and the ships were rowed safely to land.'

That was Indonesia's first confrontation with Singapore.

The crownless king's conviction that he had landed on a special kind of island was confirmed by his first sight, a strange and beautiful animal which moved with spectacular speed and grace. It had a red body, a black head and a white breast, and it was strong and agile. The court pondered over this animal and Sri Tri Buana's chief minister recalled that ancient stories told of such a beast, calling it Singha. Sri Tri Buana hearkened to the call of history and named his island Singha Pura – City of the Lion. Stamford Raffles, like many other colonial administrators, liked to dispense with an Asian syllable or two whenever necessary, and his child grew up as Singapore. One hundred and forty years later, as a minor concession to historical nationalism, Lee Kuan Yew was to restore the last syllable and make Singapura the official name of his new republic.

For Sri Tri Buana, Singapore was simply a pleasant place to set up court. With the arrival of European mariners in search of oriental wealth, its location at the far end of the Malacca Straits became its main attraction. With Singapore at one end of the straits and Penang at the other, Britain could command the sea-routes of the Far East. After leasing the island from the sultan of Rhio-Johore in 1819, Raffles assumed full sovereignty for Britain in 1824. The Dutch accepted this in return for a British withdrawal from Sumatra. It was not without reason that an

Economist article in 1971 described Raffles as 'a young visionary, self-confident enough to fly in the face of stuffy superiors and unscrupulous enough to do a bit of meddling in local politics'.

With the British came a problem which was to grow into a nightmare for Lee Kuan Yew: racial communalism. Sri Tri Buana's Singha Pura was an unpretentious fishing village inhabited by a hundred Malays. As Raffles began to mould it for a place in the empire, he was able to report that 'my city of Singapore is already attracting the peaceable, industrious, thrifty Chinese'. These were mainly poor peasants, fishermen and artisans from Kwangtung and Fukien provinces. They came in large numbers in the 1850s when China's Tai Ping Rebellion made emigration a pleasing proposition. Britain encouraged them, partly to counterbalance the Malays, partly to get for Singapore an industrious, economically productive people.

By the end of the nineteenth century a third national element had appeared – southern Indian labourers imported by the British to work the first plantations. It was simply sound rubber economics; in the golden age of colonialism no one paused to think of such things as the long-term implications of ethnic incompatibility. Indeed, Britain served its imperial interests by diligently keeping the three groups separate. Chinatowns bloomed in Singapore until much of the city fused into one big Chinatown. Serangoon Road was and is a little India, Gaylang a Malay pocket. According to the historian Victor Purcell, it was Raffles's declared policy to organize 'native divisions of the town' and earmark separate areas to the Chinese, the Malays, the Bugis and so on, stipulating that 'the first in importance of these is beyond doubt the Chinese'. Each cultural group naturally grew up in isolation, widening and confirming the inevitable racial schisms in an immigrant population. In time Lee Kuan Yew would try all known methods and then some to instil among these people a sense of national identity – only to discover how thankless it is to swim against the current of man's ethnic instincts.

Racial divisions received another boost with the arrival of the Japanese. During the occupation, from February 1942 to September 1945, the Japanese assiduously cultivated the Indians and befriended the Malays, singling out the Chinese for contemptuous treatment and persecution. That policy did not contribute to Chinese friendliness towards the Indians and the Malays. More Chinese than any other ethnic group died fighting

the Japanese in Singapore. It was a blood pledge, a Chinese
commitment to the city. Every layer of history seemed to be
adding to the problem which was to haunt Lee Kuan Yew.

As long as British rule lasted, the problem remained well
below the surface. Britain made Singapore a flourishing centre
for Southeast Asian trade, and political importance followed.
Singapore became the seat of the Straits Settlements government and the heart of operations when Britain decided in 1874 to
'inaugurate the policy of intervention in the Malay states'.

The Malays, the original inhabitants of Singapore, could not
have been happy at the inferior status to which they were reduced.
But they could hardly do anything about it for the partnership
between the British authorities and the Chinese traders was strong.
It became a common jibe in Southeast Asian drawing-rooms that
Britain ruled Malaya for the protection of the Malays and the
benefit of the Chinese.

And, it should be added, for the safety of Empire. Long after
Raffles became no more than a statue attracting dutiful sightseers,
Britain still looked upon Singapore as a strategic military post.
To keep it thus, she separated Singapore from Malaya after the
Second World War. Lee Kuan Yew called this one of Britain's

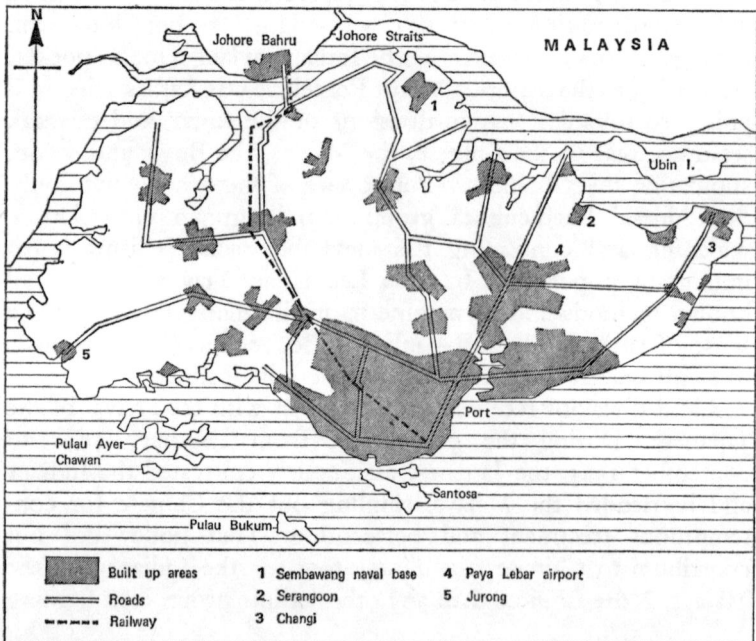

Map legend:

Built up areas

Roads

Railway

1 Sembawang naval base
2 Serangoon
3 Changi

4 Paya Lebar airport
5 Jurong

biggest mistakes. 'For eighteen years it went on, from 1945 to 1963, until the two territories were brought together again [all too briefly, as it turned out]. The problems we are facing today need never have arisen if that artificial political division had not taken place. If the British government had not been persuaded that it was possible to hold this island base for perhaps three, four or more decades, then Malaya would have had to learn to live with Singapore much earlier and all our problems, which are merely problems of adjustment today, would have had to be faced in 1945, 1946, 1947 or 1948. Much greater stability would have resulted.'

It was the First World War which convinced Britain that it was imperative to build up a naval defence scheme in the East. By the time Lee was born, in 1923, Singapore was already blossoming into Britain's biggest base in the region. But the Second World War ended all that. A power distant, yet seemingly invincible, now lay humbled before the Japanese. Japan knew the importance of Singapore: its conquest put all of Asia at the mercy of Nippon. More significantly, the Japanese relished the opportunity to humiliate the white imperialists in full view of the natives. They renamed the island Shonan, City of Lights, and they ruled it ruthlessly.

History soon caught up with the Japanese, but it caught up with the British, too. In three and a half years of occupation the Japanese had effectively destroyed the concept of Western imperialism in Asia. Lord Louis Mountbatten was a picture of imperial dignity when he accepted the Japanese surrender in Singapore in a military ceremony, but Britain's prestige had vanished. The British Military Administration governed a Singapore now vastly changed, under profound communist influence and its ethnic groups conscious of political rights and economic directions. Restoration of civilian rule in April 1946 began the inevitable process of transforming Singapore's colonial pattern into a national political system.

Parties and politicians sprouted. First on the scene was the Progressive Party, which represented middle-class opinion in the conventionally colonial Legislative Council set up under the constitutional plan of 1948. The election seven years later – under laws which restricted the franchise to British subjects by birth or naturalization – limited voting rights to some 300,000 people and excluded the bulk of the local Chinese.

Lee Kuan Yew was nineteen years old when the Japanese occupied Singapore. He watched British prestige crumble and then, with growing fascination, perceived British attempts to usher in a parliamentary system of government. He saw the dawn of a new era and never doubted his role in it. He moved.

Of the three parties which emerged in time for the 1955 election, one was the People's Action Party. It was formed by Lee Kuan Yew with a handful of English-educated left-leaning friends. The other parties were the Labour Front and the Democratic Party. Lee knew 1955 was David Marshall's day, and that the colonial constitution would give elected representatives no power anyway. He put up only four candidates. Three, including himself, were elected. The rise to power had begun.

David Marshall's chief ministership was an honorific position with Britain showing no sign of relinquishing command until constitutional talks had run their full tortuous course and the country had been fully prepared for the responsibility of independence. There are many who believe that Britain was interested in prevaricating until the unpredictable David Marshall could be edged out of the scene, enabling someone with a 'safe record' to fill his place.

The waiting period was filled with recrimination and agitation. Chief Minister Marshall struck out for immediate self-government, but his prolonged discussions in London brought nothing but frustration until he resigned in disgust. Outside the assembly, pro-communist leaders wielded power through their strong trade unions under the umbrella of Lee's People's Action Party – PAP.

Lee Kuan Yew had one foot in the Legislative Assembly and another firmly in the trade union movement as the respected counsel for a number of militant unions. From within, he watched the operations of parliamentary and extra-parliamentary groups, and drew valuable lessons from their mistakes.

Perhaps to dull the edge of the communist challenge, perhaps to speed the transfer of power, Britain negotiated a new constitution after Marshall's resignation, envisaging full internal self-government by an elected cabinet responsible to a parliament. Elections under this constitution were held in 1959. The People's Action Party received support from the pro-communists because it was vociferously leftist at the time, and from the establishment because Lee had already made firm contacts with the British. It romped home with forty-three of the fifty-one seats.

Lee was only thirty-six when he became prime minister. No Asian leader had reached the top so young.

Both before and after his rise to power, Lee devotedly backed the Greater Malaysia scheme. Once he was in a position to do so he pushed it through with ramrod efficiency. For a start he built up an elaborate bogy of international communist conspiracy in Singapore and kept it going at red heat until both Britain and Malaya began to think it would be safer to make post-colonial Singapore part of a larger whole so as to keep the communists well under co-ordinated control; in security terms Britain was already treating the two units as one.

Lee then held a referendum in Singapore on the issue of merging with Malaya. It was widely recognized as a shotgun referendum, but what mattered was that Lee won the day. As he himself told an interviewer: 'I played ju-jitsu and I won.'

Singapore became part of Malaysia in September 1963 and its colonial status ended. In the event the shotguns failed to hold the federation together. Lee's policies, especially his decision to fight the 1964 Malaysian elections in the mainland constituencies in violation of an earlier agreement not to do so for at least five years, generated strong anti-Singapore reaction among the Chinese as well as the Malays of Malaya, and in August 1965, barely twenty-three months after union, Singapore was 'expelled' from the federation. On the same day, August 9th, Singapore proclaimed itself 'forever a sovereign democratic and independent nation, founded upon the principles of liberty and justice and ever seeking the welfare and happiness of her people in a more just and equal society.'

Some nations are born sovereign, some achieve sovereignty, some have sovereignty thrust upon them. For Singapore it was clearly a case of the last. A pocket republic of only 224 square miles with no natural resources, Singapore should logically have become at best a satellite, at worst a faceless also-ran in the surrounding Asian morass. Instead it became a model of efficiency and forward planning.

The British had built Singapore into a strategic base and a thriving entrepôt city. Lee gave it a political dimension. After his plans for a federated existence in Malaysia foundered on the rocks of Malaysian suspicions about his motives, Lee's task became one of shaping a political rationale for his tiny city-state forced now to live by its wits.

CHAPTER TWO

The Making of a Man

*I am no more a Chinese than President Kennedy was an Irishman.
Slowly the world will learn that the Lees, the Tohs, the Gohs, the Ongs,
the Yongs, the Lims in Singapore, though they may look Chinese and speak
Chinese, they are different. They are of Chinese stock and not apologetic
about it. But most important, they think in terms of Singapore and
Singapore's interests, not of China and China's interests.*

LEE KUAN YEW in America, 1967

Stanley Baldwin was prime minister of Britain, President Harding
had just died and 'Honest Cal' Coolidge had moved into the
White House, Mussolini's Italy had occupied Corfu and enraged
Europe, fascists had risen in revolt against the monarchy in
Spain, Germany was sinking into a financial crisis, the months-old
Union of Soviet Socialist Republics was seeking recognition from
the British Government, India's nationalist leaders had called for a
boycott of British goods, Sun Yat Sen was leading his troops in
the Yellow River campaign, a typhoon and earthquake had
wrought unprecedented devastation in Japan and the Singapore
Cricket Club was about to begin work on its stadium when Lee
Kuan Yew was born on Sunday, September 16, 1923.

The big news of the weekend in Singapore was the outbreak of
faction fights among rival clans of rickshaw pullers – serious
enough for the British garrison in the city to be put on the alert.
Hundreds of coolies were injured and many killed. Finally the
rioters were dispersed by Indian policemen under a European
inspector assisted by Malay constables. It was a curiously
appropriate manifestation of the racial juxtaposition in Singapore
to herald the birth of a man who was soon to become the messiah
of multiracialism.

The Lees are Hakkas. And that is worth remembering. Hakkas
originally were northern Chinese who moved south to escape the

Tartar and Mongol invasions. In modern times they have been known as southern Chinese with Kwangtung province as their stronghold. Probably because of their background, they are an adventurous wandering people; Hakka means guests or sojourners. They are strong individualists, known for their pugnacity. The men are reputed to be courageous fighters and the women vigorous workers. Those who know Hakkas already know a great deal about Lee Kuan Yew.

By the time Kuan Yew was born, the Lee family had been in Singapore for almost a century. The family history in the island began with his great-grandfather, Lee Bok Boon, who moved to Singapore soon after Stamford Raffles arrived. He returned to his native Kwangtung province in China to die, leaving his wife and son, Lee Hoon Leong, in Singapore.

Hoon Leong made good. After an English education, he became a 'chin chew' (sub-agent) with a big shipping line. He later moved to another shipping company where he rose to be secretary, then manager and, finally, managing director. Trading mostly with Indonesia, Hoon Leong married into the Indonesian Chinese community. Doing business in the British colony and spending much time at sea, Hoon Leong grew to venerate the British, to respect Britannia's power over the waves. He lived to see the back of that power broken. His greatest shock came when little Japanese-made aircraft flew in and sank the mighty *Prince of Wales* in Singapore waters.

Hoon Leong's son, Lee Chin Koon, departed from the trading tradition of the family and joined a petroleum company. Foreign commercial firms enjoyed tremendous prestige in Singapore, as in other colonies, and a job with one of them was equated with high social status – the ultimate in security. That seemed to suit the quiet and self-effacing Lee Chin Koon. He stayed with the foreign oil company for thirty years and on retirement joined a Ceylonese-owned jewellery firm as a salesman.

Lee Chin Koon married young. His wife was Chua Jim Neo, a pleasant, colourful and independent-minded lady, known as a great mixer and talker. Her great-grandfather had married a Malay and the family thereafter was culturally Malay. This would explain her being completely racially unconscious and her prowess as a teacher of Indonesian-Malay cooking.

Chua Jim Neo had strong views. According to some relatives, she admired the British and maintained it was a good thing for

Chinese girls to marry Englishmen – a somewhat unusual view since, traditionally, purity of the blood line is important to Chinese. But she considered Americans inconsistent and unreliable, their university degrees not worth much. The seeds of Kuan Yew's multiracialism might have come from his parents, with Malay blood on the mother's side and Indonesian Chinese on the father's. The Indonesian Chinese community as a whole is heavily intermarried with Malays.

His parents had very little to do with Lee Kuan Yew after he became prime minister, certainly had no influence over him and no ability even to introduce people to him. The mother was full of admiration for him and recalled that, as a boy, he always wanted to take care of Singapore. She believed he was Singapore's saviour and that those who did not co-operate with the government should be arrested. She was said to have accepted that it was not easy for her and her firstborn to live in the same house because they were both headstrong. It has been Lee's habit to visit his mother only once a year, on Chinese New Year, because a visit means the police sweeping the whole area and that would be a waste of manpower.

Chua Jim Neo was only sixteen and Lee Chin Koon twenty when Lee Kuan Yew was born. Official records specify the precise address at which the birth took place – 92, Kampong Java Road, Singapore. But there are people who believe that Lee was in fact born in Indonesia. This titbit found its way into print in January 1971 when an Indonesian newspaper, *Sinar Harapan*, published a series of articles on Singapore: a photograph of Lee Kuan Yew accompanying the series carried a caption which pointedly declared that he 'was born in Kudus [Java]'. It is not impossible that Kuan Yew was born in Indonesia; the family already had close links with Indonesian Chinese and his father had been posted to Indonesia for a period by the petroleum company employing him. The theory is that, for political reasons, Lee has chosen to sidestep his Indonesian origin: it could become a factor in charges that Singapore has shown favouritism towards Indonesian Chinese immigrants and it could further complicate Lee's none-too-smooth relations with the Indonesian government.

Lingering uncertainty over even such a simple matter as the prime minister's place of birth, and the difficulty in clearing up this uncertainty is typical of Singapore under Lee. Most people do not know 'these unnecessary details'. Those who do are unwilling to talk.

Kuan Yew grew up as Harry. In all probability the parents followed the common overseas Chinese practice of giving children two names – one English, the other Chinese. Lee dropped his English name only after he became a politician.

The birth of the first child was a major event in the Lee family. Particularly excited was grandfather Lee Hoon Leong who, it has been reported, looked proudly at the bonny baby and said he should be educated to become the equal of any Englishman.

Kuan Yew's parents never forgot that instruction. With his mother in particular it became something of an obsession. Her own inclinations were in a similar direction. Apparently believing that Malay-Chinese stock produced only small shopkeepers and minor officials, she was determined to make a break from this pattern by making her sons professional gentlemen in the best English tradition. She raised the children on the English language, carefully following the common Chinese custom of skimping a little on housekeeping to save money for their education. Supplementing her savings with her earnings as a cooking instructor, she worked towards the objective of giving each of her sons, as they set out on their own, 10,000 Straits dollars as their start in life.

The elders' yearning to make model Englishmen of their children was typical of the times. The British were the ruling class, the fount of all power and therefore the repositories of all wisdom. They lived in style and brought their own language and literature with them. The closer the Asian got to the standards and style of the Englishman, the better would be his position socially and economically. To be English-educated meant to go up in life; to be educated in England itself meant becoming part of the truly privileged set, having the world at your feet. The Dutch found or created this attitude in Indonesia, the French in Indochina, the British in India, Ceylon and Malaya. Lee Hoon Leong was acknowledging the deep cultural impact of colonialism when he proposed a model English education for his grandson.

Given their notions of what made for success, Kuan Yew's parents raised the children on the pattern of the 'King's Chinese', a community of Chinese in Penang who had been under the British Crown for one and a half centuries, had largely lost contact with China and had developed their own style of living. They were considered particularly loyal to Britain and did in fact express specific patriotism to the Crown. In his childhood, on festive occasions Kuan Yew was decked out in traditional Chinese costume – brocade jacket, mandarin cap. He was sent to a small Chinese kindergarten near the Lee home. Otherwise, little Kuan Yew, which means Light that Shines, rarely came in contact with Chinese customs and Chinese society. His present command of the Chinese language is that of a man who learnt it as an adult.

His regular schooling began when he was eight, at the Telok Kurau English School. There were plenty of Malay boys in this school and Kuan Yew's friends were mostly Malay. Teachers of the time remember him as a lively boy, not over studious, but quite bright. Already, his strong point was English. He was a 'good mixer'.

Four years later, at twelve, Kuan Yew moved to the Raffles Institution. This school, founded by Stamford Raffles with the declared objective of making Singapore Southeast Asia's intellectual entrepot, had always been the most important educational institution in the city. It was synonymous with aristocracy, prestige and power. Everybody who was anybody in Singapore went to Raffles. It had to be the school for Kuan Yew, marked out from birth for the best England itself could offer.

At Raffles, Kuan Yew began slowly developing the qualities which were to become familiar in later years. He was no longer the non-studious type but developed into a hard worker. He was inclined to insist on having his way over other boys. Academically he was top of the class, his main areas of interest being arithmetic and English. A teacher wrote in his record that 'he is likely to attain a high place in life'.

On the playing field Kuan Yew was noted as an aggressive competitor, although he does not seem to have attained extraordinary proficiency in any particular game. He played cricket. He also began to join in literary activities and made little speeches in Malay. People who knew him at this stage say that although he looked very Chinese he seemed more Malayan in his ways.

Raffles Institution prepared boys for what was then known as the Senior Cambridge examination. After passing it one went straight to university. Kuan Yew finished his course in 1939 with medals and honours. This was the time the parents had chosen to send him off to England. Mother Chua Jim Neo had her savings ready and Father Lee was all set to take an advance against his pension from the oil company.

War intervened. With Europe in turmoil there was no question of sending the boy on the perilous journey to England. So he entered Raffles College, later to become the University of Singapore. He read an unusual combination of subjects – economics, mathematics and English literature. He also took an active part in union debates, impressing his teachers with his ability to make speeches in English. The ground work was being laid for what was to become one of the more important political assets of Lee Kuan Yew.

When he passed his school-leaving examination, Kuan Yew attracted public attention by emerging among the top and winning a scholarship. A little later a bright-eyed girl from the Methodist Girl's School, called Kwa Geok Choo, gained similar attention by standing first in all Malaya and winning a scholarship to Raffles College. The two merit scholars met at Raffles. They were impressed by each other's academic record; affection began to develop. Geok Choo, three years older than Kuan Yew, was to graduate from Raffles with distinction, win a Queen's scholarship and proceed to Cambridge at the same time as Kuan Yew. At Cambridge their affection grew into love.

Kuan Yew had entered Raffles College only to bide his time until the world situation improved and he could go on to England. But his waiting period turned out to be longer than expected. It also proved harrowing. For the Japanese came to Singapore in 1942.

The Chinese had long looked upon the Japanese as their natural enemies and the Japanese were ready to play this role to the hilt, as the Chinese of Singapore soon discovered to their consternation. Lee Kuan Yew was to recall many an atrocity committed by the occupation army on the local population, and especially on Chinese. There is no independent record whether Lee personally was ever a victim, but he has described one narrow escape. Every now and again the Japanese would herd Chinese youths into trucks, drive them to some convenient spot and shoot them. Once Kuan Yew, queuing up at a concentration camp, was ordered to make the death trip. He asked to be allowed to go home to collect his belongings and was lucky enough to be permitted. He never returned.

The war was a traumatic experience for Kuan Yew. He was a

naturally sensitive boy and he was an impressionable nineteen when the conquerors arrived. He was to say many years later that the Japanese 'never knew what they did to a whole generation like me. But they did make me, and a generation like me, determined to work for freedom from servitude and foreign domination. I did not enter politics. They brought politics on me.'

While the Japanese were in Singapore, however, young Kuan Yew decided discretion was the better part of valour. As an able-bodied man he found it best to get down to some kind of work that would keep him out of trouble. He began with the local defence organization and became a mobile medical orderly. But this still was not entirely safe. He then learned Japanese and obtained work as a translator in the official Japanese news agency, Domei.

The fact that this bright Chinese youth took the trouble to learn the Japanese language must have made a favourable impression on his masters. Perhaps his brief brush with journalism also gave young Lee abiding notions about the craft. During his years in power he has shown a pronounced contempt for Singapore's journalistic fraternity and has ensured that newspapers in the island were run much as Domei was run by the Japanese army.

In wartime, though, the news agency job was a convenience. It gave Kuan Yew an opportunity to find out what was happening in the world. Reports which he translated – and which, of course, the agency never passed on for public consumption – told him the allies were winning and that the Japanese would not be in Singapore for ever. It helped keep his morale up – and enabled him to plot his own course of action so that he could pick up his interrupted life again. One day in 1945, sure in the knowledge that the Japanese were on their last legs, he slipped away from the news agency and fled Singapore. He waited in Malaya's Cameron Highlands until the British returned to Singapore.

The war's end found Kuan Yew a young man suddenly in a hurry. He was conscious of lost time and was anxious to make up for it. His experience during the war years seemed to have given him clear ideas about what exactly he wanted to do with his life. Things were in a mess, however, and there was no indication when British universities would be back on their feet. Even finding a passage on a ship was almost impossible.

Kuan Yew, determined to lose no time, tried to organize a sort of private college in his house. He asked his old Raffles

College professor to go there and give him lectures so that he could surround himself with 'an atmosphere of study'. The single-mindedness and determination had already set in.

Finally the time came for his parents to realize their long cherished dream. Shipping services had not yet resumed, but they found accommodation for their boy on the *Britannia*, then a troopship. Kuan Yew sailed for England in September 1946.

In view of the strict regulations at the time against allowing civilians on troopships, the British were doing a tremendous favour to Lee Kuan Yew when they gave him a berth on the *Britannia*. There were altogether a dozen civilians on the ship, all students like Lee, and all presumably scions of highly connected families in the region. The Lee family was not particularly notable, certainly not politically influential. How then did Kuan Yew come to be among the chosen few?

A leading British journalist working in Asia raised the interesting question, during conversation with the author, whether Britain was compensating young Lee for services rendered during the war. After all, he speculated, no one knew the nature of Lee's association with the Japanese during the years of occupation; what made him take the trouble to learn Japanese, how he could escape from Singapore so easily when he decided to do so, and how he managed to hide successfully in Cameron Highlands. Against the background of his latter-day relationship of trust with Britain, it was not illogical to surmise that while in the employment of the Japanese, perhaps Lee was also in contact with the British. The information gaps in his career have not helped to remove such impressions.

One of Lee's shipmates, a Chinese from Hong Kong, remembers the voyage well and recalls how Kuan Yew made a distinct impression on others as a brash young man who knew exactly what he wanted and did not bother what others said or thought.

'Fresh water was strictly rationed,' he recalls. 'We were six to a cabin and the steward would bring in three buckets of water early every morning, half a bucket for each person. But Harry would rise as early as five or six o'clock and use up all three buckets in his cabin for himself and then go over to the other cabin for more. This of course made him quite unpopular, but he didn't seem to care. We all thought he was a spoiled boy and quite selfish.'

Card games kept the group engaged and they played for small

stakes. Harry played well and at the end of the voyage a soldier owed him about £20 sterling. He asked for the money but the soldier was in no position to pay up. The other students suggested Harry forget it and he did. 'That was the only incident which gave us a feeling that after all he had a sense of fair play in him.'

The *Britannia* dropped Kuan Yew at Liverpool. He didn't like what he saw. Liverpool was devastated, cold and drab. London was the same. The London School of Economics was a Mecca for young Asian and African idealists and Kuan Yew had gone there, as many a socialist visionary before him, to get creatively honed by Harold Laski's pristine precepts. But the atmosphere of the big metropolis upset him. He later wrote: 'The idea of rumbling down the tube from Swiss Cottage to Holborn, and dashing round from Holborn to Aldwych, and popping up at Aldwych and running across to go down to the London School of Economics and getting out to catch I don't know what number of bus to University College up King Street and then back again to King's College frightened me. This wasn't my idea of university life.'

He spent one term in London, then managed to get admission to Cambridge. The quiet pace of the ancient university town was just what he wanted. Besides, bright-eyed Kwa Geok Choo was there already, a Queen's scholar at Girton College, her academic brilliance still hanging like a halo over her head. She was to pass with first class honours in only two years. Kuan Yew courted her assiduously at Cambridge and they decided to marry as soon as they returned home.

As a student at Cambridge, Kuan Yew was lucky in his tutors. He found them intellectually stimulating and personally kind. The interest they took in him and the understanding they showed made a lasting impression on him. This was one of the influences which contributed to his development as an Anglophile.

It also made him in later years an ardent advocate of the tutorial system of education. Commending it to a group of teachers in Singapore, he once recalled that although he had heard many brilliant lectures while in Cambridge 'it was the man with whom I sat in a tutorial afterwards and discussed the problems, and in particular one who in bouts of asthmatic fits used to take out his apparatus, inhale deeply and then back into the intricacies of Roman Law, who made an impression on me which is indelible.'

The years at Cambridge were rewarding. He read widely,

enjoyed long discussions with friends and teachers, established contacts with socialist thinkers, visited London often and toured England and the Continent when he could. He took to golf, attended a club for Chinese known as the China Institute, and became known as a nationalist with leftist leanings. He did extremely well in his studies, coming first in the honours list in the final examinations. Naturally his self-assurance grew apace. Years later he was to tell a group of civil servants in Singapore: 'I speak to Harold Macmillan and Duncan Sandys as equals. At Cambridge I got two firsts and a star for distinction. Harold Macmillan did not.' (Macmillan went to Oxford where, unlike Cambridge, there are no 'starred' firsts . . . but the boast could still fairly be made.)

It was clear by now that Lee Kuan Yew was definitely planning on a political future. The youthful idealism, already sharpened by the Japanese, grew stronger by exposure in England to liberal and socialist thought. He also came in close contact with other idealists from other lands.

Student groups from the different British colonies had their own associations in Britain. Those from Singapore and Malaya congregated under the banner of the Malayan Forum which had been set up by Tunku Abdul Rahman, the prince from Kedah who was to become prime minister of Malaysia. It served as a platform and training ground for a number of future Singapore-Malaysia leaders. In Malayan Forum discussions Kuan Yew would emphasize the particular responsibilities of people like himself who went to England for an advanced education. As he saw it, these students had a privileged position and, rather than settle down to a life of ease, they had a wider responsibility to their countries. He observed that in all the Asian countries which had achieved independence since the war, the returned students had led the nationalist movement. Kuan Yew was seeing his own path clear.

He was seeing it in ideological terms too. In the course of a political speech before the Malayan Forum in 1949, he examined the question of whether the returned students would find a place in the new Malaya.

'At the moment it is clear that the only party organized to force the British to leave, and to run the country, is the Communist Party. Theirs is a tightly knit organization making their bid for power. It is this element of international communism which I fear makes the pattern of development that has unfolded in India, Burma, Ceylon, etc., unlikely in Malaya. In all these countries the leaders from the educated classes, the returned students, had time to organize and were already organized, like the Indian Congress Party, before communism became a force in the political life of the countries. But this does not mean that communism is not a force in these countries. It is, right now, the biggest threat to the newly established governments of Asia. How far these governments can counter the appeal and force of communism will depend on how far they are bold enough to carry out social reforms in the teeth of their own vested interests ... whether they can, without the communist religion, do all that a communist state can do for the masses.'

Exactly ten years after making this assessment, Lee Kuan Yew was to become prime minister of Singapore and set out to do what he preached. During the next decade he would eschew the communist religion and, in the process, make a religion of anti-communism.

His studies completed, his mind made up and his line of action chalked out, Lee Kuan Yew returned to Singapore on August 1, 1950. The first item on his agenda was his wedding. His friend and intellectual comrade of many years who was now the holder, like him, of a distinguished law degree, became his wife on September 30.

They chose an English-style wedding reception, complete with a four-tier cake. Lee Kuan Yew was twenty-seven.

As far as his parents, brothers and other relatives are concerned, Lee Kuan Yew is extremely distant in family relationships. He even tries to avoid contacts with them. To his wife and children, however, he is a devoted husband and father. Two years after their marriage, a son was born, Lee Hsien Loong. In 1955 daughter Lee Wei Ling arrived and two years later another boy, Lee Hsien Yang. The brilliance of the parents shows in the children. In his early teens Hsien Loong, for example, became adept in Russian, English, Malay and Mandarin and his active interests ranged from music to nuclear physics. Lee really relaxes only when he is home with his family. They often play golf together; Lee's handicap is a flattering nine.

Unlike the father, the children were not marked out for an education that would make them models of English perfection. The age which justified those values was gone and Lee, as a political leader, did not wish to set examples which would be open to misinterpretation. In his own case, he seems to have doubted the wisdom of his parents going out of their way to make an English gentleman of him. He has no doubt profited from it, but his political instincts put it in a different perspective. 'At the end of it all,' he once said, 'I felt the whole set of values was wrong – fundamentally and radically wrong.' He said his son was going to a Chinese not an English, school. 'He will not be a model Englishman . . . he is going to be part of Asia, part of Malaysia.' He eventually followed the father to Cambridge.

As he began to weld a family and a state according to his ideals, Lee Kuan Yew began to mould himself into a highly disciplined individual. Like Jomo Kenyatta with his fly whisk or Sukarno with his general's baton, Lee adopted a personal symbol: a thermos flask. It contained Chinese tea which he sipped throughout the day as he trudged from labour meeting to court appearance to press conference to political council. To this day Lee is afraid of catching a chill and avoids cold drinks.

That is only part of his health fad. He is sensitive in a hundred different ways. Careful about his weight, he has given up an early indulgence – beer – and is never seen to drink hard liquor. Once a pipe-smoker, he now detests all tobacco. He rarely eats the Chinese staple diet of rice and avoids bread. His breakfast is spartan, and the principal meal, dinner, is light. He is fussy about keeping his nails trimmed and filed, washing his hands several times a day, polishing his shoes to a dazzling shine, changing his vests and shirts whenever the temperature fluctuates. Air-conditioners are adjusted to keep his bedroom temperature at 66° Fahrenheit, the office temperature at 72°. He exercises religiously with a morning round of press-ups, skipping and weight-lifting. He has a penchant for all kinds of pills. The only health rule he does not observe now is the early to bed and early to rise bit. He rarely retires before 1 a.m. and often has to be woken seven hours later.

His austerity extends beyond physical matters to his habits of mind. He never listens to music, sees no movies, reads no novels, has no hobbies – golf is his only indulgence. To some people his uprightness and singleness of mind are positively alarming. He is the only Asian politician about whom no personal scandal has ever been published.

Pictures of Kuan Yew as a child show him as a charming little Chinese doll. By the time he reached Cambridge his face was beginning to become bony and was gaining a set expression of aggressiveness. Then, as his life's pace accelerated, his appearance began to reflect the stresses within and upon him.

⌐Today, approaching fifty, Lee is a man with a trim physique. The Chineseness of his face has become accentuated by little bags of flesh round his classically narrow eyes. Lines have developed round the mouth and the lower lip protrudes in moments of reflection. The large ears vie for attention with the enormous forehead which looks, in profile, as though taking off at a tangent all its own, stopped in its flight only by a full head of tough hair laced with grey. The face is pockmarked, which adds to its stern ruggedness. It bears the scars of many a remembered victory. Lighting-up time comes when he smiles and transforms his forbidding countenance into a toothy, translucent triangle of charm under a canopy of dancing eyebrows.

When relaxed, Lee is handsome. But moments of relaxation are rare. When he first saw himself on television, he was appalled by what he called the 'gangsterlike look' and asked his aides to do something about softening his image.

But in 1950, with marriage over and the political issues and opportunities he had analysed while in England suddenly becoming reality, it was a time for hardening.

It can easily be seen that Lee's background is of a kind to isolate him. Born into a Chinese family and inheriting many Chinese characteristics, he was brought up not to be an ordinary Chinese. Equipped with English as his first language, with easy access to English culture and style of behaviour, he is not English. He once described English-educated Chinese as a devitalized people, speaking and thinking in a language which was not part of their being – and his problem is that he himself is one of them, yet cannot quite identify even with them because of the special circumstances of his career.

The society in which he lives is predominantly Chinese, but very complex: the Singapore Chinese consist of many different dialect groups with totally different manners. Although all of the Chinese community in Singapore derives sustenance from the same basic culture, it is diverse, atomistic and mutually uncomprehending. Its most important division is into two main streams, the Chinese-educated and the English-educated. Lee Kuan Yew rode to power on the backs of the first and has increasingly sought to buttress his position with the backing of the second, but he has never won the complete trust of either.

The Chinese-educated are so much a world apart that he has never fully understood them. Throughout Southeast Asia Chinese schools teach Chinese *mores*, Chinese nationalism, Chinese patriotism. China is projected as the mother country, and this has not been affected by the Chinese Revolution. People raised in this way have been steadily alienated by Lee's policies of decinization, and consider him simply anti-Chinese. The other main stream, the English-educated, has certainly appreciated Lee's modernity and has provided the sinews of his establishment, but it is not quite free of suspicion. People in it remember that when Lee was on the way up he relied heavily on the Chinese-educated, and that after he was made he rejected them; others remember his proclaimed socialism and have seen its eventual betrayal; yet others resent his concentration of power in himself. And he hardly endeared himself to this stream in May 1971, during the crisis over his suppression of a newspaper, when he remarked derisively 'the English-educated do not riot'.

Outside Singapore the pattern of isolation is similar. Strangely, Lee is despised by the Malaysian Chinese (which indicates, incidentally, that racialism is not the issue between the two neighbours), and is the object of a great deal of personal dislike among the leaders of that community. The Chinese in China, predictably, have nothing but contempt for him, and the Chinese of Taiwan do not know what to think of him. To this has been added the political alienation resulting from the disparaging statements he makes about other Asian countries, holding them up as examples of stagnation and inefficiency. With the leaders of Malaysia, Indonesia and the Philippines he is extremely unpopular, while his relations with Thailand, Burma, India and Ceylon are no more than correct. His only friend in Asia has been Prince Norodom Sihanouk of Cambodia.

A personal and intellectual alienation completes the picture. Lee is so conscious of his intellectual superiority that others find him arrogant. Unlike most Chinese, who mask their feelings and let them leak out subtly, he is quick to show contempt. Most of those who work for him hint that he reduces them to the level of messenger-boys. His wife is perhaps the only person with whom he can drop the mantle of super-ruggedness and can communicate on a basis of mutual respect. Professor C. Northcote Parkinson, who spent a career in Singapore teaching history at the University wrote of Lee: 'Utterly without charm, his expression is one of barely concealed contempt; for his opponents, for his followers, perhaps for himself. . . . One cannot imagine that he is even capable of friendship.'

In short, Lee Kuan Yew is a man marked by the fact that he does not quite belong anywhere and has had to produce himself – his style and his attitudes – out of his own deep mind. Thus he has the unpredictability of a man with a mission but no power brakes. When he talks of creating a new Singapore, he means, of course, creating a new society which will justify his own attitudes to life. His concept of 'Singaporeanism' and of 'the rugged society' is only partly a political device to ensure Singapore's separate identity; partly it is a way of compensating for his alienation by making a society in his own image – the projection on to the national scene of an individual's complex psychological problems.

CHAPTER THREE

The Making of a Prime Minister

He is a master at building verbal bridges to span the extremes of debate, as well as concrete bridges and buildings. But standing in the middle, he is sometimes in danger of forgetting that all whose language, social position or partisan affiliation place them closer to the edge of debate are not necessarily thereby immoderate and unamenable to compromise. . . . It is unfortunate that he has seldom faced opponents with power and ability to match his own. This freedom from the necessity to engage in genuine negotiations has perhaps frozen a bit too much of the prophet Jeremiah into his political style.

PROFESSOR ROBERT E. GAMER, University of Singapore, 1965

Barrister Lee Kuan Yew set up a law firm in Singapore, Lee and Lee, but it was clear from the outset that he had no intention of making a career in law. His wife was perfectly qualified to look after Lee and Lee, as she soon proved. Today she is one of the most eagerly sought legal brains in Singapore and Lee and Lee rides a wave of fortune.

Lee Kuan Yew's own interests were different. Law was to be a stepping-stone to a career in politics and Lee knew precisely how he wanted to use it. What Singapore witnessed from 1950 to 1959 was the spectacle of one man pursuing one goal with awe-inspiring determination.

The historical setting was significant, Lee could already expect to win power in a short time. This was vastly different from the situation in most other British colonies where nationalist leaders struggled for long years with little hope of achieving independence in their lifetime. Five years after the end of the war, the only question in Singapore and Malaya was how to get the best deal out of the British – and which nationalist group was to get it.

In this, Lee had some advantages. No one else in Singapore or Malaya had his intellectual sophistication and political savvy. He was so much at home in the idiom of British politics that he could play the game in a style which impressed even the colonialists he sought to displace.

The picture that emerged as he set out to achieve his goal was composed of masterstrokes, applied slowly, methodically, deliberately. But it was not the creation of one master. Some of the bolder, more decisive strokes were carried out by the British authorities.

When he began setting his political course in 1950, Lee faced three problems. Achieving independence was not one of them, for the colonial period was ending. Britain's true intentions as seen by Malayan nationalists, however, constituted a major problem. Various British moves, including the separation of Singapore from Malaya in 1946, had given Lee the impression that the British would contrive an independence which would make Malaya free but would leave Singapore very much a British base. This suspicion was to linger in his mind, affecting his attitudes to Britain right up to the point of Singapore's independence. This might explain Lee's strenuous efforts to win British confidence on the one hand and, on the other, to insist on Singapore being considered part of the Federation of Malaya for purposes of independence. His persistent slogan up to 1963 was 'independence through merger'.

The other problems were tactical. He had to win pro-communist support without which he knew he would never get what he wanted. Yet he had to do this in a manner that would not enable the pro-communists one day to swamp him. At the same time he had to ensure that among the non-communists he would be the unchallenged leader. The solution to these problems was to employ a combination of tact, dissimulation and raw power, first through the colonial authorities, later through his own government, while all the time keeping his ultimate goal firmly in view.

The first step was to become part of the popular politics of the day. Two distinct elements then made up the vanguard of the anti-colonial movement – organized workers and students of Chinese schools. The latter, as we have seen, were outside Lee's ken, and he was not yet aware of their significance. Workers were a different proposition, for their organization was part of the Western public life he understood. Besides, he was freshly returned from England where he had admired the Labour Party and seen some virtues in socialism.

Unions needed someone like Lee as much as Lee needed the unions. They often had to conduct their business with employers and the government in English – and English-educated leaders with the right sympathies were hard to come by. In a few years such leaders would emerge from the University Socialist Club and the ranks of school teachers, but in the early 1950s the unions were glad to have a bright young barrister fresh from England willing to place himself at their disposal. Soon Lee was legal adviser to a hundred unions – and a very influential one at that.

His talks with trade unionists were not confined to legal matters. He took every opportunity to discuss the wider issues of Singapore's political future and what could be done to shape it. He was gauging the union leaders' political intentions, taking his measure of them, feeling his way.

There was a small group of personal associates with whom he discussed at length his own plans and intentions. This group had first taken shape in London. At meetings of the Malayan Forum he had come to know many compatriots who were students in England like himself, and had warmed to two in particular – Goh Keng Swee, a bright economist from Malacca, and Toh Chin Chye, a medical scientist from Perak. While in England they agreed that 'something should be done' about Malaya, a term which then included Singapore. Now back home, they began discussing what that something should be. Goh, thirty-two, was in government service and Toh, then twenty-eight, was teaching physiology at the University of Malaya.

Local men joined the group. Prominent among them were Sinnathamby Rajaratnam and Kenneth Byrne. Rajaratnam was a Ceylonese of Indian origin whose family had migrated to Singapore when he was six months old. He was thirty-five and associate editor of the Singapore *Standard* when Lee Kuan Yew started his mission. He joined the *Straits Times* in 1954 and stayed with it until he formally entered politics five years later.

Byrne was a Singapore-born Eurasian educated in Penang and Oxford. He had joined the Straits Settlements Civil Service and was holding a senior administrative position in the government when he became friendly with Lee. At thirty-seven he was the oldest member of the group; twenty-seven-year-old Lee was its youngest.

Anti-colonialism was the obvious issue which brought these men together. Idealism also played a crucial role, for they were all imbued with vaguely socialistic ideas of equality and justice. The cement that held them together was their intellectual bent of mind; they were all 'thinkers', and that appealed to Lee, who was

2

soon to establish a reputation for impatience with people of 'ordinary' mental calibre. Another noteworthy common factor was that they were all English-educated and had been raised on Western thought.

Above all, these were men who unquestioningly accepted Lee Kuan Yew's leadership. Their loyalty to him was to prove abiding and Lee would find it extremely important in some tough moments ahead.

The group met nightly at Lee Kuan Yew's home. Interminable arguments went on about strategies and tactics and the content of independence. Agreeing that the organization of workers was important, they devoted considerable time and energy to rallying workers round an anti-colonial platform and to recruiting their own cadres.

A strike by the Postal Workers' Union in 1952 gave Lee his first opportunity to catch the public eye. As legal adviser to the union he issued a torrent of statements to the press in defence of the strikers. These were supplemented by regular letters to editors. His journalist friend Rajaratnam helped obtain maximum publicity for everything Lee penned. The union's legal counsel was as much in the limelight as the strikers.

The postmen's strike also gave Lee a direct link with a group of student activists in the university which was solidly backing the strikers. These students organized the Socialist Club in 1953, then looked around for help to start a journal – and found Lee able and willing to help. This was the beginning of Lee's power base in the university. A small band of half a dozen student leaders would mobilize significant support for him and his party in the next few years. Immediately after coming to power, Lee would imprison half of them and banish the other half from Singapore.

If postmen gave Lee his first big break as a leader, students gave the second. Soon after the students started their journal, *Fajar*, it attracted punitive action under sedition laws. Later, in independent Singapore, such publications would simply go under and nothing more would be heard about the men behind them. The British had a different value system and brought *Fajar*'s young editors to trial.

The *Fajar* sedition trial became a *cause célèbre* in Singapore – and the students' lawyer was of course Lee Kuan Yew. With great panache Lee argued the case, citing every principle in the book in defence of individual liberty and freedom of expression. He dramatized the case at every possible turn – and brought off a coup by bringing D. N. Pritt, QC, the famous socialist lawyer, to Singapore for the defence. The case stayed on the front pages for many days. Pritt got the charges against the students quashed. Lee Kuan Yew was firmly established as a public figure.

On a subsequent occasion Lee forged links with the Chinese students normally outside his sphere of influence. They had rioted over compulsory national service – a sore issue with Chinese students even today – and Lee defended them in court. Once in power, he would make national service a test of patriotism and prohibit even letters to editors criticizing it.

Men who worked with Lee in those days as students now recall that his energy was phenomenal. He displayed more stamina than the younger university boys. He worked practically round the clock and did not seem to need rest or recreation.

With incessant work in support of popular causes, Lee had become a nationalist hero with strong labour and student backing when, in 1955, Britain announced plans for a limited-franchise election: Singapore's first popular election, which would give it its first elected head of government.

Singapore politics suddenly took on a different complexion, for the election plan brought with it an aroma of freedom. Parties and platforms now became significant. The Lee group realized it was time to give itself a formal political platform. Lee had already set up a small organization called the Joint Action Council with himself as secretary and Rajaratnam and Byrne as the main leaders. That was his first, somewhat diffident, attempt at organizing a party; it had its own white, blue and red flag. But it was not quite a party and it would not suffice in the emerging parliamentary situation.

Lee toyed with the idea of joining an established party. Of the two major parties of the day, one was the ironically named Progressive Party, which in fact consisted of all the extreme right-wing conservatives. It was also palpably ineffective. Lee could only consider seriously the other party – the Labour Front under the liberal leadership of David Marshall.

But negotiations with the Labour Front were abortive. The reason Lee gave later was that he found the Labour Front an election party, not a genuine socialist movement. Nearer the truth might be the reason adduced by Labour Front spokesmen – that they found Lee a difficult man to work with.

It might simply have been a case of personality clashes. Given Lee's ambitions and determination, he could only have thought of taking over the Labour Front and becoming its leader. Marshall, a leonine presence whose brilliance is matched only by his great oratorical power, is a natural leader who could not possibly have entertained any thought of yielding his position to a brash young challenger. The two men were to drift further apart as time passed, each with an increasingly dim view of the other.

Once the idea of collaboration with the Labour Front was abandoned, the Lee group had only one course: to form its own party. They chose the name People's Action Party. It appealed to them 'mainly because this political party was meant for the people'. As for 'Action', it was already a favourite term with Lee and came straight out of the Joint Action Council. Lee chose to be secretary-general; Toh Chin Chye was made chairman. They would remain permanent fixtures in those positions.

The first public hint that the PAP was in the works was a newspaper report on October 19th. It said the forthcoming election would see a new 'national group' in the arena and that it was 'being formed by the UMNO–MCA Alliance [the United Malay National Organization and the Malayan Chinese Association, the prominent parties of Malaya] and a new political party, as yet unnamed, headed by a young colony lawyer.'

The formal proposal for the PAP's formation was made by Lee at a Sunday public rally on November 21, 1954. The left-wing aura the promoters had already achieved, and the solid support given by trade unions – seven of the fourteen original conveners of the party were established trade union leaders – whipped up considerable mass interest in the rally. It was clear the PAP was going to be a party to reckon with.

On the platform, as Lee made his spirited plea for new socialist action, were representatives of Malaya's United Malay National Organization and the Malayan Chinese Association – among them the princely Malay hero Tunku Abdul Rahman himself. At the time it was an auspicious gesture signifying the essential unity of Chinese-dominated Singapore and Malay-dominated Malaya. But very soon Lee and the PAP would emerge as antagonistic to the Tunku, the UMNO and the MCA. The two neighbouring territories were to drift into distrust and enmity.

It was a good time for a new party to flex its muscles in Singapore. No doubt the new constitution was still colonial in character and the bulk of the Chinese population remained without the vote, yet it was a great improvement on the framework in which the previous election had taken place in 1948. Those Chinese who were citizens of the United Kingdom and Colonies could now vote – and that meant a chance, however limited, for popular sentiment to express itself.

Lee began to work out the PAP's electoral strategy. Some of his colleagues favoured an immediate bid for power, but Lee knew no real power was possible under the constitution. In Toh Chin Chye's words, 'If we had launched enough candidates to become ministers then we would be reduced to mere puppets of the colonialists.' Still, emergence as an opposition in the legislative assembly would give the PAP a useful platform and an opportunity to show its popular radicalism to good effect. The PAP decided to field a token number of candidates.

It decided to be spectacularly leftist in its campaign. On the basis of what Lee has said time and again after he came to power, he was strongly suspicious of communists and fellow travellers from the very outset; but in the 1950s he kept such feelings well masked and accepted all the support he could get from leftists of all hues. Ideology could wait. This was a time for common sense. And Lee's common sense told him that communists, and communists alone, were then in a position to work up mass enthusiasm for a political party.

Historical factors had contributed to the communist strength. The Chinese-constituted Malayan Communist Party had taken to the jungles of Malaya in mid-1948 and the guerilla fighting that followed had helped to glamorize the communist image. Chinese nationalism was strong in Singapore, anyway. Unemployment fanned the flames of this nationalist fervour, for vast numbers of Chinese-educated high school students and former students were frustrated to see job opportunities as well as social status going to the English-educated. Lee himself acknowledged once that 'it is easy to be called a communist in Singapore if you come from a Chinese school'.

On the other hand even non-communists, if they were anti-colonial and anti-British, faced the danger of being equated with communists in the eyes of the authorities. Most nationalists therefore preferred to lie low while others threw in their lot with the communist underground. This was one of the explanations Lee gave in 1961 for his collaboration with communists in the 1950s.

He said 'emotionally we felt more sympathetic to the communists who were sacrificing life and limb to get the British out than with the clowns and crooks who were in the open political arena'.

Being no clown, Lee worked himself into a unique position: he was in the political arena as well as in touch with the communist underground. He knew that some of the trade union leaders with whom he was working were members of the banned Malayan Communist Party. He needed their backing and thus he used his position as legal adviser to persuade several key unions to take communist sympathizers as secretaries and leaders.

As soon as the PAP was launched, Lee came in intimate contact with communist systems of organization. Hitherto his work in the unions and attempts to recruit cadres were confined mainly to the English- and Malay-educated sectors. The year the PAP was formed he suddenly came face to face with the Chinese-educated world. Some years later he described this as 'a world teeming with vitality, dynamism and revolution, a world in which the communists had been working for the past thirty years with considerable success. We were latecomers trying to tap the same oil fields . . . our initiation into the intricacies and ramifications of the communist underground organization in the trade unions and cultural associations had begun.'

Lee was impressed by what he saw, for he was to employ the same methods to spread the PAP's roots in Singapore. He also found no party could make headway in Singapore without winning over large chunks of the Chinese-educated population. As he admitted later, anybody in Singapore who wanted to carry the Chinese-speaking people with him could not afford to be anti-communist. He was already a believer in a cardinal communist principle: the end justifies the means.

On this basis the PAP projected itself as a revolutionary party. Its rallies began and ended with communist songs. Speakers invariably shouted stirring anti-colonial slogans with clenched fists. The party's demands were all popular: repeal of emergency regulations which Britain had imposed in the wake of the communist insurrection in Malaya, independence for a unified Malaya-Singapore, Malayanization of the civil service, official recognition of Chinese and Tamil, universal adult franchise. The English press described the party statements as 'nicely calculated to attract the unthinking, a feast of promise with little regard to the facts'. Lee must have quietly chuckled over that, knowing popular sentiments were unmistakably with the fiery, left-wing, trade-union-backed, student-supported PAP.

Of the four candidates put up by the PAP, two were from the Lee group and two were pro-communist. Only one lost – Devan Nair, then a militant communist sympathizer. After a term in Changhi jail, he became an ardent follower of Lee and now acts for him on the labour front. Among those who won were a young, soft-spoken revolutionary with a very agile mind called Lim Chin Siong – and Lee.

Though the PAP had only three seats in the assembly against the Labour Front's ten, Lee was now the leading opposition member. He filled the role with ability and acumen. The assembly was a very different platform from street rallies, and Lee seemed to enjoy it. His speeches were in the best British parliamentary tradition. They showed up that quality again when Lee later played opposition in the parliament of Greater Malaysia in Kuala Lumpur. As a member of the opposition Lee Kuan Yew was a great parliamentarian.

A special advantage he enjoyed in the assembly was that he had two ready targets of attack: the colonial rulers and the Labour Front government. Chief Minister David Marshall was an easy target because the British seemed to oppose him even more than Lee did. He was a Singapore-born Iraqi Jew, English-educated like Lee, but unable to hit it off with the British. He was known at the time, and is still revered, as being too much of a liberal and a gentleman for the hurly-burly of politics; and this, together with his failure to be seen as 'one of the chaps', put him at a disadvantage. Contemptuous of Marshall from the start, the British harassed him by denying him even an office or staff. He asked for four assistant ministers and the British refused. After he had threatened to set up an office under a tree he was granted rooms under a staircase, and an office boy.

The British attitude only made Marshall more belligerent. A scintillating debater and great individualist, he was rather naive in political infighting. He was naturally defiant and the British found him quarrelsome. He persuaded the assembly to vote for immediate self-government, but Britain frustrated him at every turn.

Marshall's period in office was picturesque, but his Labour Front ministry lasted only fourteen months. He led an all-party delegation to London to negotiate transfer of power and six months later resigned in disgust over the lack of progress. For ever after, Lee Kuan Yew was to pour ridicule on him. In fact Lee's future tasks were considerably eased by Marshall's work and Lee's government later would have gained much from an infusion of Marshall's humanism. Although Marshall failed in London, he had begun a process which could not be stopped. As Ronald Mckie observed, 'for the first time in the history of Singapore, one man, an Asian Jew, stood up to the British, demanded a ruling on the status of his chief ministership, forced a governor to lose face, called for self-government, began the Malayanization of the civil service, reached out for independence.' A Yale University scholar, Thomas Bellows, put it thus: 'The Labour Front years were the years of greatest political freedom and debate in post-war Singapore. By yielding office once defeated, the LF confirmed and implemented a rule of the game central to the functioning of a pluralistic party system. The willingness to yield to new élites and to eschew the arbitrary and repressive measures that might have enabled the LF to remain in office possesses a significance for Singapore that only history can fully credit.'

Marshall's successors would use repressive measures to remain in office; when defeated they would not yield. But Marshall was a sportsman to the core. History can give him credit for preparing the way for freedom and Lee.

All through Marshall's chief ministership the PAP did a great deal of rabble-rousing in its bid for popularity. Marshall blamed it for the student riots which shook Singapore during the period. Lee never batted an eyelid. An extremely radical public stance was what he needed then and he worked for it energetically.

But in his own mind there could have been no doubt about the radicalism being no more than a ploy. Indeed, within months of the PAP's formation, and more particularly after the 1955 election, it became clear that Lee was also deftly trying to win British confidence so that the British would consent to the PAP becoming the government of Singapore when the time was ripe. This could be done only by stretching principles. Critics called it cheating, admirers called it flexibility, neutrals called it political opportunism, but the fact is that it was a competent display of sustained dissimulation lasting nearly seven years. And it was successful.

Evidence suggests that the Lee group, while publicly working hand in glove with the pro-communists in the PAP, was in fact persuading the colonial authorities to clamp down on them. The

British, facing an emergency in Malaya, were very sensitive about communists in Singapore and any assistance received from the Lee group would have made them favourably disposed towards members of the group. At the same time the Lee group would have been making its own future secure by keeping the pro-communists under a colonial clamp without incurring the odium of doing so directly.

In his meticulous dissertation on the PAP, Thomas Bellows mentioned 'the growing pro-communist conviction that the non-communists (inside the PAP) were assisting the government in its periodic security sweeps against the pro-communists'. Among other things he cited a memorandum by Dr Goh Keng Swee in which the PAP leader referred to a Special Branch recommendation that three hundred pro-communists be put in prison. But David Marshall 'refused to accept this professional advice' and detained only seven – an action Goh called 'feeble and lamentable in the extreme'. The Special Branch of the police was a British responsibility at the time and obviously the PAP's non-communist hierarchy was on its wavelength.

The pro-communists were in fact active leftist trade unionists, men who had deep roots among the masses. The leadership consisted of the 'Big Six' – Lim Chin Siong, Fong Swee Suan, Sandra Woodhull, James Puthucheary, Jamit Singh and S. T. Bani. Lim and Fong represented the Chinese stream and were mass leaders wielding great influence. The others came from the English-educated stream. There was never any evidence, except Lee Kuan Yew's word, to show they were card-carrying communists. Their advocacy of workers' rights and a socialistic economy was communism enough for Lee. While using their undeniable mass base for the benefit of the PAP, it was Lee's perennial preoccupation to prevent the party from falling into their hands. He let them have the run of trade unions, but insisted that the party machinery was his domain.

Often they came close to capturing the party – only to be thwarted by the government of the day. After David Marshall was replaced as chief minister by Lim Yew Hock, who proved to be a pliable British instrument, Lee found his path being cleared by bolder governmental action at some critical moments. On more than one occasion it was executive action that saved him from being ousted from PAP leadership.

The first crisis came in 1956. Newspaper headlines were already calling Lee the 'PAP boss', but his subtle swing to conservatism was disturbing left-wing trade unionists in the party. They knew, however, that the following enjoyed by the PAP at that time was demonstrably left-wing, so they planned to use this strength to curb Lee's influence on the party leadership.

The PAP's supreme decision-making body was the central executive committee. At the time of the party's formation there were only three leftists, or pro-communists, on this twelve-member body; in 1956 their strength rose to four.

In this election Lim Chin Siong received more votes than Lee Kuan Yew, and Chinese schoolboys with red arm bands were prominent as security guards. Following this election, the leftists pressed for a new party constitution which would give them added weight. They put their brightest theoretician, James Puthucheary, on the sub-committee appointed to redraft the constitution. Puthucheary clamoured for a constitution which would allow party branches to nominate members to the central executive. This would have given the leftists, who were in a position to control most of the party's branch units, the opportunity to send their own men to the executive.

Lee and his associates had little chance of blocking the passage of the new constitution, for in any trial of strength they would be swamped by the massive pro-communist membership of the party. But the Lim Yew Hock government suddenly decided on a 'communist purge' and most of the active trade unionists were arrested. As Lee recalled later, 'that was the end of their attempt to rewrite the constitution and capture the PAP.'

The arrests did not diminish the popularity of the leftists. In fact rioting and arson broke out as they were led to jail. At the 1957 party conference the leftists put their popularity to good use. In a veritable coup six of their members were elected to the central executive – achieving parity with the Lee group.

That was virtually a takeover and Lee faced his second party crisis. With half the seats of the supreme body in their hands, the leftists could have a decisive voice in all policy matters and prevent the PAP from going blue under Lee. It appeared the PAP would at least become entrenched as an aggressive extreme-left mass party.

But ten days after the party election the Lim Yew Hock government suddenly ordered another purge. Five of the six newly-elected leftist members of the central executive found themselves in prison. A government statement implied the men were arrested to prevent a communist takeover of the PAP. That was a touching piece of solicitude from a government led by the rival Labour Front. To cushion the embarrassment Lee said the arrests were made because the leftists were attempting to capture the Trade Union Congress founded by Lim Yew Hock.

Whatever the motive behind the arrests, the gainer was not Lim Yew Hock but Lee Kuan Yew. Flabbergasted by the capture of six seats by the pro-communists, the Lee group had preferred not to take over the other six seats it had won in the central executive rather than to 'lend cover' to the pro-communists. Now, with the inconvenience neatly lodged in jail, Lee and his men 'were able to retrieve the party and rebuild', as they later put it.

Repeated government intervention to ensure Lee Kuan Yew's political survival confirmed the feeling that Lee was by now Britain's chosen man for Singapore. Thomas Bellows wrote: 'Sir William Goode had been inaugurated as governor of Singapore on December 11, 1957. He had previously been appointed as colonial secretary in 1953 (the title later changed to chief secretary), a position he held until governor. As chief secretary, one of his duties was supervision of the Special Branch. Goode was described to the author as a person who knew Singapore politics "to the fingertips". For at least twelve months before the May 1959 elections, Goode had maintained close contact with Lee Kuan Yew. What covert assistance Lee received in the form of information during these talks is not a matter of public record. However, it has been stated on good authority that, in specific instances, Lee used information against the Labour Front to which only the Council of Ministers were supposedly privy. British interest and influence in the political process were still considerable, if not crucial. The sum result of these factors was that by mid- or late 1958 the non-communists in the PAP were willing to seek an absolute majority of the seats in the May 1959 elections.' Lee himself later gave 'a personal tribute' to Goode and implied that Goode's reports when he was in charge of the Special Branch had helped him. (See Chapter Nine.)

Apparently Lee knew and accepted the fact of secret British backing. 'He justified government action against the left group in the PAP when he came to talk to us in prison,' said Sandra Woodhull, for long a close associate of Lee as university activist, trade unionist and PAP leader until he joined the opposition and eventually was exiled from Singapore. Lee's argument before his own colleagues was that Lim Yew Hock wanted to wipe out the PAP and get it banned and that was why he (Lee) should have 'the Brits on his side'. According to Woodhull, the liaison officer between Lee and the British administration was the police superintendent, an Englishman.

Governor Goode understood his task was to hand over power to leaders who were not communist or pro-communist and Lim Yew Hock, as chief minister, knew that the governor was in constant touch with the Lee group. Nevertheless, his own apparent rejection by the British must have galled him and the thought of having been the instrument to rescue Lee Kuan Yew from certain political eclipse must have grated.

In the 1959 assembly debate he took his revenge – almost. He referred to the subversive clause which had been written into the Internal Security Ordinance during the constitutional talks in London in 1958. This had made the ordinance an effective instrument to prevent pro-communists from coming to power legally or illegally. Lim alleged this was Lee's work. He said: 'The truth shall be told. If one side can play dirty and begin to be dirty, I shall play the same game and do it too and let the country and the world and God decide. The subversive clause was put in as a result of the Honourable Member (Lee Kuan Yew) and I seeing the Secretary of State for Colonies. . . .' At this point Lee sprang to his feet with a vehement 'That's an outright lie' and the speaker closed the discussion. Investigating in Singapore many years later, Thomas Bellows said: 'Lim's statement was accurate.'

In his years of power, whenever the Internal Security regulations were used to put away political opponents, Lee would say this act was not of his making. The role he did play in making it could only be hinted at – because of the speaker's intervention – by the other actor in the drama. Lee clung to what he disowned and used the extra-parliamentary powers with far more deadliness than the colonial authorities did.

Lee's own decision on a change of PAP tactics became apparent on his return from London after the first constitutional talks in 1955. The British stand had frustrated Marshall, but the effect on Lee was very different. Sensing power, he began to change the PAP's make up, highlighting its conservative respectability. The difference between the English-educated and the Chinese-educated was made subtly clear. Among the leaders the Chinese-educated were identified as the radicals while the English-educated stood out as moderates and liberals – precisely the kind of men Britain might support, even welcome, in a self-governing Singapore.

Under Lee's deft management, the PAP became 'democratic, non-communist and Malayan'. It was the beginning of the PAP's transformation into a catch-all party – pragmatic, non-ideological and very much an Asian banyan tree under which nothing else would grow.

It also became wedded to an 'iron law of oligarchy'. After the 1957 intra-party 'coup' was aborted by an obliging government, Lee carried out his own constitutional reform, making two classes of members, ordinary and cadre. Admittance to each was preceded by a period of probation. Elections to the central executive were restricted to cadre members – and cadre members were chosen strictly after screening by Lee Kuan Yew. As Lee himself once justified it, 'The Pope chooses the cardinals and the cardinals elect the Pope.'

The by-laws framed then still govern the PAP. Barely one per cent of the party's membership rise to be cadres. The exceptional ones must not only prove their loyalty to the leadership over a period of years but must subject themselves to more than one security investigation before they are admitted as cadres.

And then they must keep their cadre status secret. Lee takes no chances. A board of selection, set up ostensibly to 'cope with the work of promotion of members and appointments within the party', acts as an iron curtain protecting the inner reaches of the party for Lee Kuan Yew.

To Lee's credit, while successfully manœuvring these advantages, he maintained his public posture of identification with the pro-communists. Because their leadership was in jail or, more likely, because they realized that independent existence would only invite British proscription, the pro-communists were reluctant to break with the PAP. This suited Lee.

After the leftists were arrested in the 1956 and 1957 purges, Lee continued his contacts with them. Normally, under the British colonial system, a lawyer visiting his clients in prison was allowed only to discuss legal matters connected with their case, but apparently Lee was no ordinary lawyer. He was allowed to see the leftists in prison and to discuss party and political affairs with them. 'I had the singular advantage of arguing their appeals, seeing their captured documents and special branch reports on them.'

He had long political arguments with them, 'they trying to convince me that the bourgeois democratic system was no good and I trying to prove that whatever happened in China, we were living in Malaya.' This was the official British line at the time and Britain must have felt gratified at Lee's willingness to carry it to his colleagues in jail.

Towards the end of 1958 Lee was discussing with the prisoners whether the PAP should fight the general election the following year. This was to be a very different kind of election from the 1955 exercise which had put David Marshall in the chief minister's chair. This time a new constitution had come into being and Singapore was going to have a fully elected government for the first time. Supreme power would still be with Britain, which would look after defence and foreign affairs and have a major say in internal security. But it was self-government all the same. Singapore was to have a prime minister.

This was the opportunity Lee Kuan Yew was waiting for. He did not of course doubt that he was the best man for the job. He remarked later that 'to lose would mean that a bunch of rogues would form the government and ruin the country and also fix the PAP'. It was a characteristic comment which summed up Lee's own personality – his self-assurance, contempt for others, tendency to equate himself with the country and above all his fear that, given half a chance, his adversaries would be willing and able to 'fix' him. By the same token it indicated Lee's readiness to 'fix' others once he got hold of the reins of power.

They were now well within reach. In five years the PAP, largely powered by the popularity of the leftists in trade unions and Chinese schools, had come a long way. In 1957, despite the internal dissensions, the party had succeeded in the municipal elections and made one of its leading members mayor of Singapore – the ebullient Ong Eng Guan whose iconoclastic mayoral style had added considerably to the party's appeal. An organizational infrastructure had been formed and some familiarity with effective electioneering had been gained. Above all, the British had kept the pro-communists in jail on one hand and encouraged the Lee group on the other. It was reasonable to consider 1959 as the PAP's year.

But Lee had a serious reservation: Lim Chin Siong. Although Lim was in Changhi prison, Lee knew this was one case in which stone walls did not a prison make. Lim was then a PAP luminary.

He had been secretary of the powerful Factory and Shop Workers' Union, member with Lee Kuan Yew of the 1955 legislative assembly and member of the PAP's central executive committee when he was arrested in one of the purges that saved Lee's position.

Lim was a meteor. When the Second World War ended he was only twelve years old. When he entered the assembly he was an impressive twenty-two. He was a man of tremendous drive, resolve and vision. Avoiding routine work in school, he had read Turgenev and Dostoevsky in translation. In jail he continued his reading of classics, studied *Dr Zhivago* several times over. Now at twenty-six, he was already a charismatic mass leader.

Lee was afraid. Lim Chin Siong had qualities that made him a formidable political rival, and he was superior to Lee as a human being. First, his charisma and mass appeal were embellishments evidently beyond Lee Kuan Yew's reach. Second, his interest in general reading despite his lack of Westernization was in marked contrast to Lee's inclination then and now to avoid everything that was not immediately and directly relevant to his job (some say he stopped reading when he left Cambridge). Third, Lim was widely recognized as being utterly selfless.

Lim was also believed to be a communist – in Lee's words, 'the most important open-front leader the Malayan Communist Party had built up'. In the circumstances then prevailing, this only added to Lim's mass popularity. His quiet manner and human qualities might have even made his communism seem acceptable to many.

Lee Kuan Yew knew that he could not yet do without Lim Chin Siong's hold on the masses. At the same time he feared that such a hold might prove fatal to him and to his leadership once the PAP formed its own government. For Lim, however, this was a minor issue compared to Singapore's freedom. During one of the prison discussions with Lee Kuan Yew, he offered to go away to Indonesia if that would lessen Lee's fears.

But Lee had a better solution. He kept it to himself for the present.

The decision taken, the PAP plunged into the 1959 general election campaign. Lee drummed up a platform which was so communistic in its appeal that some Western countries regarded him as a communist and thought Chief Minister Lim Yew Hock was Singapore's best hope. The British also appeared to take this line, but must have known full well that Lim Yew Hock was a lost cause. This public stand by forces associated with colonialism strengthened Lee's credibility with the electorate.

There were as many as fourteen parties in the field, but the PAP stood far above the others. Masses of voluntary workers from the trade unions and Chinese schools manned barricades in a hectic campaign which did everything short of setting the Singapore River on fire. The Malayan Communist Party had issued instructions to its members to back the PAP. Through a front organization it fielded four token candidates against the PAP, and Lee made speeches underlining the differences between the PAP and the communists, but the collaboration was unaffected and there were many who believed Lee had struck a deal with the Malayan Communist Party.

Through it all Lee Kuan Yew with deadly seriousness was drawing up the policies a PAP government should follow. In a series of pamphlets called *The Tasks Ahead*, he spelled out party policy on the economy, on education, on health. A common market with the Federation of Malaya was envisaged. Sweeping changes in the educational system – a favourite Lee subject – and the establishment of an industrial court with full powers to arbitrate in labour disputes were promised, with equality for women and the eradication of communalism.

The most decisive election promise was that the PAP would assume office only if Lim Chin Siong and seven other leftist trade union leaders were released from prison. Lee by then had worked out his strategy to meet the challenge of Lim and was ready to have him freed. In any case, the PAP, if returned to power could not countenance the continued imprisonment of Lim and the others who were leading PAP members. The first PAP statement on the demand for release of the trade unionists even said it had come from 'Comrade Lee Kuan Yew'.

But the comrade was playing a game. 'Lee came in to work out a conduct code for us after release,' said Sandra Woodhull, one of the eight whose freedom was being demanded by the PAP. 'One of our conditions was that within one to three months woman political detainees should be released, followed by all other rank and file. When we pressed him on this, he said we should go and explain to the other detainees why certain things had to be done for form's sake. These prisoners had been moved from Changhi to the isolated St John's island where, Lee said, things like food and service were better. Lee said he also had arranged a day's boating for the prisoners and had told the British to provide all comforts. The detainees were out in the sea the whole day and at night we were sent into their cells to talk to them. After we all retired, about midnight, one detainee suddenly felt there was a snake on his roof. There was a continuous hissing sound. He woke up everybody and called the guards. There was a great deal of commotion and a thorough search. Finally we discovered the cobra – a microphone. When the chaps were out on their picnic, the whole place had been wired.'

The episode convinced the leftists that Lee, not yet in power, was preparing a dossier against them while publicly professing solidarity with them. It also showed the extent of Lee's collaboration with the colonial authorities.

At the time nothing of this was known to the public. The PAP was glamorous with its profoundly leftist image and Lee had clinched victory by steadfastly insisting on the release of leftist leaders as a pre-condition for responsible government. The party put up candidates in all the fifty-one constituencies: forty-three won landslide victories. The party received fifty-four per cent of the total votes cast.

The PAP was home but Lee Kuan Yew suddenly faced an unexpected obstacle. When the central executive council of the party met to choose a prime minister several members shocked Lee by showing a preference for Ong Eng Guan, the celebrated mayor.

Ong, an amazingly popular man, was an Australian-educated accountant. He was a non-communist and as such belonged to the Lee group in the PAP, but he was firmly identified with the Chinese stream in Singapore which made him essentially different from Lee and his close lieutenants. While other non-communist leading lights had to work as second strings to Lee, Ong was in a position to operate on his own. Alone among them, he enjoyed the elusive quality of charisma which put him in the same class, personally if not ideologically, with Lim Chin Siong.

It was Ong's appeal to the masses that made him the natural choice for mayor when the PAP won municipal elections in 1957. Chinese multitudes loved his childlike face and his extreme informality. He elevated to a fine art the classical politician's hand-shaking, baby-kissing routine. A colourful man, he became a legendary mayor. He had little political substance, no philosophy

of his own, but his ways were winning. On the day of his inaugu-
ration he set off fire crackers in front of the City Hall and was
arrested. To the delight of the people, he threw off the anglicized
symbols of office such as the wig, and chaired meetings in cotton
trousers and shorts. An American researcher, Willard A. Hanna,
called him 'a sort of PAP Huey Long' and said Ong 'shortcuts the
niceties by shouting at those who would prolong a discussion he
would rather see closed, favouring such succinct phrases as "shut
up", "sit down", "get out", or just "Blab, blab, blab, blab".'

Lee Kuan Yew had used Ong's popularity to the PAP's advantage. In fact, as Thomas Bellows noted, Ong was 'groomed to
project the type of appeal which would replace the attraction of
Lim Chin Siong after Lim's detention in 1956 – specifically, to
appeal to the non-English educated, China-oriented, more anti-
British strata of the population.' In other words, Lee's plan was to
use Ong's ability to attract strong communal loyalties and thereby
keep under leash those sections of the voters he and his Western-
oriented friends felt unable to reach.

Obviously Lee did not expect that Ong, propelled by his mass
popularity, would emerge as a challenge to his own leadership.

In the general election Ong won the highest popular vote of any
candidate – seventy-seven per cent. Still riding the crest of the
wave when party chiefs met to choose a leader, Ong received half
the votes of the executive members. Lee was saved this time by
his old friend Toh Chin Chye. It was reported that Toh voted
twice, first in the original vote leading to a tie, then again to
exercise his casting vote as chairman of the party.

Lee would make a note of Ong and take the first opportunity
to deal with him decisively. What mattered now was that he had
become, by the skin of his teeth, prime minister of Singapore.

An ordinary man would have taken a day off to relax and cele-
brate. For Lee Kuan Yew there was no let-up. He took his position as a matter of right. Driving his own two-tone Mercedes, he
went to Government House to meet the governor. Two years later
he was to tell a group of students: 'I was entrusted with leadership
some six years after I left the university and I became prime
minister some eleven years after I took my first degree at the
University of Cambridge. It is unheard of in other parts of the
world.'

In Singapore itself people seemed to have known what to
expect. Vernon Bartlett, the distinguished British journalist who

was then a columnist on the *Straits Times*, wrote in the midst of Lee's campaigning that 'Mr Lee Kuan Yew's attitude to press criticism is sinister'. On the eve of the election he referred to Lee's statement that the ultimate fight would be between the PAP and the communists and wrote that Lee 'cannot afford to imitate the anti-democratic methods of the communists'. Bartlett grossly underestimated Lee Kuan Yew.

So did Cassandra of the *Daily Mirror*, who likened Lee Kuan Yew to Goebbels. The *Daily Express* angrily editorialized: 'To such men Britain entrusts independence. Greedily they seize their new freedom for themselves and deny it to the people for whom it was intended.'

As the dogs barked, the caravan moved on.

One of the first things Lee did on becoming prime minister was to call his parents and brothers around him and tell them that from then on they should expect no special consideration from him, that they were entirely on their own as ordinary citizens of the state.

Prime Minister Lee Kuan Yew was setting his style.

CHAPTER FOUR

The Battle for the People's Minds

*Lee Kuan Yew has induced the British to imprison his more disloyal
supporters, publicly protesting against this violation of the rights of man.
He has used the Federation of Malaya to counter-balance the Singapore
trades unions. He has used the mob to intimidate the merchants and the
merchants to influence the Colonial Office. He illustrates perpetually
the principle that it is better to have two enemies than one.*

PROFESSOR NORTHCOTE PARKINSON, *A Law Unto Themselves*

Asian leaders coming out of colonialism into the first flush of
independence were usually inclined to lace the burdens of office
with its pleasures. Not the new men who took over Singapore.
They were cotton-shirts-and-trousers men, at their desks at eight
in the morning, sinking a third of their salaries in the party,
shunning pomp, graft and public-expense junkets abroad. They
were Lee Kuan Yew's ministers – accessible to the people,
champions of redress.

Unlike most other newly triumphant leaders, Lee never had a
'honeymoon' with his people. Setting an example in hard work,
thrift and dedication, he drove them hard from the very start. In
the first days of his administration he took executive decisions
which left no doubt about what Singapore could expect of him.
Civil servants' salaries were cut. Employers were threatened with
imprisonment if they 'frustrate Government's policy of industrial
peace'. Workers were given a similar warning. The university was
asked to cut academic salaries and protesters were attacked for
insubordination. Newspapers were told that anyone souring
relations between Singapore and Malaya 'will go in for subversion'. The *Straits Times* shifted headquarters to Kuala Lumpur.
The *Tiger Standard* closed. A virulent campaign was launched
against 'yellow culture', banning striptease shows and girly
cabarets with a view to 'eliminating sex-obsessed culture and all
activities which are detrimental to the growth of a healthy society

and culture'. On his first day in office eight 'yellow culture' publications were banned. Other chores on that first day were equally revealing: a two-hour inspection of security arrangements and a conference with the police commissioner and the director of Special Branch.

These were clear enough indications that Lee was not going to think twice about abridging democratic rights, and of his reasons for doing so. He has never taken such action for his personal advantage, but always because of his conviction that his plans for Singapore were valid and that Western-style democracy would only interfere with their implementation. Lee had, and has, ideals, and was not going to be one of those intellectual politicians who pursue them only to find themselves powerless to practise them. From the outset he believed in assuming all the power necessary to translate his ideals into reality.

Lee became an inveterate speaker, meeting groups of people one after another. He spoke to workers, business tycoons, University of Singapore graduates, Nanyang University students, law students, civil servants, English journalists, Chinese journalists, foreign correspondents, Muslims, Indians. His theme was constant: forget separate identities; think of Singapore; co-operate with Government.

Co-operation was not requested as a favour or canvassed as a recognition of merit. It was demanded as proof of patriotism. This was to be the hallmark of Lee Kuan Yew's premiership. He seemed convinced from the outset that anyone who opposed him was an enemy of Singapore.

Given this outlook, the elimination of opposition became an early preoccupation. In the first years of self-government, while Britain still retained political supervision, the game had to be played by the rules; but this was no problem, for Lee knew the rules better than his adversaries.

The first three years in office were full of booby traps. On several occasions the prime minister was on the point of being toppled. There were humiliating electoral reverses which left him crushed and despondent. What pulled him through these crises and ultimately fortified his position was a fortuitous set of circumstances. On the one hand, he enjoyed the unalloyed loyalty of the original Lee group in the PAP – Ton Chin Chye, Goh Keng Swee and Rajaratnam. On the other, his adversaries were to prove men of limited political expertise. Lee's political luck was that he never had to meet opponents of calibre. Even the pro-communists, some of whom were leaders of great talent, were in a state of confusion and diffidence until it was too late. Eventually he solved the problem by getting rid of them all one by one. Above all he received decisive help from Britain.

Lee had known all along that assumption of power would soon be followed by mortal combat with the communists. This he had prepared himself to face. But the first threat to face him did not come from the left wing of the PAP. It came from a man identified with his own moderate wing – Ong Eng Guan, now smarting under a sense of having been cheated out of the leadership by Lee and his cronies.

After Ong almost became prime minister in the leadership election, he was appointed minister of national development, but both Ong and Lee knew this was merely the first move in a power game. The sides were unevenly matched. Lee, now assessing the Ong character afresh, apparently decided that all he had to do was to give his colleague enough rope to hang himself. Ong, perhaps realizing the prime minister was out to get him, decided to strike first. He neglected his portfolio, tried independently to build up support at the lower levels of the party and, at a party conference in June 1960, fired his first salvo.

The PAP branch at Hong Lim, Ong's constituency, brought up sixteen resolutions to improve the party. The gist was that there was no democracy within the PAP, that the party was moving more and more towards the right and that it was being run by a ruling clique.

Ong was clearly staking a claim for leadership on the basis of his mass popularity. But he betrayed a lack of political instinct in the process, misjudged his support within the party's higher echelons and reckoned without his adversary's gift for manœuvre.

Lee decided to destroy Ong in a style that would set an example to other would-be challengers. At the party conference Chairman Toh Chin Chye refused to admit the resolutions, arguing that the issue at the moment was that the party's collective leadership had been challenged.

What followed was a discussion not on the sixteen resolutions but on Ong Eng Guan. The party's inner group argued that the resolutions were a plot by Ong to divert public attention from his own anti-party activities and his failure as mayor and minister. They accused him of slandering his colleagues, of building a personal empire in the party.

Evidently the inner group was following a concerted plan of action orchestrated by Lee. A historian of the party, Pang Cheng Lian, remarked: 'From the minutes of the meeting on 20 June 1960, it does appear that the subject of Ong's anti-party activities had been discussed before. At the party conference the leaders took the same line. . . . Apparently the leadership had come to the conclusion that the time had arrived to reveal the "blunders" of Ong to the public.'

The meeting was tense and action-packed. As one after another of Lee's supporters was called on to speak, Ong protested that the meeting was being converted into a trial; if he had known about this he would have come prepared with evidence in defence. He said secret police with guns had been posted in and around the meeting place to intimidate party men. 'This is not the first instance of cloak and dagger plots in the party and it will not be the last.'

What Ong called the 'pre-planned' character of the meeting prevented his getting support from anyone other than his own Hong Lim delegates. The leadership got the conference to endorse unanimously a recommendation to expel Ong. He was first suspended as national development minister, then officially dismissed from the party by the Central Executive Committee for 'attempts to disrupt party unity and destroy collective party leadership'. Two of the forty-two PAP Assembly men backed Ong and were promptly expelled from the party. The Hong Lim branch committee itself was suspended for putting up the rebellious resolutions.

Ong moved to the opposition side of the Assembly as an independent, but the fight was not over. Ong thought he could still fall back on mass support; Lee was not going to rest until Ong's destruction was complete.

Ong himself provided the setting for the next act in the drama. Defeated in the party, he took the fight to the Assembly. He levelled serious allegations against the PAP, charging the prime minister with nepotism. In December, six months after the party conference, Toh Chin Chye moved that the Assembly condemn Ong for 'dishonourable conduct'. The resolution said Ong 'repeatedly used his privilege in the Assembly as a cloak for spreading malicious falsehoods to injure unjustly innocent persons both inside and outside the Assembly'.

Seeing the noose tightening round his neck, Ong resigned from the Assembly on the eve of the special committee meeting to consider the charges against him. Lee would not let him escape that easily. He set up an inquiry commission and personally participated in its proceedings. The commission exonerated Lee and the government of all the charges levelled by Ong and strongly condemned Ong, describing him as a person not to be believed, and his allegations as untrue, groundless and reckless. The attempt was not merely to liquidate Ong politically but to expose him socially as well. Ong's private linen was ruthlessly washed in public and allegations were made that he was a bigamist and a liar.

This was something new in Singapore. In Chinese society one is expected to observe certain rules when fighting and always to leave an escape route for one's opponents. One must give one's enemy a chance to save face. The Chinese in Singapore seemed dumbfounded by the PAP leadership's 'utterly European' style of fighting.

This had its backlash when the Hong Lim by-election necessitated by Ong Eng Guan's resignation fell due in April 1961. It was a straight fight between Ong and the PAP's Jek Yuen Thong, a Chinese-educated activist who later became minister for culture. It turned out to be Singapore's most spectacular election campaign, spread over seven weeks. Lee Kuan Yew threw everything into the contest, seeing it as a test of whether he could survive more than one election. He received a windfall when the pro-communist forces decided for their own reasons to rally round the official candidate. The entire resources of Lee's establishment and of the pro-communist forces were thus pitted against one man.

The man triumphed. Ong Eng Guan did not simply win, he won with an incredible 73·3 per cent of the popular vote.

The scale of this victory dismayed Lee more than the victory itself. His immediate and characteristic reaction was to set about learning Hokkien, the dialect in which Ong Eng Guan had spoken to Hong Lim voters while he watched helplessly. (He also learned Mandarin, his ancestral Hakka still being unfamiliar to him.) But this doggedness did not conceal the bitterness of the defeat and Lee and his colleagues even considered resignation.

For Ong, though, it was a swan song. His victory vindicated him in his fight against Lee, but he seemed to have lost much of his political potency. Denied a proper party platform, he soon found himself reduced to a Hong Lim local chief. Four years later he resigned from the Assembly again because, the PAP alleged, some people connected with the government in Kuala Lumpur had promised him shares in a tin mine. Thereafter Ong gradually disappeared from public life.

The Ong episode once again showed that his opponents' miscalculations helped Lee Kuan Yew as much as his own prowess. If Ong had joined forces with the left-wing trade unionists in the PAP, Lee would have been ousted from the leadership. But Ong did not directly seek leftist support, hoping that some of his sixteen resolutions would automatically attract it. The leftists considered him an opportunist and decided to withhold their support. As some of them later said, the story of Singapore would have been different if Lim Chin Siong, instead of Ong Eng Guan, had brought up the resolutions. Even when Lee thought of resigning in the wake of the PAP's Hong Lim defeat, the leftists urged him to stay, for they were afraid the successor government would suppress them. They seemed to have had little inkling of what the Lee government itself had in store for them.

Quick to learn and to profit from experience, Lee did not waste too much time licking his Hong Lim wounds. One consolation he could derive was that his remaining adversaries within the party, the leftists, were even more discomfited than he. They thought if Hong Lim was a sign of popular rejection of the PAP government, they would be rejected too for being identified with it. Perhaps they should hitch their wagon to a mass hero like Ong? The left-wing leadership did not know which way to turn.

While this confusion among the leftists was a good augury for Lee, he himself saw a chance to squeeze some advantage out of the Hong Lim setback. This was to play on Ong Eng Guan's reputed support for the theory that an independent Singapore should emerge as a 'Third China'. Lee could use this to intensify his appeals to the leaders of Malaya and Britain for Singapore's merger into an independent Malaysia. That would give his government a great new political theme to pursue and, with luck, a chance to take on successfully the PAP pro-communists whose position on merger was full of contradictions.

Lee lost no time in adopting this line of policy. His argument was that if proponents of an independent Singapore were allowed to gain strength, the island would become a pawn in the hands of communists and neither Malaya nor Britain would be able to meet the security threat that would follow. It was a taste of the Lee dogma soon to become part of the Singapore way of life.

At the height of the Malayan emergency, it clicked. A month after Ong Eng Guan's triumph, Malaya's Tunku Abdul Rahman made a speech in Singapore in which he proposed a Federation of Malaysia comprising Malaya, Singapore, Sabah, Sarawak and Brunei. The Tunku was probably influenced by the Lee government's threat to resign, and its warning that its place would be taken by an extreme left-wing group. 'I don't want a damn Cuba at my feet,' he told an interviewer.

It was the first time Malaya had responded favourably to an idea Lee Kuan Yew had assiduously plugged for many years. The inclusion of Sabah, Sarawak and Brunei in the scheme changed the perspective significantly; nevertheless, it must have been a moment of great satisfaction for Lee. Historically it promised the removal of the last vestige of colonial rule. In terms of power politics, he could now take the first opportunity to tighten the screws on the pro-communists.

The opportunity came unexpectedly with the sudden death of the PAP Assemblyman from Anson. As preparations were made for the by-election, Lee decided to take full advantage of the merger issue which he was convinced was popular with the people. It followed that he could also challenge his pro-communist adversaries to a trial of strength. It was a cardinal principle of Lee's politics to provoke political confrontations on issues of his choice at historical moments of his choice and, calling the shots, to benefit from the confusion and tensions in his adversaries' ranks. In this art of manipulation he was unrivalled then, as now. Having worked closely with the pro-communists for a decade, he chose the Anson by-election as the moment of confrontation.

As Lee no doubt intended, it caught the pro-communists off guard. Anson had followed close on the heels of Hong Lim and the leftists were in no position to put up an independent show. Nor could they join hands with Ong Eng Guan, who seemed strangely uninterested in striking while the iron was still hot. Reluctantly they once again cast their lot with the PAP leadership and faced Anson. That was when Lee decided to isolate them.

He based his strategy on the leftists' fears about the merger scheme. Unity of Malaya and Singapore had always been an article of faith with the leftists, but Tunku Abdul Rahman's sudden espousal of the cause and the attendant circumstances created by the security bogy made them extremely suspicious. They saw Lee Kuan Yew and the Malayan leaders combining to 'wipe out the left-wing forces in Singapore and thus save the PAP leadership from being defeated in the next elections'. They were clearly afraid that a government in Kuala Lumpur would be more repressive than a government led by the PAP of which they were a part.

Lee skilfully played on these fears. He simply kept the leftists in the dark about the merger discussions he as prime minister was holding with Malaya. He let them suspect the worst – that internal security in the federal set-up would be in the hands of the central government in Kuala Lumpur. Lee evidently was forcing the leftists to break with the official party line and adopt an anti-merger position which would contradict their own earlier stand and thereby confuse their ranks.

Coincidentally or otherwise, British policy once again seemingly ran parallel to Lee Kuan Yew's. As Lee later related the story for public consumption, it was a big British plot to subvert the PAP. He said the British lion was up to all kinds of mischief in the official residence of the British High Commissioner in Singapore. He described how his detectives had discovered leading pro-communist office-bearers of the PAP going into the British residence for 'wining and dining'. In fact, it took no detectives to discover the meetings Lim Chin Siong and his colleagues held with the British High Commissioner, for their faces were well known in Singapore and they went in to the residence through the front gate, in daylight.

Sandra Woodhull, one of the participants in the talks, recalled that the meetings with the British High Commissioner were the result of a 'friendly warning' by Lee to his leftist colleagues that if they pressed demands for self-government on their terms he would resign and then the British would wipe out the entire left group. Lee said, according to Woodhull, that the British had told him so themselves. The leftists saw this as a critical situation and were inclined to withdraw from party politics altogether if such indeed were the British plan. But they decided to ascertain the truth from the High Commissioner personally, hence the 'wining and dining'. Woodhull remembered the High Commissioner telling them that his job, as Her Majesty's representative, was to ensure they carried on their activities peacefully; he would inter-vene only if there was any threat to life and limb.

Lee touched it up with a conspiratorial flourish when he gave his own account of the meetings later. According to him, Lim Chin Siong and his friends were led to believe that if they obtained power by constitutional means, so long as the military bases were left untouched, the British would be quite happy to let them run the island.

In arranging the meetings, perhaps the British had their own objective: gauging leftist thinking and finding out who exactly would stand up and be counted with them in a crisis. Always suspicious, Lee obviously resented the direct contacts between the leftists and the British, but the net result was a tactical gain for him. The talks had the effect of encouraging the leftists to go their own way, thereby facilitating Lee's own efforts to isolate them and force a showdown.

Frustrated by Lee's non-co-operation, concerned at the pros-pects of Kuala Lumpur queering the pitch for them, and en-couraged by British assurances of constitutional propriety in treating with them, the pro-communist leaders finally made up their minds to break with Lee.

Their disenchantment with him had been growing steadily ever since he became prime minister. Many of their colleagues, imprisoned by the previous Lim Yew Hock government, were still behind bars despite Lee's pre-election pledge to release them. Others, though released, had been deprived of their citizenship under a new bill Lee pushed through. At the same time, the Lee government had refused to unify the trade union movement while the PAP was trying to set up its own trade union hegemony in opposition to the leftists. The government was also thought to be unduly restrictive in its policy towards Chinese education. The last straw for the pro-communists was the Lee-Tunku 'collusion' on merger.

Hardly realizing that this was a straw deliberately chosen by Lee himself, the leftist forces suddenly stopped supporting the official PAP candidate in the Anson by-election. As a PAP spokesman put it, seventy to eighty per cent of party workers 'just laid down their tools and left the place' half way through the campaign, though they did not yet quit the party.

Lee achieved his objective of forcing the pro-communists to defy the party. But, as in Hong Lim, his basic calculation went wrong. The supposed popularity of the merger issue was not enough to carry the PAP to victory. The leftists proved conclusively that without their backing the PAP had little electoral appeal. On election day – July 15, 1961 – the official candidate, a former bus conductor named Mahmud bin Awang, received barely thirty-seven per cent of the popular vote. The victor was David Marshall who had received the tacit support of the leftists at the eleventh hour.

Two major defeats in three months: the fortunes of Lee Kuan Yew and his PAP had reached their nadir. The Anson débâcle was particularly galling, first because Lee had fought it on the issue of Singapore's merger with Malaya; second because he had deliberately chosen to break with his pro-communist colleagues; third, because he had hinted that a defeat at Anson would make his continuance in office amoral. On the eve of the by-election the official party organ had recalled the Hong Lim verdict and written that 'a democratic government, whether good or bad, which has lost its moral authority to rule, cannot in the long run be effective. The primary aim [in Anson] is to satisfy ourselves that by and large we have the people's approval.'

When Anson proved otherwise, Lee adroitly changed tactics. The line now was that 'we are resolved not to abdicate our position in order that the party and the government does not pass into the hands of people who intend to use it for purposes for which the people did not vote the PAP in'.

Morality was a fine thing, but Lee knew that even a temporary fall from the seat of power could be politically fatal to him in the circumstances that developed after 1959. He sat fast – through Hong Lim, Anson and all – until the system reached a stage where it was unable to unseat him.

Following the Anson defeat, Lee decided to take the intra-party feud over merger into the Assembly. The leftists could have forced the issue in the party forum where they enjoyed the support of a vast majority of the branch committees. By contrast, Lee could be sure of majority support in the Assembly. It was Lee who had the sagacity to see this and take the offensive.

He was after more than a favourable vote in the Assembly. He wanted to create public mistrust and fear of the leftists so that he could move massively against them when the time came. He opened the debate with the 'bombshell' accusation that the British government was plotting with the pro-communists to overthrow the PAP government. Simultaneously Toh Chin Chye gave a sop to public sentiment by announcing that the remaining detainees would be released in batches. Also released was a purportedly secret document showing that Lim Chin Siong was a communist front man.

These moves had the effect of sensationalizing Lee's crusade against the leftists. With his penchant for seeing himself in perennial combat with conspirators, Lee was in great form. He made great play with dark hints of a 'plen' (a characteristic Lee coinage for plenipotentiary) pushing a sinister Peking plot in Singapore. He gave dramatic blow by blow accounts of subversive plots and of communist agents and British secret service men behind every bush in Singapore. He never stopped to think of the absurdity of suggesting that Britain would seriously consider handing Singapore over to communists on a platter.

Nor did his party men. In the fifty-one-member Assembly twenty-seven voted for the government's action. The significance of the voting lay not so much in Lee's victory as in the fact that his plans to isolate the leftists could now move on to their logical finale. Having disagreed with the official PAP line in the Anson by-election, they could not support the government in the confidence motion though they were still sitting on government benches. Thirteen men, including the core of the leftist faction in the PAP, abstained.

It was the first formal break between Lee and the men who had given him political muscle during his climb to power. Now they were out of the PAP fold for good. Now Lee could clear the deck for a great crackdown and the final consolidation of his power.

At the moment of defection the leftists convincingly demonstrated their strength. On July 26, 1961, they formed a new party called Barisan Sosialis with Lim Chin Siong as secretary-general. A virtual landslide in favour of the new party followed. As much as seventy per cent of the PAP's rank and file membership left the party to join the Barisan. Control of almost all PAP branches fell into Barisan hands. In the PAP headquarters only three or four staffmen remained, some thirty joining Barisan. What was left of the PAP was less than a skeleton. But that did not bother Lee Kuan Yew. He had a more effective organization at his disposal – the government.

In the months that followed, the line dividing the party and the government became invisible. The cadre character of the party was jealously preserved, but functions normally carried out by organizations began to be performed by government departments. After the 1961 split with the leftists, Lee's PAP never even attempted to become a popular political party in any realistic sense of the term. Lee needed no such party.

It was different for Lim Chin Siong and his Barisan colleagues. The least of their problems was to explain why they had helped prop up Lee all this long time. In a letter published in the press immediately after Barisan's formation, Lim said 'once and for all' that he was neither a communist nor anybody's front man. He charged that Lee was trying to isolate him (Lim) from his colleagues by smearing him as a front man on the one hand and, on the other, asking him to join the government as parliamentary secretary to show the people that he was identified with the Lee government. 'Having denied me any participation in the party and government, I was still to be used as political secretary to give the impression that the workers and government were one.'

Lim said such a deception could not go on for long. But he hardly seemed to realize it had already gone on too long. It was Lee, after using Lim and other leftists shrewdly, who had cut them loose. He now had executive power to use against the leftists in addition to his proven superiority over them as a tactician.

It soon became clear that the Barisan's only strength was its mass popularity; at the leadership level it lacked both experience and shrewdness. One of the founders said 'the story after the formation of the Barisan is a story of our retreat'. As the party lost itself in the constitutional labyrinths of the merger move it showed up inconsistencies which the alert prime minister was quick to exploit to the hilt. At the same time Lee projected an image of profound consistency, fortifying it with effective governmental performance. The Barisan's only hope was to wait till the next general election, due in 1964, and see if its mass appeal could be converted into power.

But Lee Kuan Yew had other plans. His advantage of the moment was the vote of confidence he had won in the Assembly. It was necessary to press home this advantage. The PAP leadership thought of a referendum on the issue of merger. When Malaya and Britain made a joint announcement that the Federation of Malaysia would be formed in August 1963, Lee decided it had to be now or never. He fixed September 1, 1962, as the date of the referendum.

The publicity campaign that followed took Singapore by storm. Ministers and assemblymen held nightly public meetings to explain the importance of merger. Lee himself gave a celebrated series of twelve radio talks in less than a month, revealing dramatic encounters with communist agents, details of the communist underground, the PAP's internal feuds. It was, as he repeatedly stressed, a battle for the people's minds, an open argument of who was right and who was wrong. And in large measure that *was* what it was – with the important qualification that the means of mass communication were confined to one side. Most of the press had already been tamed and the radio was a limb of the government. Only the PAP possessed weapons with which to fight battles for the people's minds.

Even so, both Malaya and Britain were upset by Lee's decision to hold a referendum, for they feared the heavy Chinese majority in Singapore might repeat the Hong Lim pattern and vote against any suggestion that they merge with the Malays.

In the end the Chinese didn't have a chance. Lee had learned his lessons from Hong Lim and Anson and had no intention of allowing the ballot box to stand again between him and his objectives.

What transpired was not a referendum in the usual democratic sense of the term; not quite cricket, as a PAP leader later put it. Lee confronted voters with three choices which, cleverly, fused into just one proposition. The choices: merger under the terms of a Singapore government white paper giving Singapore autonomy in education and labour; merger which would give Singapore the same status and citizenship provisions as the component states of Malaysia; merger on no less favourable terms than those given to the Borneo territories.

The proposition, it turned out, was not after all to be 'merger or no merger'. Of the three choices, the third was automatically ruled out since the terms for Borneo had not yet been worked out. The second was essentially the same as the first. Singaporeans were simply being told to vote for the government white paper.

And voting was mandatory. Those who disagreed with the government had only one alternative: to record blank votes – and Lee said all blank votes would be counted as votes for the government. Further, as the Barisan alleged, 'through an organized whisper campaign the PAP passed the word round that all those who cast blank votes would be found out by the government later and they would get themselves into trouble'. This allegation rested on the fact that a system of numbering ballot papers and retaining them for a period of six months after polling day made it theoretically possible for the government to trace how each citizen voted. On no occasion has the government been known to resort to this underhand method, but the mere existence of the possibility was enough to spread among the electorate a sense of intimidation. This has continued all through the Lee years, the secrecy of the ballot remaining suspect among a people constantly worried about attracting the displeasure of the government.

In the event the government, of course, had a walkover in the referendum. Of the 417,482 marked votes, 397,626 favoured the white paper. But Lee was incensed by the discovery that as many as 144,077 people dared to cast blank votes despite his warnings. He forthwith jailed 133 people – political workers, university activists, journalists, public men – who had through the limited constitutional methods open to them opposed the idea of merger. Some of them are still in jail, though merger itself is dead. Both the conduct of the referendum and the repression that followed showed that after two years in office Lee was now ready openly to discard democratic niceties to get things done his way.

This is a process hard to stop, once it has been begun. In the days when Lee was in opposition, in 1956, he himself gave a vivid description of it. 'I'm told it is like making love – it's always easier the second time. The first time there may be pangs of conscience, a sense of guilt. But once embarked on this course, with constant repetition, you get more and more brazen in the attack and in scope of the attack.' He became, and has remained, a striking example of what he was then condemning.

Lee bided his time to use executive powers for the suppression of Barisan leadership as a whole. And with good reason. During the no-confidence debate and his famous series of broadcasts in 1961 he frankly explained why he did not 'deal firmly' with Lim Chin Siong and other pro-communist stalwarts. It was not because summary arrests were undemocratic or detention without trial repugnant to the Rule of Law. It was because to detain political opponents when Britain still held ultimate power in Singapore would be to attract the odium of acting as Britain's stooge. The previous Lim Yew Hock government had done just that and had failed in the eyes of the people.

Lee might also have thought the leftists were trying to create

3

precisely such a situation. 'So long as British power is supreme in Singapore,' he said, 'in any conflict between armed communists and armed colonialists we must opt out. Violence and unrest which the communists can well mount on a scale that will require the intervention of British troops and the taking over of command by a British general must mean that we abdicate, otherwise we can be labelled stooges of a colonial regime.'

The success of the referendum, such as it was, shored up Lee's confidence. The Hong Lim and Anson humiliations were forgotten. The hectic publicity campaign preceding the referendum had made for a highly charged atmosphere and the arrests of the anti-merger activists had given him the first real opportunity to draw blood. Now he was itching for action. Three days after the referendum Lee went on radio and said: 'Before September 1st, firmness would have been misrepresented as fascist repression. After September 1st, I'm sure you will want me to do what is right for the security and well-being of all in Singapore and Malaysia.' He had obviously concluded that he could not wait until Britain relinquished ultimate power in Singapore.

His mind made up, Lee started by advancing the general election to September 1963. He might have calculated that Malaysia would be formed in August of that year as announced, and an election immediately after it would be best for the PAP. In fact Malaysia was proclaimed in September and the election took place four days later.

The experience of the referendum also emboldened Lee to repeat the tactic of denying the opposition a sporting chance to campaign. If anything, Lee could less afford to take chances in this election than in the referendum, for this was the first time he would be openly fighting these same leftist forces which had swept him to victory in previous elections. It was going to be a straight fight between the PAP and the Barisan. This was no time for democratic nonsense. This was a time for consolidation of power. Already, in 1960, he had declared in the Assembly that 'all this talk of democratic rights, laissez-faire liberalism, freedom and human rights, in the face of the stark realities of an underground struggle for power, can only confuse the English-educated world'. He was not one to add to that confusion.

In this frame of mind the prime minister laid down the ground rules for the 1963 election which had the cumulative effect of not only reducing the Barisan to impotence, but also of quickly leading to the eclipse of the parliamentary party system itself. Official campaigning was to be limited to the constitutional minimum of nine days. This effectively tied up the opposition. To make things double sure, the government ordered festivities during the nine-day period to mark the proclamation of Malaysia. This reduced electioneering days available to the opposition to four and a half days.

The PAP was above these restraining factors. In his capacity as prime minister, Lee Kuan Yew began, as early as November 1962, a tour of Singapore's constituencies. The ostensible reason was 'to ensure that performance of the Singapore government is kept up to the best possible level of achievement', but everyone knew they were political expeditions. Lee covered all fifty-one constituencies while the Barisan Sosialis was barred by the election law from doing anything of the kind.

There were other practical electioneering techniques brought into play. Almost all printing facilities in Singapore were blocked with government orders connected with the celebration of Malaysia Day. The opposition found it impossible to get any election literature printed, while the PAP, tipped off in time, was able to get its own literature neatly printed in Hong Kong three months ahead. Blocked too were nearly all public squares and halls where Barisan could hold election meetings. When Barisan asked for the necessary police permission to put up election banners, the usually efficient government suddenly became red-tape conscious.

Preparations did not end there. 'Unofficial' pressure was put on the Barisan printer to cease publication of the party organ, *Plebeian*. Three days before nomination day the Registrar of Trade Unions ordered the freezing of the bank accounts of the three largest Barisan unions. Later two of its most popular ancillary organizations, the Singapore Rural Residents' Association and the Singapore Country People's Association, were to be dissolved by government order. A year earlier the government had asked employers to dismiss nearly four hundred key Barisan trade union cadres. It was, as a Barisan leader put it, like tying up the opponent's hands and legs and putting him in the ring to box according to the rules of the sport.

Even Lee's erstwhile enemy Ong Eng Guan came in handy. Politically liquidated by Lee's sustained tirade, he had formed the United People's Party as a personal platform. His national significance had vanished, but he still enjoyed enough support in Hong Lim to be able to split leftist votes. Under unknown pressures, the United People's Party refused any electoral pact with the Barisan and went its own way. Pang Cheng Lian wrote in her dissertation on the PAP that 'rumour was rife that Ong had gone to Japan and received money from the Americans to split the left-wing votes and thus prevent a Barisan victory'.

Rumour is a familiar weapon at election time in Singapore. Its efficacy is extraordinary because it often smacks of official parentage. In the 1963 election the rumour that proved perhaps the most effective was that a Barisan victory would bring in Federal troops and that Kuala Lumpur would then rule Singapore.

With all these insurance measures, Lee still did not underestimate the Barisan's voter-appeal. He had seen too much of it to be complacent and he could not afford to make a mistake this time. So, early enough in election year, he administered the *coup de grâce* by imprisoning all opposition leaders of any potential. In the wee hours of February 2nd, the government launched the aptly named Operation Cold Store and more than a hundred men found themselves suddenly in jail. Among them were leaders of the Singapore Association of Trade Unions, Nanyang University and Rural and Country People's Associations.

In this operation the important figures, of course, were the Barisan's Lim Chin Siong, Fong Swee Suan, Sandra Woodhull and James Puthucheary. With them put away the Barisan became a headless body. Lee Kuan Yew had come into his own.

Back in 1959, when Lee was making his first bid for power, Lim Chin Siong and other leftist leaders were in jail by courtesy of Britain. Their physical absence had made Lee rival-less while their mass popularity had brought him votes. Lee had personally told Lim of his reservations about the leftists and Lim had offered to banish himself to Indonesia.

When Lee insisted on Lim and his seven trade union associates being released before the PAP would take office, he probably had his line of action already mapped out in his mind. Publicly he sought credit for playing fair by his colleagues, claiming repeatedly that he had not betrayed the pro-communists, that it was his action which had brought them out of jail. But the released men had been persistently watched and rigorously harnessed as second-class citizens. Before their release Lee had made them sign a political manifesto categorically pledging support to the PAP, yet they were barred from becoming cadre members. They were also denied citizenship papers. They were placed as political secretaries in the various ministries, but denied access to important papers so that they could do no 'harm'. From the outset Lee acted in the full knowledge that one day soon he would have to take them in and keep them there. Now Operation Cold Store achieved just that. It was a more reliable solution than letting Lim Chin Siong go in freedom to Indonesia.

Unseen, unheard, denied trial or the right of appeal, Lim was to stay in Changhi jail for seven years. His morale shattered by solitary confinement, this once brilliant man was to come near to suicide. Political insiders in Singapore and Kuala Lumpur were to claim that Lim was fed drugs which induced depression and self-destructive tendencies. Finally he was to write an abject letter of apology and beg his old comrade-in-arms for mercy. In 1969, reduced to a vegetable, Lim was to be released, after his letter of recantation and apology had been given full publicity. He was to be taken from Changhi prison straight to England, in utmost secrecy, and there allowed 'to continue his studies', presumably under surveillance.

When the axe fell in 1963, Lim was not unprepared. The tough mood displayed by the prime minister in the wake of the referendum had alerted the Barisan. In Singapore and Malaya as a whole, tension had arisen following government allegations that an elaborate *coup* was being planned by rebels. This was based on the adventurist dream of A. M. Azahari who thought he could seize power in Brunei. Azahari's bubble burst as soon as he declared himself prime minister from the sanctuary of the Philippines, but the general tension generated by the episode gave Lee the opportunity he was waiting for. He alleged that Lim and his associates were conspiring to organize an uprising in Singapore to coincide with the Azahari rebellion in Brunei.

Action was taken against the opposition in Sarawak and Malaya in December 1962, and Barisan knew its turn would be next. Leading cadres began to sleep in different places each night. Lim Chin Siong and other leaders made a habit of going to late cinema shows on Saturdays, for they knew police raids usually came in the small hours of Sundays.

The British-trained intelligence network in Singapore – one colonial organization which Lee Kuan Yew has preserved in all its pristine efficiency – was equal to the task. It kept track of the different places where cadres slept at nights, their movements during the day, their habits. Surveillance was thorough. In dead secrecy Operation Cold Store was mounted from Johore. Lim Chin Siong and other top leaders were caught in the drag-net. But the Barisan's precautions were not totally useless; many middle- and lower-echelon cadres escaped arrest.

With all holes blocked, Lee expected the election to be a foregone conclusion. Yet the PAP received only 46·9 per cent of the popular vote though it amounted to thirty-seven seats in the fifty-one-member Assembly. Headless, denied campaigning facilities, the Barisan won 33·3 per cent of the popular vote, amounting to thirteen seats. If the contest had been on fairer terms, it was estimated that the Barisan would have won between twenty-one and twenty-seven seats.

By now democratic norms were not even of academic interest to Lee Kuan Yew. Convinced that he alone was capable of leading Singapore correctly, his objective was to make the PAP invulnerable to assaults from the hustings. This was achieved through the election techniques he devised and the incarceration of opposition leaders. The 1963 election was the last significant attempt by opposition parties to challenge the PAP through constitutional means. After that the Lee techniques did not give anybody any chance. The present chairman of the Barisan, Dr Lee Siew Choh, summed up these techniques in an apt phrase: 'Legal fixing'. In subsequent elections Lee would get embarrassing 99·9 per cent majorities and not a single opposition member would be seen in the Assembly. Lee would profess injured innocence and publicly bemoan the absence of men who could oppose the government responsibly.

Barisan's own mistakes helped the decline of the opposition. It depended exclusively on its trade union base. It made no real inroads into the English-educated classes. Identified with extremist policies, it did not attract support from the middle class and the moderates. It tended towards 'tailism' as opposed to the 'commandism' Lee preferred. It failed to employ sophisticated methods of party penetration in which Lee excelled. Above all, in Woodhull's words, 'we under-estimated the British. They would never tolerate a left-wing government. They foisted Lee up. Lee knew everything was on his side.'

Barisan's weaknesses were only one element contributing to the PAP's emergence as Singapore's dominant party. Another important factor was the integrity and efficiency of Lee Kuan Yew's administration. In performance no one could fault the government. Lee's method of mobilizing popular loyalty was not through conventional party organisation but through providing a palpably achievement-orientated government. He sought to create legitimacy through prolonged effectiveness.

The question remained whether high performance alone could have given him invulnerability. A leader more steadfast to the principles of socialism and democracy learned in the best English tradition might at least have given the possibility a fair trial. But Lee obviously thought otherwise, hence the free employment of authoritarian methods to eliminate all opposition. In Lee's reckoning no one else in Singapore was, or could be, right. What he achieved in the process was a one-man party and a one-party state.

Consolidation was complete. It was barely four years since Lee became prime minister. Singapore was not yet the sovereign republic it was to become. But already Lee Kuan Yew's was the kingdom, the power and the glory.

CHAPTER FIVE

Marriage and Divorce

He is a little like the small man who makes a lot of noise to divert your attention from his sixty-two inches.

RONALD MCKIE, *Malaysia in Focus*

The taming of the opposition in Singapore moved to a climax in September 1963, along with Lee Kuan Yew's wider plans for a finger in the Malaysian pie. Lesser men might have hesitated before embarking on two complex manœuvres at once. But Lee flourished in crises. Besides, merger with Malaysia was an integral part of his elaborate scheme for the consolidation of his power base. The lasting achievement of the Malaysia episode, nightmarish as it was to everyone else in the game, was that it brought sovereignty to Singapore on the one hand and consolidated the PAP's position on the other.

More than any other episode, the Malaysia interlude highlighted Lee's genius at provoking a crisis and profiting from the tension generated. From beginning to end Malaysia was pure politics – and Lee the master craftsman. It was the high-water mark of Lee's evolution as boss of Singapore.

Many reasons have been adduced for Lee's deep interest in the merger of Singapore and Malaya. The one most widely promulgated – that he wanted to be prime minister of a regular-sized country rather than of a mere city – is too simple to be the whole truth. Whereas the persistence with which he denigrated leaders of Malaya even before the merger went through lends some credibility to the theory that Lee was pushing the merger idea only as a means to the end of achieving sovereignty for Singapore. According to this theory, it was a heads-I-win-tails-you-lose proposition: if merger brought only the independence of Singapore it was gain enough; if it somehow ended by propelling the PAP to the top of the heap it would be a still bigger gain. As always, Lee was smartly keeping open more than one option.

The objective of outsmarting the British was important. It was known that Britain was inclined to want Singapore independent only if its internal security was enmeshed with that of the larger whole of Malaysia. Otherwise, it was considered best to retain Singapore as a British military base; when merger collapsed in 1965, Lee was momentarily afraid that the British would resurrect this plan and retake Singapore. In the light of these fears 'independence through merger' was more than a slogan for Lee. During the 1962 referendum the PAP's most telling argument was that 'the alternative to immediate Malaysia is the continuance of British rule'.

But it would be wrong to suggest that cynical considerations alone influenced Lee in his Malaysia policy. There was substance in his argument that if Singapore was left outside the Federation it would grow into a communist bastion, a Cuba of the South China Sea. He believed that colonial territories lingering in a state of semi-independence were grist to the communist mill. He said 'the only chance of survival and success is to unite the one strong and potent force that will overcome both communists and the British, namely Malayan nationalism'.

It is true that Singapore was a very important element in the revolutionary calculations of the Malayan Communist Party. But the weakness in Lee's building the party up into a bogy was that he was ignoring his own capacity and plans to take care of the communist threat. In fact, his programme for the containment of communists was already nearly complete by the time Malaysia was proclaimed. The prospect of a 'Cuba' off the Malay peninsula was the primary reason for Kuala Lumpur's acceptance of the merger idea. Once this threat vanished due to Lee's own handling, Malayan interest also diminished. This Malayan feeling that it was no longer necessary from the security point of view to prolong merger with Singapore was a key factor in the dissolution of the marriage two years after it was contracted.

Undoubtedly Lee was intellectually satisfied that, though politically apart, Singapore and Malaya were socio-economically inseparable. In the early stages of his career he believed that Malay peasants, not Chinese traders, held the key to socialism in Malaysia. He saw Singapore as just another urban concentration in the peninsular region while progress and development could come only on a regional basis. He always remembered that 80,000 British troops in Singapore had to surrender ten days after the

Japanese captured the water supply in Johore. When he repeatedly said, during his campaign for Malaysia, that merger was as 'inevitable as the rising and setting of the sun' he was clearly alluding to the economic interdependence of the two territories. Lee was practical enough to recognize Singapore's need for a hinterland and conscious of the ephemeral character of what he called 'our shop window economy'.

After the end of merger Lee rose to the occasion and made a success of Singapore's economy, developing an independent industrial base and conceiving Singapore as a global city with the world as its hinterland. This was a tribute to his administrative leadership. But, for all their mutual antipathies, both Singapore and Malaysia carefully avoided any move that would seriously hurt each other's economy. Each was aware of its need of the other. Lee was justified in first describing the idea of an independent Singapore as 'a political, economic and geographic absurdity'. It was his innovative leadership that transformed an absurdity into a possibility.

In the end, however, valid socio-economic arguments mattered little. What clinched Malaysia was Lee's lurid painting of a communist dragon with its head firmly planted in Singapore and its vicious long tail about to whack Malaya and the rest of Southeast Asia. As his Assembly speeches and radio exposés rose to a crescendo of bogy-building, goose pimples grew in Whitehall as well as in Kuala Lumpur. The referendum came as a *coup de grâce*. Shotguns blazed, but so did statistics enabling Lee to proclaim that merger was Singapore's collective tryst with destiny. Fifteen days after the referendum Singapore was precisely where Lee wanted it – in the Federation of Malaysia.

Never was there a more tumultuous political marriage – the wonder was that it held for twenty-three months. Lee Kuan Yew did not even change his title of prime minister, indicating that he wanted Malaysia to adjust itself to him rather than he to it. It was his aggressive tactics that had made Kuala Lumpur initially resist, then accept, merger, and which finally made it abhorrent to his thoroughly confused partner.

Malaya's nationalist leaders had already worked out their own neat formula for communal co-operation. Under the benign leadership of Tunku Abdul Rahman, the United Malay National Organization (UMNO), the Malayan Chinese Association (MCA) and the Malayan Indian Congress (MIC) had come together under the umbrella of an Alliance which would rule Malaya for a long while. UMNO suspicions of the PAP had begun early. In the Singapore City Council elections of 1957 the two parties had collaborated and immediately after the PAP victory, Chairman Toh Chin Chye had announced a proposal for the PAP to join UMNO. But UMNO immediately said any coalition between the two parties was unimaginable. As UMNO saw it, the PAP was a predominantly Chinese party and, under Lee Kuan Yew's radical stance of the day, was championing the cause of Singapore's militant chauvinistic Chinese middle-school students. Worst of all, the PAP's official party organ, *Petri*, was carrying in its Chinese edition anti-Alliance articles which its English edition omitted – no doubt with Lee's knowledge if not under his guidance.

As Lee Kuan Yew's campaign for merger gathered momentum, these UMNO suspicions grew. A curious feature of the Malaysia interregnum was that Lee, personally above racialism, often sounded in his speeches like a champion of Chinese nationalism. A definite outcome of his actions and attitudes at that time was the inflammation of racial emotions to such an extent that the first racial riots in the history of Singapore broke out in 1964, a year after Malaysia was formed. Lee blamed it on Malay extremists, but the record shows that the grist for the extremists' mills was often supplied by Singapore.

Many of the speeches Lee was then making offer examples. As late as in September 1963, with only days left for the official proclamation of Malaysia, he was ridiculing leaders of Malaya by saying power had been handed to them 'on a silver platter with red ribbons by British Royalty in uniforms'. The Malayans, naturally, were deeply offended and UMNO's secretary-general prophesied: 'If this be the attitude of our new friends who join the Malaysia family ... I am afraid that we will face more difficulties and problems.'

The Malays also found some of Lee's general theories unacceptable and provocative. He propounded, for example, that no one of the three major racial groups in Malaysia – Malays, Chinese or Indians – could claim to be more native to Malaysia than the other two, for all their ancestors had come to the region not more than a thousand years ago. This was an obvious rejection of the fact that Malaya, after all, had become the home of the Malays; that its very name indicated the special position of the Malays in comparison with that of the Chinese and Indians, who had their own countries to their names. Lee was out to establish that the Malays were on a par with the Chinese and Indian immigrants.

If it had been the Malays and their UMNO alone who were annoyed by Lee's denigration, his repeated assertions that Malayan opposition to Singapore stemmed from racial considerations might have appeared justified. In fact the MCA was even more stridently anti-Lee.

This was due mainly to Lee's ill-concealed attempts in the initial stages to get the PAP to replace the MCA as representing the Chinese in the Alliance – again a curious objective for an anti-racial leader and a non-communal party. Lee reserved his harshest phrases for MCA leaders. In his most notorious attack, he described them as political eunuchs. He called them greedy and inept and said they were expendable. No wonder those Malaysians who personally hated Lee the most were to be found in the top echelons of MCA leadership.

In addition the MCA probably suffered from an inferiority complex before Lee. None of its leaders came anywhere near him in political savvy. They had necessarily to play second fiddle to UMNO in Malaya while the PAP was supreme in Singapore. Jealousy probably combined with fear to make the MCA extremely resentful of the PAP – and UMNO, too, was evidently afraid of the PAP's potential. With its proven efficiency and thoroughness, the PAP could dent the Alliance in the long run. If PAP representatives were given ministries in the Federal government, they could use them to establish an effective party infrastructure in the peninsula. In time the PAP's socio-economic appeals, backed by its exemplary performance record in Singapore, might even win over peninsular Malays. UMNO, comfortably ensconced in its easy-going Alliance set-up, had every reason to be suspicious of the aggressive, modernistic thrust of the PAP.

Lee seemed unconcerned about UMNO suspicions as well as MCA resentment. All through the Malaysia years of 1964 and 1965 he was crusading like a man on fire. Relentlessly he pursued the aim of getting the PAP accepted as a partner in the Alliance government in Kuala Lumpur, be it as a replacement for the MCA, or on the basis of federal elections, or even as insurance for communal peace.

Lee's speeches harped endlessly upon the dangers of communalism, the need to curb 'ultras', even to restrict liberties in order to ensure multiracialism. Obviously these appeals were high-minded and sensible, but Lee laid it on so thick and made it so aggressive a campaign that the practical impact was exactly the opposite. He spread an atmosphere of impending catastrophe. The sheer emphasis he placed on the dangers of racialism turned people's minds in that direction. Steadily a deep communal consciousness was generated among the masses on both sides of the causeway, and *Utusan Melayu*, the often extremist mouthpiece of Malay nationalism, called Lee 'the father of communalism without parallel in Malaysia'.

Even the benign Tunku was disturbed. In one of his rare moments of bluntness he told a public rally in Kuala Lumpur in January 1965 of some politicians 'whose minds are obviously distorted, polluted. Their thoughts and talk appear to be so. They talk of Malaysia with gloomy forebodings. They talk of strife and strain, of trouble and bloodshed ahead, they talk of war, they talk of calamities. They strike fear and despondency in the hearts of men who hear them, though with their high office, they should be talking of peace and happiness. . . . I say shame on them.'

For the soft-spoken, fatherly Tunku, these were harsh words indeed. They highlighted the contrast between two approaches to the same problem. The Tunku was as deeply wedded to multiracialism as Lee, and personally as racially unconscious. But the two men were otherwise poles apart. The Tunku was simplicity personified, Lee highly complex. The Tunku cherished mass popularity, Lee spurned it. The Tunku was sincere to the point of being embarrassing; Lee was all cleverness. The Tunku's responses sprang from the heart and from his identification with the people, Lee's from the mind and his studied aloofness from the crowd. The Tunku was utterly human, Lee a machine.

Lee's style of posing the problems was intellectually appealing: 'Would a multiracial Malaysia be achieved more quickly and better through communal bodies meeting at the top or through interracial political organizations meeting at all levels?'

But in so posing the issue, Lee was ignoring the fact that Malaya's ruling groups enjoyed traditional legitimacy and identification which were non-existent for the PAP in Singapore and that therefore the realistic question was whether it was politically wise to seek changes 'more quickly and better'.

While 'multiracialism now and here' had an obvious liberal appeal, the Alliance had consciously chosen a different policy approach articulated by its house intellectual, Home Minister Dato Dr Ismail. As he put it: 'There are two ways of establishing

Malaysia. One, the platform of the PAP, imposes non-communalism right away. The other is the Alliance method which is, first, to achieve interracial harmony between racially organized groups and, secondly, the ultimate stage of non-communalism. It is this difference in approach that has disturbed the hitherto comparatively tranquil political scene in Malaysia. The PAP has no experience of politics in a multiracial society because Singapore is a homogenous society with some racial minorities. Probably, like mediaeval men, it is easier for them to destroy than to understand a phenomenon which is strange to them.'

Tun Abdul Razak, the Tunku's deputy and since 1970 prime minister of Malaysia, returned to the theme in 1966 when he claimed that the Alliance had, since its 1956 education report, moved in the direction of a united nation of Malaysia. 'The difference is that we want to create a united nation gradually and not by force.'

Whether the leadership in Kuala Lumpur was making real progress towards multiracialism was a moot point. What was relevant was that Lee Kuan Yew would not entertain the possibility of any approach other than his to the achievement of a multiracial society. As one who had developed his whole political style on the basis that democracy itself should be adapted to suit the socio-economic reality of Asia, he should have appreciated the value of hastening slowly and solving communalism through methods adapted to the reality of Malaysian traditions. However, he preferred in this case to superimpose a Western liberal mind on an Asian environment. What was thought dangerous for Singapore was good for Malaysia.

As UMNO saw it, Lee was crying himself hoarse over potential race trouble only to create a situation where, for the sake of peace, the Alliance would agree to take the PAP into the Federal government. The extremist elements in UMNO spewed venom against Lee and the PAP. As Lee said, every copy of the *Utusan Melayu* 'pumped poison into the Kampongs'. Appeals went out asking Malays to unite. Lee was called an enemy of Malaysia.

Lee for his part now cajoled, now ridiculed, now threatened: 'Supposing we real, virile Chinese unite, there would be trouble in five or ten years, because there are five million Chinese, forty-two per cent of the population.' If some Malay leaders were intemperate, Lee was belligerent.

The running battle reached its first climax with federal elections

in April 1964. In November of the previous year, Lee had told a
PAP meeting that the party would confine itself to Singapore and
not participate in elections on the mainland for five years after
merger. Realizing that without a base on the mainland and participation in the federal cabinet the PAP would be reduced to a minor
local grouping, he switched policy seven months after merger. He
put up PAP candidates in urban centres where the MCA was known
to be strong. It was a bold move to prove to the Alliance leaders
that the MCA 'will be finished in the towns'.

It was the PAP that was finished. Ten of the eleven candidates
fielded by the party lost heavily. The solitary victor scraped
through on a minority vote. Peninsular Malaya where the PAP
could not command the government support it enjoyed in
Singapore was not available for the asking.

But the PAP incursion seriously bothered UMNO as well as MCA
leaders in Kuala Lumpur. In the Singapore elections the previous
year the MCA had sent two representatives to canvass support for
its party and the move had been strongly resented by the PAP.
That the PAP should consider Singapore its sacred territory and the
mainland a sort of no-man's-land annoyed the Alliance. Apart
from the breach of confidence of which they accused Lee,
Alliance leaders were anxious to prevent the highly effective PAP
cadres from gaining a foothold in the peninsula.

A dangerous intensification of mud-slinging between Malayan
and Singaporean leaders followed. Speeches of the extremists and
writings in *Utusan Melayu* reached fever pitch. Cries rose for the
arrest of Lee.

One of the theoretical possibilities which Lee had to live with
following merger with Malaysia was of course the use by the central government of its constitutional prerogatives. It had the
right to detain him or suspend the Singapore constitution and
rule the island directly from Kuala Lumpur. While provoking a
political confrontation with the Alliance government, it was
important for Lee to avoid pushing it too far.

There were Malay extremists insisting that the central government should use its powers and call the Lee bluff. There were
widespread rumours, too, that it had drawn up plans to do just
that. Chances were that the rumours started in Singapore. While
Alliance leaders denied any knowledge of plans to arrest Lee, the
PAP said it had prepared counterplans. These called for several of
Lee's colleagues to escape and set up a government in exile in

Cambodia. Lee himself would submit to detention 'because', he said without elaboration, 'I cannot run away'.

There was melodrama from the Singapore side over the arrest – Lee speculation, but never any hint of action from Kuala Lumpur. Singapore's interest was understandable because the rumours played an important political role when a second by-election came up in Hong Lim in July 1965, following Ong Eng Guan's final exit from politics. The PAP dinned it into Hong Lim voters – who had earlier trounced its candidate – that they would dig their own political grave if they rejected its nominee this time. A PAP defeat, it was argued, would be seen by Kuala Lumpur as evidence of people's loss of confidence in the Lee government and therefore justification for it to arrest Lee and establish direct central rule.

The PAP candidate won a convincing victory with 59·8 per cent of the popular vote. Hong Lim was safe for the PAP.

While talk about plans to arrest Lee were to pay political dividends in Singapore in 1965, it marked a dangerous escalation of the hate campaign with Kuala Lumpur in 1964. Soon UMNO officials in Singapore were exhorting Malays to unite to defend their special rights. Lee was accused of trying to damage the religion of the Malays. A dangerous edge to this campaign was provided by Sukarno's Indonesia which had launched a policy of *konfrontasi* to scuttle the Malaysia merger, which it called a neo-colonialist plot against the people of the region. Indonesian propaganda projected a vision of the Malay minority in Singapore being hounded out by the island's Chinese-dominated government. Although Kuala Lumpur was as much a victim of *konfrontasi* as Singapore, Malay extremists in the Alliance Party took full advantage of the Indonesian propaganda. The fires of communal hatred raged.

The climax came suddenly. July 21 was Prophet Mohammed's birthday and at noon Malay Muslims in Singapore took out a religious procession. According to one version of what happened during the procession, a Chinese policeman pushed a Malay steward. According to another, given by Lee himself, a Chinese member of the Federal Reserve Unit (the riot police) asked a group of five Malays who were straggling away from the procession to return, and the Malays, instead of obeying him, set upon him. In minutes the procession turned into pandemonium.

For the next six hours Singapore was the scene of pitched battles. Violence spread from the Malay-dominated Geylang area to nearly every part of the city. Groups of armed youths roamed the streets, wrecking shops, overturning cars, throwing cycles and rickshaws into storm drains. A curfew kept the night relatively trouble-free but sporadic fighting continued for two and a half days. More than twenty people were killed and 450 injured. Two months later there was a repeat performance, following the murder in Malay-dominated Geylang market area of a Chinese trishaw rider – a crime now commonly attributed to local thugs hired by Indonesians. This time trouble lasted five days but claimed fewer lives.

Although Lee put considerable blame for the riots on Indonesia's belligerent policies, the *konfrontasi* between the Alliance Party and the PAP was evidently more to the point. This was underlined by the differing reasons the two parties gave for the outbreak of the violence. In a television broadcast Lee bluntly stated there was organization and planning behind the riots. He left no doubt about his conclusion that Malays had started it; he said his Special Branch officers at the July religious rally had noticed thirty Malays in black wearing Malay warrior hats. He clinched his account by saying that at 'about seven in the evening the Chinese hit back'.

The next day Malaysian Acting Prime Minister Tun Abdul Razak gave a very different account of the incident. He flatly rejected the suggestion that the riot was pre-planned. According to him, the trouble started when a 'mischief-maker' threw a bottle during the procession. And he was in no mood to accept the implication that the Malays had ruled the roost for six hours before the Chinese hit back.

Significantly, after each outbreak of violence, Lee urged Tunku Abdul Rahman to take the PAP into the Federal government. Each time the Alliance rejected the request. In a subsequent account of the events, Tun Abdul Razak noted that Lee tried every possible stratagem to get into the Federal government. 'This was,' Razak wrote, 'despite their propaganda that the Alliance government was a "feudal, reactionary and corrupt" government and that they, and they only, represented the Chinese in Malaysia. When they found they were unsuccessful in persuading UMNO to accept them, the PAP started to criticize and attack UMNO and Malaysia. In this way they hoped to coerce UMNO to accept them.'

Lee denied all these charges hours after Razak made them. He quoted from his own notes and said the idea of PAP joining the

Federal government was raised by British Prime Minister Alec Douglas-Home to the Tunku in London, and that he himself had agreed to it only if the Tunku were to desire it.

That Britain was in favour of an Alliance–PAP coalition was known. Lee also tried to get Australia and New Zealand interested; he made a successful public relations tour of the two countries in March-April 1965. But the Alliance did not yield.

Alliance leaders must have found it particularly galling that Lee Kuan Yew sat as government leader in one of the federating units and as opposition stalwart in the national parliament. Lee's professed parliamentary role was that of 'a friend, loyal opposition and critic'. This might have been in order according to the textbooks, but it was anomalous according to the Malayans. As Lee attacked the Federal government policies – from budget to political philosophy – Alliance leaders were convinced that he was simply using parliament as another forum for his anti-Alliance campaign.

It did seem extraordinary that throughout the Malaysia period Lee Kuan Yew insisted on retaining the designation of prime minister. Leaders of other federating units were known as chief ministers. Lee's unique practice meant that in the national parliament there was a prime minister who sat on the treasury benches and another in the opposition.

It is not clear why the Alliance government at the centre did not use its constitutional authority to overrule Lee on this question at the outset. The point was not lost on Prime Minister Tunku Abdul Rahman. He said in an interview in February 1967 that Singapore went out of the Federation 'because the prime minister of Singapore wanted to be a prime minister. There can never be two prime ministers in one nation.'

Lee not only retained the status of a prime minister but toured the world as such as often as he could. The ostensible purpose was to convince world leaders that Malaysia was not a neo-colonialist plot. With his sophisticated style and Cantabrigian articulation he proved an excellent ambassador, but it was clear that he was intent on building up his own international image in the process. At the height of the Malay ultras' tirade against him, he told a group of religious leaders in his office that the continuing racial tension in Singapore was unfortunate because 'my position with the Muslim leaders of Africa will be somewhat embarrassed'. Lee's international posturing only added to the suspicions generated in Kuala Lumpur by his domestic politics.

By early 1965 it had become doubtful whether the marriage could last much longer. As extremists in Kuala Lumpur clamoured for Lee's arrest, moderates argued that if only Lee would resign as prime minister other Singapore leaders could save the situation.

The British also were working overtime to devise a formula to make the Federation work. Their thoughts seemed to run parallel with those of a moderate group in Kuala Lumpur which was willing to accept a PAP-Alliance coalition government with Goh Keng Swee and Finance Minister Lim Kim San representing Singapore, if Lee Kuan Yew would go to the United Nations as the Malaysian ambassador.

The idea had some merit. It would satisfy Singapore by giving the PAP a prominent slot in the national government. It would also set Kuala Lumpur's fears at rest by removing Lee Kuan Yew's volatile personality to a safe distance. The Alliance leaders were worried that Lee, with the United Nations for his stamping ground, would make his own foreign policy. But they were reportedly willing to settle for it as a lesser evil than having him in Malaysia.

But the plan reckoned without Lee's own ambitions.

Lee insisted that he would accept the ambassadorial assignment for only two years. That would have meant his returning home just in time for the 1967 Federal elections – and it would be a Lee glamorized by the United Nations and firmly established as a world figure. The very thought scared the Alliance leaders, and the plan fizzled out.

Meanwhile, Lee was working out some plans of his own. The federal elections had boomeranged on the PAP and riots had failed to bring the party any nearer power. Lee now turned to organizing a grand opposition which would make up for the PAP being a local Singapore party and enlarge the scope of his challenge to the Alliance. In May 1965 his official residence, Sri Temasek, became the venue of what was called the Malaysian Solidarity Convention (MSC). Within days it grew into perhaps the most important of the many reasons why Singapore went out of the Federation.

Nominally two small parties from the Malay Peninsula and two from Sarawak attended the MSC, but it was a PAP show through and through. Its objective was to organize a 'loyal united opposition' to fight external aggression and internal dissension. In other words, the PAP was to make a strategic semantic withdrawal from peninsular politics and operate henceforth under the label of the

MSC with other groups from outside Singapore filling the flanks. In fact the MSC exacerbated communal antagonisms. This was not because Lee or the PAP deliberately sought to do so; any suggestion that they did would be untenable. It was simply that the MSC naturally brought non-Malay elements together so that the confrontation between them and the Malays became emphasized.

The MSC harped on two slogans, 'Malaysian Malaysia' as distinct from a Malay Malaysia, and '40–40–20', a reference to the country's population ratio between Malays, Chinese and others. The constant repetition of these slogans invested them with distinctive communal connotations. In popular imagination the MSC became synonymous with 'doing away with the special privileges of the Malays' and 'protecting Chinese education'.

'Tragically the MSC became only a slightly more subtle form of communalism than that preached by the Malay ultras. The MSC succeeded in accentuating the social system's vertical ethnic cleavages and in the process, began to eliminate overlapping cleavages and realign the cleavages so that they all became mutually reinforcing: non-Malay/Malay; urban/rural; traditional/modern. . . . The MSC was eroding what confidence and trust the various communities had in one another. Social cleavages were progressively being reinforced by political divisions and the entire Malaysian social and political system was being threatened with dire consequences' (Thomas Bellows).

It was typically Lee Kuan Yew. Intellectually well-reasoned and objectively valid, his policies have often ended up as counterproductive because they were unrelated to the human factors surrounding them. Lee might have been entirely sincere in trying to provide the Malaysian voters with a democratic alternative to the community-conceived, UMNO-led Alliance, but the total effect of the MSC was communal. Lee said later it was after the thrust of the MSC developed fully that the Malays decided to stop him at all costs.

What Lee meant by the thrust of the MSC was perhaps the arithmetic of parliamentary politics on which apparently he was basing one of his strategic options. Soon after the MSC blossomed, Lee was in a position to count on sixteen seats from Sabah and thirty-four from Sarawak in the Federal parliament. Singapore's thirteen were with him. He could also expect the fifteen-member Malaysian opposition to back him. He was only short of a bare dozen to attain a majority and become prime minister of Malaysia. The Alliance leaders had reason to stop him.

MSC politics also tended to confirm the impression in some circles that Lee had seriously considered another option: setting up of a rival federation with Singapore as its epicentre. This would have been the Three-S Federation comprising Singapore, Sabah and Sarawak. It was pointed out by political commentators that ninety per cent of the Chinese in Sarawak were Hakkas like Lee. It would have been a truncated country, but a country nevertheless, and a reasonable substitute for Greater Malaysia. Lee even thought that urban centres of Peninsular Malaya, where Chinese are in a commanding position, might join the Three-S Federation in course of time. He said publicly at one stage that 'those states that want a Malaysian Malaysia can come together. I can think of three straight away – Sabah, Sarawak, Singapore. I can think of a few others like Penang and Malacca. I can even believe that Johore would be one. . . .'

The scheme clearly was to engineer the disintegration of Malaya into numerous pieces and then gather the pieces in a new pattern round Singapore. But the idea never germinated, perhaps for want of time. Soon after the MSC was formed, Tunku Abdul Rahman moved for divorce.

The Tunku had carried on with Singapore for nearly two years, hoping the storm would blow over, pleading with extremists on all sides to exercise restraint, counselling patience. Finally his own patience gave way.

Lee's barely disguised contempt for the Tunku made for strained relations between the two. His inability to get on with Chinese as well as Malay leaders of the Alliance added to the Tunku's worry. The PAP's effective containment of pro-communist elements in Singapore had removed the rationale for merger in Kuala Lumpur's eyes. Now the Tunku shared the general Malayan resentment of Lee's aggressive campaign to get into the Federal government. He felt Lee was always shouting, and the shouting in turn was aggravating the very racial dangers he was decrying. As racial tension rose steadily under the impact of Lee's campaign, the Tunku began to wonder if he had done right in proposing merger in the first place. As the meaning of the Malaysian Solidarity Convention revealed itself, he had little doubt left.

By May anti-Lee emotions reached a climax in Kuala Lumpur. Information Minister Inche Senu said Lee was 'drunk with flattery showered upon him by the foreign press'. Finance Minister

Tan Siew Sen described the PAP as a party which shouted 'Fire, fire' while committing arson. Home Minister Dato Ismail compared Lee to Dr Jekyll and Mr Hyde – spreading fairy tales about PAP reasonableness abroad and engaging in ruthlessness at home. Even the usually restrained Deputy Premier Tun Razak said: 'If the people of Singapore wish to maintain this relationship with us they must find another leader who is sincere. Mr Lee does not care what happens to the people as long as he can get into power.'

Towards the end of June, recuperating in a London clinic, the Tunku reached his decision: if there could be no agreement with the PAP on calling off the intense politicking which already had led to communal bloodshed and could lead to more, then Singapore must go out of the Federation. When he returned to Malaysia a few days later, the Tunku already had a separation bill drafted.

On August 1, a Sunday, Lee Kuan Yew went to the cool resort town of Cameron Highlands with his family for what he 'called the annual breather. On Friday his finance minister, Goh Keng Swee, telephoned him from Kuala Lumpur and asked that he go to the capital post-haste. Lee left the same afternoon and reached Kuala Lumpur around dinner time. There Goh told him: 'This is it'. On Saturday Lee met the Tunku and signed a separation agreement, but the world knew not a word of it. The *fait accompli* hit the world only on Monday, August 9, when the Federal parliament met and passed the bill – without Lee and his cabinet colleagues being present in the House; they were already back in Singapore. The Tunku told a hushed House there were only two courses open to the country: to take repressive measures against, or to sever all connections with the Singapore government which had 'ceased to give even a measure of loyalty to the central government'. The Tunku preferred the latter course, although the ultras in UMNO had wanted the government to take the former – and some of them resigned in protest when it did not.

Parliament passed the bill – and the curtain was rung down on a tumultuous tragi-comedy.

Though Lee had been the most eloquent advocate of merger, he never really gave Malaysia a chance. For one thing, he pushed the Malayans too hard; had he pitched his campaign an octave or two lower he could have been more effective. For another, many of his actions – from the retention of the prime minister's designation to unilateral forays into foreign policy – suggested that he did not intend giving up his posture as a national leader in his own right. Though many states came together to form the Federation, Lee saw to it that Singapore was more equal than the rest. It was as though he would only have Malaysia if a pre-eminent position accrued to him and to his party. Not even for a short while did Singapore become truly integrated; even fiscal and defence policies found Singapore pulling in a different direction from Kuala Lumpur. No thought whatsoever was given to evolving the joint economic policies which the PAP had always held up as the main reason for advocating merger. For Lee merger was merely a catchword written on the wind of *realpolitik*. And when it ended his main concern was to move heaven and earth in a whodunnit controversy to prove that Singapore had been 'expelled' by Malaysia.

The sentiments expressed in Kuala Lumpur and Singapore at the time of separation indicated the divergences in the attitudes of the two countries as well as the deep antagonisms which two years of togetherness had generated. Both Tunku Abdul Rahman and Lee professed profound sorrow at the collapse of the Malaysia dream. In his parliament speech announcing the separation, the Tunku also bitterly decried Lee's actions and speeches of the previous two years.

Suggestions that the Alliance leaders found Singapore unacceptable because of its progressive profile had evidently stung the Tunku. He said: 'It was suggested that our quarrel with the PAP was due to the fact that we are afraid of the far more advanced and enlightened socialist government of Singapore. They [the foreign press] appeared incredulous when I informed them that there are socialist parties in the mainland and other parties who are opposed to our party and the PAP contested our election without success and that the only party we ban is the Communist Party. I also informed them that most of these parties are made up mainly of Chinese whose number will exceed that of Mr Lee Kuan Yew, and to suggest therefore that Mr Lee Kuan Yew represents the Chinese and at the same time represents the only left-wing party in the country is wrong.'

Lee Kuan Yew's representation of any left-wing party at all was by then, in fact, part of Singapore's buried history. After 1960 the PAP's socialism and progressivism were highly debatable features, for in Singapore itself Lee fully equated economic progress with capitalism, and state planning with denial of civil liberties. Only in Kuala Lumpur, because he chose to sit with the federal opposition, did he strike the left-wing pose of his pre-power days. Evidently this rankled in the mind of the Tunku.

He referred to what was perhaps even more of a sore point when he said: 'There has also been certain inclination on the part of some countries to look upon the prime minister of Singapore as an equal partner in the government of Malaysia and to encourage him directly to assert his authority, and this has made the situation rather awkward for us. In a nation there can only be one national executive head. The illustration which I saw in one of the British papers depicting a cartoon of Lee Kuan Yew and myself over the map of Malaysia, and with the caption "too many cooks", is to the point. This is a situation we must avoid. There can only be one prime minister for the Nation, and so the best course we can take is to allow Lee Kuan Yew to be the prime minister of independent Singapore in the full sense of the word, which otherwise he would not.'

The Tunku went on to specify issues on which Singapore had refused co-operation to the Federal government: fitting the port into the national economy, contributing to the Federal budget, meeting its share of national defence and security expenditure, honouring a provision in the Malaysia Agreement which had called for a five-year loan from Singapore for the development of Sabah and Sarawak.

For his part, Lee Kuan Yew made a much more emotional speech before television cameras to mark the separation. He described it as a 'moment of anguish' for him, and declared he had spent all his adult years working for the unity of Singapore and Malaya. As if to prove his anguish, he broke down and wept before the cameras, and the press conference had to be postponed for fifteen minutes to let him recover his composure. The Tunku later expressed surprise at the TV tears and remarked: 'I don't know why Mr Lee acted like that. . . . He was quite pleased about it.'

In fact the dominant emotion in Lee was anger rather than anguish, as some subsequent speeches showed. Three days after separation, he hinted that he believed the Malaysian government headed by Tunku Abdul Rahman would be toppled. As a result of this, he said, 'Singapore and Malaysia will come together in the end – and the end is not very far away.' A month later, addressing the Printing Employees' Union, he viciously lashed out at the

Alliance leaders. 'If they think they can squat on a people,' he said bitterly, 'I say they have made the gravest mistake of their lives. And I know why they are doing this. They must do this. They want to slow down our pace so that their society – a medieval feudal society – can survive. Because if we surge forward at the rate we have been doing, in five or ten years there would have been an even greater disparity and contrast between an effective open society and a closed traditional society. Here if you want to stand up or if you don't want to stand up, that is your business. But nobody crawls. But I will tell you this: this is what hurts them – fear. It is not so much envy as fear.'

The speech brought forth a formal note of protest from the Malaysian government – which only made Singapore hand Malaysia its own protest over newspaper reports of allegations made against Singapore by the chief minister of Sarawak. It was revealing that Lee should have called Singapore an open society while seeing Malaysia as a closed one. This was in 1965, when every leading opposition politician in Singapore had been either imprisoned without trial or banished permanently, the press had been brought effectively under control, trade unions had been 'officialized' under the auspices of trusted PAP men and the universities were being systematically brainwashed. Malaysia was never a shining example of the open society but it did have an edge over Singapore, however slight; critics of the government were not all in jail and political prisoners were brought to trial now and again. Lee's tendency not to see the beam in his own eye perhaps suggested that he sincerely believed the propaganda he put out about himself, his party and Singapore. The self-righteous never see themselves as others see them.

For all his anger and frustration over Malaysia, Lee was a preoccupied man at the moment of separation. He and other PAP stalwarts did not attend the parliament session in Kuala Lumpur which passed the historic separation resolution. They were busily mapping out Singapore's immediate strategy. Highest on their list of priorities was the question of ensuring that independence was not snatched out of their hands at the very moment of its dawn. Lee laboured under the apprehension that Britain might intervene and re-take Singapore. Britain had not been informed or consulted about separation by either Kuala Lumpur or Singapore. Lee Kuan Yew's way to avert the worst was to put on a virtuoso performance of toughness before the British High Commissioner for Malaysia, Lord Head, and pressurize him for immediate recognition.

To begin with, Lee played hard to get. When the High Commissioner telephoned his office for an appointment, Lee's secretaries told him he was not available. Several calls later a night meeting was fixed. What happened later was described by Lee himself to a group of British correspondents on August 30. 'The first question I asked him, "Who are you talking on behalf of?" And he said, "Well of course, you know I am accredited to a foreign government?" I said, "Exactly. And have you got specific authority to speak to me about Singapore's relations with Britain?" He said, "No". I said, "Well then, this is a *tête-à-tête.*" He said, "Well, if you like to put it that way." And it *was* that way. And he took it very nicely. He is a toughie, you know; a brigadier in the army, former defence minister. . . . But he never showed the mailed fist, except for this flag.

'I went out, sent him to the door after one hour, and I looked at the flag. If he is not accredited here, what is the flag doing there? Who is he to fly the flag? . . . He knew exactly where I stood. He knew it was not the time of day or the part of the world to do a Cuba: the Bay of Pigs was not possible in Singapore. Or the whole thing would have come crashing down. And I said to him: "You know of course, as far as I am concerned, I will prefer my first recognition from an Asian country such as India. And if I were you, I would get in touch with the British High Commissioner in India, Mr John Freeman, of whom I happen to be a friend, and tell the Indian government that the British really cannot intervene. Once the British say that, the Indians will recognize me." He did not do that. He whipped back to Kuala Lumpur. I do not know what signal he sent to London, but within seventeen hours I got recognition from the British government. Mind you, if it were a Tory government it might have been a bit delayed because I think they would have just toyed around with a few ideas like – supposing the brigadier has a *coup* – not the British brigadier, mind you – the local brigadier. . . .'

Evidently Lee was convinced that the all-important British recognition came – and came in time – primarily because he anticipated a possible conspiracy and took appropriate timely action to avert it. However, he may have been tilting his lance at a windmill. No evidence came from any quarter to show that Britain in fact intended to reassert itself in Singapore at this late stage. If it did, it is unlikely that a toughie high commissioner would have taken Lee's bullying lying down. In the event, British recognition was followed by British efforts, official and otherwise, to build Lee up as a leader of world stature, even to the extent of making Alliance leaders complain that Britain was more sympathetic to Singapore than to Malaysia.

Lee found not only Britain but also Indonesia strengthening his sovereignty. The break-up of Malaysia was seen in Djakarta as vindication of its policy of *konfrontasi*. President Sukarno rejoiced: 'There is no force in the world which will be able to maintain the existence of Malaysia – neither the Tunku, nor Britain, nor America, nor even a thousand gods from heaven!' He saw the break-up as one more piece of evidence of the failure of Britain's neo-colonial policy and of a piece with the failure of the West Indies Federation, the Central African Federation and the South Arabian Federation. Indonesia offered immediate recognition to the new Singapore, while Lee spoke of his willingness to trade with the Devil if necessary.

There was one devil with whom he was not prepared to have any dealings – the United States. He declared that, should Britain withdraw its security umbrella from Singapore, he would never permit the Americans to step in. Referring to American reactions to this sentiment, he later told correspondents: 'From the responses of the British and Americans to what I said, you can judge the quality of the two different administrations, and if I may add, the two different peoples and their civilizations. . . . You are not dealing with Ngo Dinh Diem or Syngman Rhee. You do not buy and sell this government. . . .' It was a time not only to be independent but to be seen to be independent.

For Lee Kuan Yew the loss of Malaysia was only the loss of one option. He now fell back on his other option: the elevation of Singapore to a country and the swallowing of his own earlier dictum that island states were a political joke. The days of running were past. The pro-communists were all put away and the PAP was unassailable. The self-government phase was over. The Malaysian experiment had yielded sovereignty. Now he was in the United Nations in his own right. Now he was in a position to tell reporters, 'Singapore is the owner of the British base. I could give the British twenty-four hours' notice to quit.'

At forty-two Lee Kuan Yew was home.

CHAPTER SIX

Strategy for Progress

The reasonable man adapts himself to the world, the unreasonable one persists in trying to adapt the world to himself. Therefore all progress depends on the unreasonable man.

BERNARD SHAW

Instant evolution into being an independent republic marked the end of two years of bitter feuding. It also signalled the beginning of a new problem: how to make a minuscule city into a credible country. Raffles' Singapore had had a great time of it, playing to perfection the leisurely role of a commercial and imperial capital. Out of it grew Somerset Maugham's Singapore, a romantic cavalcade of characters trooping through the inscrutable Orient. Lee Kuan Yew's Singapore had to be altogether different. A capital, certainly; leisurely, no; romantic, never.

But Singapore was too tiny to show up on maps of Southeast Asia. On one side was a bulging peninsula of more than 50,000 square miles and eight million people – and that was only half of Malaysia – and on the other side was the sprawling archipelagic hulk of Indonesia, 576,000 square miles and 120 million people. Here was Lee with a flock of two million faithfuls on an island of just 224 square miles – at high tide: 227 when the tide ebbed.

Hong Kong was the only other Asian 'country' in a comparable situation. But the Crown Colony had the full weight of Britain to carry it to commercial glory and keep it there.

Of course Singapore was better off than the Principality of Monaco which was only 0·6 of a square mile in size. Yet Monaco had made a go of it with a casino, an oceanographic museum and the sale of stamps. That was encouraging.

Another European model was the Grand Duchy of Luxembourg – although that was five times the size of Lee Kuan Yew's island. Even so it was good to know that Luxembourg could maintain a status among the steel producers of the world and had made a great success of its commercial radio station – an indication of what imaginative little countries can do to hold their own. Then there was the Principality of Liechtenstein, offering a somewhat more realistic European model with at least sixty-one square miles of territory. True, Liechtenstein had handed over to the Swiss the running of its telephones and postal service, but it could still sustain a prince in his magnificent hill-top castle on the strength of a delectable wine and a range of products from precision instruments to pottery. Singapore was not alone.

What eventually made the mini republic go was not casinos or commercial radio or steel mills, but the dynamism which Lee Kuan Yew began, with independence, to display. He evolved his own philosophy of development, identified his priorities, assembled the expertise required and, with zealous determination, applied himself to achieving visible results. Which followed in quick succession. The philosophy lay wide open to question, as did the methods adopted for its implementation, but no one could deny that Lee achieved the targets he set for himself. He made independence workable.

The foundations had been laid well before Singapore attained sovereignty. It was pure Lee Kuan Yew that some of the most far-reaching instruments of development were forged in the midst of the biggest political crises in which Lee and his party were caught. The Economic Development Board, which was to become the cornerstone of Singapore's industrialization, was established in August 1961 – one month after Lee's numbing defeat in the Anson by-election. A few days later, in September, the first government bulldozer moved into Jurong, the mangrove swamp in the western corner of Singapore which in a few years was to blossom into Southeast Asia's biggest industrial estate and a throbbing town.

It was part of Lee's political style to ensure that performance would be such as to speak for itself. Now he hit his opponents below the belt; now he worked up a confrontation where none existed; but always he insisted that the government not only did its job well but was seen to be doing so.

The result was that, unlike that of many other Asian countries, the government of Singapore really governed. Preoccupation with politics never interfered with the nitty-gritty of administration. Indeed, strong administration was woven into the fabric of politics. Within a decade of independence, the little country stood apparently transformed into an industrial power-house, a major financial centre, a model of low-cost housing and medical services, an example in city planning. Achievements on each of these fronts were accompanied by some dubious side effects and some questionable compromises, but these remained largely unknown or, when known, were successfully projected as consequential on the larger scheme of things.

Never one to hide its light under a bushel, Singapore broadcast its achievements stage by spectacular stage at every opportunity. In a speech to mark the second National Cake-Making Exhibition and Competition organized by the Women's Subcommittee of the People's Association in September 1970, Minister of State for Labour Sia Kah Hui said: 'In this particular field of cake-making I think we Singaporeans are the most fortunate. I had travelled round the world twice and I can say as far as cakes are concerned, not many places can claim to be on par with Singapore in the variety and excellence of cakes available. I am sure that permutation of ideas of people from different cultural backgrounds may yet produce new varieties in time to come.'

Such comic relief notwithstanding, Singapore's development began to be carefully chronicled – with the outstanding exception of trade with Indonesia. The government's unconvincing reasoning was that inconsistencies with Djakarta's trade figures would be used by the press to exaggerate the extent of illegal trade. Smuggling flourished in the penumbra of statistical silence. Indonesians claimed that Singapore's Jurong barter centre had in fact encouraged contraband because it was worried about a shortage of raw materials and semi-processed goods. Illicit trade long remained one of the sore points between the two neighbours

However, the figures that Singapore did publish told a story of success under Lee Kuan Yew's tight management. The total value of goods and services produced in Singapore more than doubled between 1959 and 1969, the first decade of Lee's power. The long-time finance minister and an architect of Singapore's economic philosophy, Dr Goh Keng Swee, proudly noted this in his budget speech surveying the achievements of the decade. He rightly stressed that 'the doubling of the Gross Domestic Product during the 1960s was not due to discoveries of natural resources as these were virtually absent. It was the result of the growth of trade on the one hand and the growth of industry on the other with tourist development providing a small but welcome increment. In other words, it was largely the result of greater human effort.'

The growth of trade was helped, of course, by what may be considered Singapore's one natural resource – geography. It was geography which 'sold' Raffles on Singapore in the first place. Sitting right on the main Europe–Far East shipping route, Singapore became the natural converging point of some fifty maritime nations and more than two hundred shipping lines. In Lee Kuan Yew's first decade the number of ships and the volume of cargo doubled. Singapore became, in one of the catch-phrases of the time, the world's fourth busiest port.

Oil did much to push the youthful republic to that position. Indeed, Singapore was one of the few places in the world to grow oil-rich without producing a drop of its own. What it lacked in resources, it made up by developing phenomenally as an oil refining and distribution centre, the largest in Asia. Four modern refineries and offshore mooring systems processed crude imports from the Persian Gulf and shipped them to a massive market stretching from Indochina to Japan and Australia. The oil trade accounted for upwards of seventy-five per cent of all cargo handled by the port of Singapore.

The forward thrust of the port itself was a major feature of the saga of development. The Lee government always looked at the port as a lifeline and gave it special attention. The result was that the port was in a perpetual state of expansion and modernization. It was no surprise when it built Southeast Asia's first containership terminal. And it was in character that it should have introduced twenty-four-hour berthing service to speed turnrounds. The dominant objective was always clear; what trade demanded, Singapore provided.

When Britain decided to close its enormous naval base in Singapore, the Lee government panicked momentarily. But, quickly regaining its drive, it began converting the dockyard into a veritable commercial bonanza. Enlisting the active involvement of British and Japanese companies, Singapore became the best ship-repair centre between Japan and Europe. The shipbuilding and repairing industry alone kept expanding at the rate of thirty per cent a year.

Emphasis on developing Singapore as a servicing centre flowed from another pragmatic reading of the situation by Lee and his men: that Singapore could not depend for long upon its traditional entrepôt trade. Malaysia, remembering the Lee politics that led to the demise of merger, could not be expected to cherish the idea of its trade being in the hands of middleman Singapore. Indonesia, resentful of the smuggling that ate cancerously into its economy, was certain to want Singapore out of its hair.

Singapore's response to this anticipated resistance from its neighbours was to explore possibilities of restructuring its basic economic pattern. It had time on its side. Neither Malaysia nor Indonesia was in any position to force the pace in the absence of business and communication facilities anywhere near those of Singapore. Nor did they have organizers and salesmen of Lee's calibre, or a single-minded team of ministers and officials such as Lee had gathered around him.

The team began a planned diversification programme. By 1964 entrepot trade had yielded place to manufacturing as a contributor to the Gross Domestic Product: it accounted for only ten per cent while manufacturing contributed twelve per cent. In the years since then entrepot trade has been kept deliberately stagnant between ten and eleven per cent. However, some experts have questioned these official claims, pointing out that the government has provided no separate re-export figures.

Nevertheless it remains clear that Lee had started planning for progress well before complete independence. One of the first jobs the PAP government tackled immediately after coming to power in 1959 – and in the midst of the intense behind-the-scenes politicking that was going on between the Lee group and the leftists within the party – was a detailed perspective study, by a United Nations committee, of Singapore's industrial potential. The mission's report provided the framework for the policies that followed. After the mission had completed its task, Lee independently retained the services of the Dutch economist who had headed it, Dr Albert Winsemius. Year after year, Dr Winsemius visited the island at regular intervals, keeping an outsider's objective eye on the direction in which progress was being made, and advising the policy-makers on when and how to make in-course correctional moves. It was a simple device to ensure that the Lee government did not get stuck in its own rut and that detached expert advice was available with the added advantage of continuity. It was another example of Lee Kuan's Yew's characteristically pragmatic approach to achievement.

The strategy initially adopted under the Winsemius plan was to go all-out for foreign investment and industrialization under the centralized guidance of a powerful Economic Development Board. The board was packed with recognized experts of long experience. A string of industrial estates began to develop, and incentives such as tax concessions were liberally offered to all comers. It was a period in which Singapore's ministers really went to town, drumming up investment capital from anyone who had a spare dollar. Even the privilege of citizenship – carefully denied to PAP activists whose loyalty to Lee was suspect – was extended to anyone willing to invest S$500,000 at first, later S$250,000, in an industrial project. Snide jokes spread among critics about Lee's cut-rate nationalism, but foreign investment flowed in.

Singapore was often a 'second choice' location for international corporations in Asia because countries such as Taiwan and South Korea offered cheaper labour. Yet many shifted their Asian operational headquarters to Singapore for a variety of reasons. The island's work force was familiar with English and Lee's policies ensured the continuance of this advantage. The efficiency of the infrastructure services that Singapore offered was matched in the Orient only by Hong Kong. There was relative freedom from red tape. Above all, Singapore was nearly always free of graft.

By the end of the 1960s Singapore was in a position to change course and turn choosy about the kind of investment it would accept. No longer was the incentives carpet rolled out for everyone who came along. Now new criteria were drawn up: export potential, development of worker skills, scope for progressive growth in technological content. The simpler sweat-shop industries were no longer receiving the nod: now the spotlight was on high-technology industries such as quality cameras, electrical components and machine tools. The bustling Jurong industrial town was programmed to have 12,000 acres of developed land by 1975 and the majority of its 500 factories would be capital-intensive and technologically sophisticated.

At this level the wooing of investors continued assiduously. Official government advertisements in London and elsewhere went for the hard sell: 'Singapore is where it's happening. . . . Yesterday shakes hands with tomorrow and it's yours – today.'

In June 1970 Dr Winsemius, the grand old Dutchman still on the job for Lee, saw the vision of Singapore emerging as a fully developed industrial nation in six to eight years and striking out

4

into 'the fourth dimension of exporting brain services'. He said: 'The unemployment situation which created the need to indus-trialize has been mastered. Soon an investment of, say, S $25 mil-lion in a university or technical institute would be much more important to Singapore than a new factory.'

Graduation to this status had become an economic necessity, for it was the only way Singapore could achieve the viable export-orientated economy it was seeking. It was true that industrial exports had grown faster than exports as a whole. But the largest items on the export account were still oil products. It was slippery ground.

And there was a political factor with which to reckon. Partly because of nationalistic pride and partly because of their resent-ment of Lee's abrasive posturing, Malaysia and Indonesia were increasingly unwilling to fit themselves into Singapore's industrial master-plan. They did not want to play the role of 'rural hinter-land' where the more labour-intensive components required for Singapore's industries would be obtained cheaply. Nor were they prepared to act as a market for Singapore's products, so manu-facturing operations in the island predicated on marketing potential in Malaysia ran into protective tariffs and import con-trols imposed by Kuala Lumpur. Both Malaysia and Indonesia began putting heavy pressure on foreign firms, especially the petroleum cartels, to invest directly in their territories if they wanted to distribute their products in these markets. Obviously both countries had strong anti-Singapore sentiments, perhaps sea-soned with a dash of jealousy, certainly rooted in their national desire to be free of traditional middlemen.

But this was the kind of challenge on which Lee Kuan Yew flourished. He took warning noises from Kuala Lumpur and Djakarta with his customary cool, confident in the knowledge that he would always be able to keep several steps ahead of his giant neighbours when it came to manœuvring. It was clear, any-way, that Singapore would do best to shake itself free of over-dependence on the Malaysian–Indonesian market. This was what made Lee's Singapore develop the concept of the world as its hinterland. Resented by its neighbours, it would reach the world beyond through skill industries that the world needed.

There was, however, a serious labour problem to cope with. Not that the Lee government was ever bothered by the usual kind of labour problem created by aggressive unions; that had been taken care of early enough and the labour force converted into a docile element guaranteed to appeal to the most capitalistic bosom. The Employment Act ensured maximum labour discipline as well as maximum productivity, while wage restraints kept the average monthly industrial wage at about US$87. No profit-seeking investor could seriously complain about that. The problem was that Singapore did not have enough skilled labour. Lee personally tried to attract skilled workers from places such as Hong Kong, but with little success.

Crash programmes to turn out young men with the necessary skills were part of Lee's eventual solution to the problem. Already suspicious of the liberal arts as subjects to be taught to the young, he began putting more emphasis than ever on technical education. The Winsemius vision of a shift in investment priorities became a fact of life. Companies were asked to share costs of training schemes. Most important, proposals were made to lower the guards on another sacred cow – immigration laws.

In his 1970 budget speech, Dr Goh Keng Swee said it was necessary 'as a matter of high priority that we should relax our immigration and work permit restrictions on the inflow of personnel belonging to categories [such as engineering and management]. At present they have to find work here before they are allowed the necessary permits. It would be a clear advantage . . . if they could be allowed here for any length of time they wish so that they can do the job-hunting and in this way fit into the best slots available to them.' For a government which usually tended to look upon an outsider as an enemy until proved otherwise, which expelled British teachers from the university for speaking outside the classroom, and which often made it unpleasant for tourists if they happened to have long hair, this was a sensational departure. It was pragmatism all over again.

The circumstances which pushed Singapore into areas of industry which did not depend on markets in its periphery and would not be labour-intensive also pushed it into the world of high finance. Helped by some American banks it became the focal point of the Asiadollar market, and that appeared to act as a financial snowball. By the end of the 1960s nearly two dozen foreign banks were operating in the little island, among them the first Soviet bank in Asia – a branch of the Moscow Narodny Bank. Depositors who chose to keep their money in Singapore included central banks of Thailand and Indonesia. In its drive to develop as a financial centre comparable to Tokyo and Hong Kong, Singapore boldly provided facilities others did not offer; it allowed free exchange of hard currencies while Tokyo clamped a maze of regulations on such transactions; it made Asiadollar deposits tax-free while Hong Kong took a fifteen per cent interest tax; and it went Swiss to provide the comforting confidence of numbered accounts. In fact, the epithet 'Asian Switzerland' was added to the stock of Singapore's publicity slogans.

During the newspaper crisis in 1972 Lee publicly twisted the arm of a powerful American bank and forced it to foreclose on a daily paper which had dared to be nonconformist. At that time doubts were widely expressed about the Asian Switzerland image. The episode did warn international bankers and investors that they were best advised to leave the prime minister's hang-ups severely alone. For the rest, though, they could have the run of the island for the glory of business. Singapore seemed confident that that was good enough.

Spectacular as Singapore's business and industrial growth was, the greatest showpiece achievement of them all was its many-splendoured low-cost housing scheme. It was this which physically changed the look of Singapore. It was what gave Lee his first opportunities to demonstrate to the people that things were being done for them. It was what made Singapore a topic of discussion round the world. It was Singapore's most publicized activity. After meticulous computing, feature after impressive feature of the housing performance was dinned into the people – such as that one housing unit was being built every forty-five minutes, one of the fastest building rates in the world. New satellite townships with rows of skyscrapers, symmetrically lit at night, bore witness to the continuous conversion of swampy fishing villages into modern urban precincts.

The Housing and Development Board which master-minded and co-ordinated the project was established soon after the Lee government assumed office. One of Lee's major electioneering points during the 1959 campaign was the ineffectiveness of the Singapore Improvement Trust with a building rate 'insufficient even to cater for the annual population growth, let alone alleviate the slum problem'. So the board was set up to provide incontrovertible proof of the PAP's capacity to fulfil its pledges to the people, and to succeed where others had failed.

It was in the same spirit that the government resolved the

initial policy question: should time and resources be spent first on research to determine the ideal type of housing required or should they be spent on building houses right away? The decision was to go ahead and build as many houses as finances would permit in as short a time as possible.

This policy subsequently touched off criticism that the apartments were stereotyped and unimaginative. It also led to the paradox of several hundred flats lying vacant each year despite waiting lists of 15,000 and more applicants. The government charged that people were too choosy and preferred to wait for something better. Half-way through the second plan the board did undertake a sociological study to see if design concepts could be improved to suit popular tastes and thereby approach the ideal-house situation in future building policy. Improvements followed.

Despite the early criticism, however, the board's build-now-plan-later policy eased the housing shortage perceptibly. Each year the target was exceeded. At the end of the first Five-Year Plan in 1965 the board had built more than 54,000 units against a target of 51,000 which was, as the board's report proudly pointed out, 'well over twice the number of units completed by its predecessor, the Singapore Improvement Trust, during its whole thirty-two years of existence from 1927 to 1959'. By then twenty-three per cent of the island's population had moved into these flats and the board was racing confidently towards its goal of resettling two-thirds of the population in its flats by 1975. The government was building eighty per cent of the total number of houses coming up in the country. Singapore became 'the public housing laboratory of the world'.

Nothing could stop the Housing Board, it appeared. It went for maximum utilization of land with buildings rising up to twenty storeys. When it was stumped for land in the tight little island, it created its own by filling up swamps and by reclaiming areas from the sea. There was a time when a Bailey bridge over the Serangoon Road was carrying a thousand lorry-loads of earth each day to the swamplands of the Kallang Basin. Nearly 400 acres were developed in this area alone, with five million cubic yards of earth. An ambitious scheme was launched to extend the eastern coastline by a thousand acres across a six-mile stretch of sea.

The Housing Board's sprawling projects were all expensive, yet Singapore completed them with its own money. Some other problems it faced had a potentially explosive political edge. Most of the fishing villages which were cleared were Malay and the cry arose that Chinese Singapore was persecuting its Malay minority and disrupting the traditional Malay kampong way of life. It was true that the kampongs were disappearing one by one, but so were some of Asia's more notorious slums. For once Lee could justifiably take comfort from the fact that modernization always brought in its wake some criticism.

Occasionally opposition to the housing projects would spill over the bounds of criticism and develop into resistance. Slum-dwellers were not always willing to give up their $7 shanty-huts for $30 Housing Board flats. But Lee was not the type to be put off by hurdles of that kind. His government tried persuasion where possible, other methods where necessary.

Sometimes nature felt obliged to help. In 1968 a major fire broke out in a Havelock Road shanty-town which had refused to liquidate itself despite constant government warnings about disease, theft and fire. It was Singapore's worst fire in seven years. It was suddenly discovered that only five engines were available to fight it. Water pressure in the neighbourhood turned out to be inexplicably low. The hydrants were insufficient, the hoses damaged and leaky. Even winds proved treacherously changeable. To cap it all the firemen did what a press report at the time described as 'rather odd target selection'. In no time the fire completed its course and cleared an area occupied by some 200 huts. Soon another high-rise building covered it.

The fire that had raged seven years earlier was strikingly similar. It too had completely razed a shanty-town and immediately made way for another Housing Board estate. There were other smaller fires in other recalcitrant slums, each followed by housing development. Singaporeans began happily talking about 'fires of convenience'.

Housing was a stone that killed many birds. It gave a spectacular three-dimensional effect to Singapore's economic progress. It gave the Lee government concrete confirmation of its concern for ordinary citizens. It helped create a tremendous building boom deliberately intended in the late 1960s as a means to get the economy going. It bought political supporters for the PAP. It provided another constraining security fence around leftist political forces; the slums had been breeding-grounds of political dissatisfaction and Lee not only removed them but ensured that the resettlement systematically dispersed ethnic and political groupings.

The unstoppable housing scheme in due course formed part of a rebuilding and renewal programme embracing the island as a whole. Lee loved long-term planning – the kind of visionary forward look which took social permanence and his own government's stability for granted. Plans for progress which sometimes spanned decades, sometimes generations, were used as further arguments for the undisturbed continuance in power of his team. The steady implementation of these plans gave such arguments strength. Singapore's renewal plan aimed at nothing less than giving the island a rebirth in the most modern and sophisticated idiom.

The pace of growth demanded such a plan. Though Singapore had scored a major success in cutting down its population growth rate, it still was expected to double its population by the beginning of the twenty-first century. Even with two million, the pressure on land was too heavy. Nearly two square miles of land was being taken up every year for public housing and industrial development. Besides, the growth of industries as well as of general prosperity threatened to bring to Singapore the evil the obsessively hygienic Lee Kuan Yew most abhorred – pollution.

In characteristic fashion, the government had five different plans prepared, each after extensive computer analysis of various concepts. The master-plan eventually chosen was a comprehensive blueprint for controlled urban growth and envisaged a belt of high-density development along the southern rim of the island from Jurong to Changhi with a ring of heavy urban development around the other three sides of the central water catchment area. The plan would not only accommodate the four million population expected around AD 2000 but would leave substantial scope for further population expansion and industrial growth.

A maze of 'complexes' – a word dear to Singapore's planners – had sprouted under the master-plan by the end of the 1960s and more were coming up: industrial complexes, shopping complexes, building complexes, office complexes. By the early 1970s work was under way on what was perhaps the most exciting part of the grand renewal programme – a new 'heart' for the city, to be called Raffles International Centre. This, said the 'complex' planners, would equal the grandeur of New York's Rockefeller Center and have the tallest buildings, the most modern transportation systems, the best drainage. It was tall talk, but in Lee Kuan Yew's Singapore, boasts had a habit of quickly growing into reality.

Rapidly becoming a reality also was a dream island for holiday-makers barely half a mile from Singapore's southern coast. The 649-acre Pulau Blakang Mati used to be a reserved area housing some defence facilities and was handed over by Britain to the Singapore Defence Ministry only in 1968. After considering eager offers by industrial interests, the government decided to use it as 'Singapore's trump card in its accelerated campaign to attract tourists'. Rechristened with the easier and more romantic name of Sentosa, a S$400-million scheme was drawn up to enrich the lush and lovely island with chalet-like hotels perched on hill-tops, an eighteen-hole championship golf course planned by British designers, a swimming–boating lagoon and various parks, beach facilities and restaurants on stilts.

The tourist dollar was contributing a negligible one and a half per cent of Singapore's gross domestic product in the early years; by 1970 it accounted for five per cent. In its bid further to boost this revenue, the Lee government was prepared to make an adjustment or two in its philosophy. For all the government's initial antipathy to 'Yellow Culture', for example, a profitably blind eye was turned to hot cabaret shows. The press could note such things as 'six busty British blondes arrive this week to wow night club audiences with a topless agogo dancing show', and could further assure the public that the dancers would not only be 'carrying a good 36 inches where it matters' but would be performing before carefully arranged mirrors which would give the impression there were sixty girls, not six. Though routine in other Asian tourist cities, in prim and proper Singapore this was a concession from the government.

Another concession, truly surprising, was over Bugis Street. This street is easily the most overt display of perversion in South-east Asia, a hangout of queers and transvestites of every description. A government which turned angrily on juke boxes left Bugis Street alone. More, the Singapore Tourist Promotion Board advertised this unique attraction in international magazines. For all the postures of uprightness the Lee government struck, it did appear on occasion that business, not principles, came first in its scheme of things.

At one stage the government drew up a plan which, among other things, sought to glorify the Japanese general who ruled Singapore during the Second World War: General Tomoyuki Yamashita. The idea was said to germinate from studies which had shown that Japanese tourists were the vacationing wave of the future and six times more Japanese tourists were going to Italy than to Singapore. The plan called for waxwork recreations of Singapore's history, among them Yamashita accepting the surrender of Singapore from the commander of the defending British forces.

Yamashita was a dirty word for Singaporeans who had lived through the Japanese occupation. His stock was no higher in Singapore than in the Philippines, where he was eventually tried and executed for war crimes. Protesters in Singapore and the US threatened to blow up the waxwork as soon as it was erected. A newspaper, which was subsequently closed, wrote that while the facts of history should be accepted, 'to erect a monument to it would be to display a weird historical masochism. And to do so for the sake of attracting Japanese tourists would be utterly obscene.' You can't hide your history, was the Singapore Tourist Promotion Board's reply.

One programme which won the unstinted praise of tourists and locals alike was the transformation of Singapore into a garden city. Like Chinatowns everywhere, Singapore, when Lee took office, was largely a photogenic cesspool. One fine morning the prime minister decided it would not do and set about to beautify the place. There was no time gap, it seemed, between decision and implementation. Overnight, as it were, squads of gardeners planted crotons at the sides of roads, tidied house-fronts, spruced up trees, converted public squares into miniature parks, installed fountains on traffic islands. Shop-owners were told to keep their frontage spotless. Littering became a serious offence. Singapore emerged 'Clean and Green', yet another slogan to its repertoire. Given its pocket size, it was an easy enough achievement. But the fact remained that no other Asian city had a mayoral mind moved to beautify it with anything approaching the same results.

An element of chance could be seen in Singapore's progress. The state came into being at a time when there was a general momentum propelling countries like Taiwan and Hong Kong towards progress. There was considerable floating capital in Southeast Asia and the region as a whole was attracting business houses and investors who were anxiously looking for safe havens in which to pitch their tents. Logical economic, geographic and geopolitical factors favourable to the launching of international business in the region made capital gravitate towards Hong Kong and Singapore. The miracle of Hong Kong was created by faceless, anonymous civil servants and bankers. In Singapore the impersonal efficiency of such men (which could have worked there as well) was overshadowed by the personal nationalism of political leaders. Considering how similar factors had made for poor management of the national economy in most other Asian countries, Lee could take credit for Singapore's achievements under his guidance. He seemed to follow the Hong Kong civil servants' pattern, keeping Singapore within an essentially colonial system of economy: means never mattered so long as the ends he desired were reached. He ran Singapore like a tightly managed private corporation, paying what he considered good dividends to the shareholders.

In 1970, according to official statistics, an individual Singaporean's income stood at an impressive S$2,620; the United Nations regarded a *per capita* income of S$1,500 as the dividing line between the rich and the poor. Singapore's 1970 status represented a seventy-four per cent increase over 1963. The World Bank placed the Republic thirty-fifth on the global affluence scale.

However, some of the crucial figures officially put out were misleading. For example, the *per capita* income mentioned in the 1972–3 budget exceeded the magic figure of US$1,000. This was so high that for the first time the finance minister felt obliged to acknowledge that the figure was accounted for by the salaries of highly paid expatriates who dominate so much of Singapore's economy. A 'genuinely Singaporean' income indicator was being worked out, he said. The question remained whether even the new indicator would reveal the gap between the genuinely Singaporean rich and the genuinely Singaporean poor.

Indeed, there were critics who took many of Singapore's claims sceptically. These were not only professed political opponents of Lee Kuan Yew such as the remnants of the Barisan Sosialis, but included Western researchers and intellectuals who, at one time or another, had spent time in Singapore and delved into the economic realities of the republic. The most formidable case from this standpoint was presented by Iain Buchanan of the University of Leicester in his book *Singapore in Southeast Asia*. The thesis which he backed with painstaking research was that the kind of progress Singapore had achieved was strictly within colonial terms of reference, leaving the exploitative character of, and the serious imbalances in, the economic system basically untouched.

After five years of a detailed run of English-language press reports, and a meticulous collection of field data, Buchanan found that Singapore's official statistics were extremely uneven and often grossly inaccurate. The fundamental point about Singapore's economy was its colonial logic. The shift of America's strategic-economic interest southwards towards Indonesia made Singapore crucial to the flow of American capital and, by the closing years of the 1960s, the republic became an explicit part of the West's economic thrust into Southeast Asia. The influences to which it was subject in this wider regional structure were those of Western and (increasingly) Asian (that is, Japanese) economic imperialism. A characteristic of this imperialism was its tendency towards selective development of resources and its use of disparities – between areas and between communities – as a means of overall control. Buchanan provided an impressive array of facts and figures to prove that Lee Kuan Yew's policies had in fact left large sections of the population in poverty while making the top ten per cent prosperous and satisfied. Official figures, as well as such spectacular features of progress as high-rise housing estates, had only hidden unpleasant facts such as, for instance, that sixty per cent of the population lived on *per capita* incomes of less than S $600 per annum, or less than one-third the national average.

Indeed, the public housing programme was an example of the dangers of adopting the approach of physical town planning towards solving what were essentially socio-economic problems. Buchanan pointed out that squatter resettlement, while successful in some respects, did not reach the heart of the matter because the slum system was only transferred from one physical setting to another, not transformed into something socio-economically less depressing to those who belonged to it. Slum dwellers who were resettled in new government estates remained apart from the rest of society; the alienation between the rich and the poor continued. If anything, the new life increased the tensions among former squatters because the estates developed a split personality; in nearly every aspect of life there was an 'allowed' way of doing things and an 'underground' and forbidden way of doing things. While the programme might have cleaned up slum areas, it had become one of the Singapore government's basic tools of political discipline. The *Economist* once quoted a British businessman as saying that the Toa Payoh housing estate was '1984 in concrete and steel'.

Buchanan's argument challenged assumptions and impressions about Singapore which, over a decade, had come to be taken for granted. The state's apparent progress was so visible that it seemed incredible that anyone should question it. Yet much of what he said had the force of logic behind it and the evidence of figures, demonstrating that while the profile of a bustling Singapore as presented by the government had some validity, there was at least another profile which remained hidden from world view. *Singapore in Southeast Asia* indicated that a considerable backlog of myth about Singapore had accumulated during thirteen years of unchallenged PAP dominance.

The PAP was too deeply committed to its particular style of government to care very much at this stage about criticism from abroad. It was a proud and obviously satisfied Lee Kuan Yew who announced new wages policies to the annual delegates' conference of the National Trade Unions Congress in March 1972. He was still in shirt sleeves but, as if in acknowledgment of the end of the age of struggle, he wore a tie, and the customary white cotton trousers had yielded to a stylish dark pair. In the ringing tones of success, he said:

'The end of 1971 marked the close of an era in our economic history. From chronic high unemployment we have entered a period of full employment. From 1961 to 1970 we trebled our GNP at constant prices. Today Singapore's position is analogous to that of Germany or Holland in the early 1960s. Then their economy was booming and they began to increase the number of "guest workers" from other countries. We have the choice of controlled and steady wage increases and real growth, or of taking quick gains in artificially high and sudden increases in wage rates and bonuses but thereby jeopardizing future growth. Unions, managements and government together will have to rethink their respective positions and roles, to reframe policies for very different social and employment conditions.'

Then the prime minister proceeded to announce special allowances to all government employees and increased provident fund contributions as first steps towards a pay rise for both the public and private sectors in Singapore. The long wage freeze thawed a little. Singaporeans in the lower income bracket could now hope for a whiff of the prosperity which had become a feature of life at the top.

Television in the living-room, a Mercedes in the garage, press-button telephones, air-conditioners for the asking – what more would any respectable citizen want? A dash of culture, perhaps?

A couple of years after Singapore's emergence as a sovereign state, a visiting Asian editor called on the PAP philosopher under whose ministerial charge fell culture. The two men were old friends, so conversation was free.

MINISTER: Well, now how do you find Singapore?

EDITOR (casually): Great.

MINISTER: What do you mean?

EDITOR: Just great.

MINISTER: I don't think I like the tone of your voice.

EDITOR: I have just come from Djakarta and Manila. Nothing worked there. Here my telephone works, my flush flushes, everything is clean and antiseptic. Singapore is simply great.

MINISTER: All right, old chap, what's bothering you?

EDITOR: Look, what does it all mean? What about people? Don't they have minds? I see no evidence of people here having minds of their own, feelings of their own.

MINISTER: They are happy. See those modern high-rise buildings? We gave them decent places to live in.

EDITOR: What have you done to their minds?

MINISTER: Well, we are thinking about it. Having given them a clean city, modern amenities and a strong economy, we are now thinking of what culture we should give them.

EDITOR (after pause): Is the culture factory also going to be in the Jurong industrial estate?

End of conversation.

CHAPTER SEVEN

Strategy for Repression

Those who profess to favour freedom and yet deprecate agitation are men who want crops without ploughing up the ground. They want rain without thunder and lightning. They want the ocean without the awful roar of its many waters. . . . Power concedes nothing without a demand – it never did and it never will.

FREDERICK DOUGLASS, 1849

The rapidity of Singapore's apparent progress and the high-powered and selective public relations which accompanied it kept the world largely unaware of parallel developments in the political organization of the republic's society. Tenement towers grazing the sky were enough to make the government seriously consider culture as a commodity to be designed, manufactured and handed down to the people from above. By the time the implications of this attitude became known outside the nucleus, the public-relations machine had come to the fore and made them appear irrelevant. Lee Kuan Yew's intellectual gifts were used to rationalize the restructuring of policy along oligarchical lines, and the West (its notions of post-war Asia swinging between anti-communism and the thirst for profitable investment) seemed grateful to Lee for what he projected as the Asianization of democracy – which in fact meant reducing people to digits; or to the letters GNP. Capitalist totalitarianism, as distinct from communist totalitarianism, became the ideal for developing societies – and Singapore was its shining example.

Lee Kuan Yew's initial image as a knight-errant of democracy and socialism played a crucial part in this ideological *coup d'état*. The image was strong in Singapore as well as in the West. Until he actually became prime minister, Lee could not have been to the ordinary Singaporean anything other than a champion of the oppressed. His time until then had been taken up in defence of workers and students, in opposition to colonialism. He was an advocate of popular causes, a progressive. This impression was reinforced during the four years he spent in opposition, facing first David Marshall and then Lim Yew Hock, with British colonial authority as an ever-popular target of attack. These years saw Lee as a parliamentarian whose astuteness was comparable to the best in Britain, where he had learned the ground rules; and as a liberal whose conscience was sensitive to the slightest sign of injustice around him.

Almost any speech he made in the Assembly between 1955 and 1959 could go straight into the liberal democrat's bedside bookshelf. The most celebrated of these – celebrated partly for the parliamentary thrust he displayed but mainly for the irony it was to provide in the years to come – was the repression-is-like-making-love speech of October 1956, quoted earlier, in which he deplored the arbitrary arrests of trade union and civil leaders. It was an outstanding example of the popular pose he struck in the years before power, and of the distance he was to travel in the years after. In other ways, too, it was an important landmark in Lee's political career.

Examining how governments could fall all too easily into the habit of suppressing the liberty of the individual, Lee said:

'First the conscience is attacked by a sense of guilt. You attack only those whom your Special Branch can definitely say are communists. They have no proof except that X told Z who told Alpha who told Beta who told the Special Branch. Then you attack those whom your Special Branch say are actively sympathising with and helping the communists, although they are not communists themselves. Then you attack those whom your Special Branch say, although they are not communists or fellow travellers, yet, by their intransigent opposition to any collaboration with colonialism, they encourage the spirit of revolt and weaken constituted authority and thereby, according to the Special Branch, they are aiding the communists. Then finally, since you have gone that far, you attack all those who oppose you.

'. . . All you have to do is to dissolve organisations and societies and banish or detain the key political workers in these societies. Then miraculously everything is tranquil and quiet on the surface. Then an intimidated press – and some sections of the press here do not need intimidation because they have friendly owners – the press and the government-controlled radio together can regularly sing your praises and slowly and steadily the people are made to forget the evil things that have already been done. Or if these things are referred to again, they are conveniently distorted, and distorted with impunity, because there will be no opposition to contradict.

'. . . But if we say we believe in democracy, if we say that the fabric of a democratic society is one which allows the free play of ideas, which avoids revolution by violence because revolution by peaceful methods of persuasion is allowed, then in the name of all the gods we have in this country, give that free play a chance to work within the constitutional framework.'

Such sentiments were not heard publicly in Singapore after 1959 – not from the intimidated press or the government-controlled radio, not from the detained political workers or the eliminated opposition. For, behind the façade of economic progress – indeed, under its pretext – the Lee government had put into effect a policy of rigorous internal repression. Systematic destruction of political opposition and suppression of the trade union movement were the outstanding features of this policy. Simultaneously, as if to round it off and ensure the total effect, the government also completely 'officialized' the education system, beat the mass media into subjection and instituted other programmes aimed at casting a generation of Singaporeans in a carefully prepared mould.

After 1959 Lee returned to the theme of democratic rights only when he sat with the opposition in the Federal parliament in Kuala Lumpur. Blithely ignoring executive actions in his own island territory, he then exhorted Alliance leaders in Kuala Lumpur to honour liberal principles, respect individual liberty and foster the great traditions of free debate.

In his first speech in the Malaysian parliament he poured scorn on the Alliance for its apparent addiction to office. 'One of the reasons why Western-style parliamentary democracy has not taken root in the newly independent countries of Asia and Africa,' he said, 'is that the government in power does not contemplate with equanimity the passing of power to the opposition'. Opposition groups in Singapore, in retrospect, would have found this laughable but for the grimness of the methods used to prevent the passing of power to them.

There was irony again in the protest voiced by PAP Chairman Toh Chin Chye in July 1965, when Kuala Lumpur expelled an expatriate Lee partisan for carrying on propaganda which the Alliance considered mischievous. Warning that the expulsion would damage Malaysia's image abroad, Dr Toh said: 'The world press will not find it hard to depict Malaysia to their readers as a growing democracy. In countries which are committed to the defence of Malaysia the question will inevitably be asked: what is it that is being defended in Malaysia – democratic freedom or a repressive ruling group?' Even as he spoke, Singapore was building up its own list of expelled journalists.

A qualitative change could be discerned in Lee's speeches even as he came within sniffing distance of power. Towards the end of 1958 he bluntly told the Singapore Assembly that a PAP government would retain emergency laws. But he still found it expedient to couch the threat in democratic clothing. 'These powers,' he said, 'will not be used against political opponents within the system who compete for the right to work the system. . . . If in using these powers you in fact negate the purpose for which you made them, then you will end up with a situation where force and more force will become increasingly necessary.' As the 1959 campaign showed the wind blowing unmistakably in his favour, Lee at last dropped his guard and began openly threatening critics in the press and elsewhere. The wise immediately fled to Malaysia, the otherwise ended up behind bars.

Lee always gave an intellectual-pragmatic justification for his moves to eliminate democracy's irksome restrictions. This rested on two principal arguments: first, that long-term governmental stability was a prerequisite to progress and it did not pay to split hairs on the subtleties of how to achieve such stability; and second, that communists followed an unscrupulous book of rules which, once they attained power, knocked out opponents once and for all and it was only appropriate that a non-communist government should also play for keeps.

At the back of it all was Lee's unshakable conviction that, he being no self-seeker, his plans for Singapore's progress were beyond criticism in every detail; anyone who disagreed with him was consequently anti-Singapore. The extent to which he could be stung even by indirect disagreement was seen when the opposition failed to support him in his vendetta against erstwhile PAP hero, Ong Eng Guan, in 1960. The opposition did not in fact vote against the PAP motion to condemn Ong; perhaps reflecting the widespread feeling at the time that Ong was being personally vilified for daring to challenge Lee, it simply abstained. That was enough to make Lee fly into a rage. 'The system of one man one vote,' he lashed out, 'which ensured that the interest of the majority prevails without having to crush and destroy all opposition, can only work if adjustments are made to preserve not the form but the essence of a tolerant political system which ensures

change in the social and economic order without violence. ...
Unfortunately most, though not all, opposition in Asia are negative in that they have no alternative policy to offer to the electorate
and oppose for the sake of opposing not only the party in power
but, as is the case of Singapore, also the institutions of the state.'
It was the first clear indication that in Singapore the opposition
had no justification to oppose and that if it did so it should expect
to be crushed.

The theme stayed with Lee thereafter. The elimination of
opposition never struck him as an exercise in autocracy, only as a
necessary measure in the interests of the people. He appeared sincere in this belief, which helped him to develop his autocratic disposition into a philosophical thesis. Always anxious to maintain
his international image as a progressive leader, Lee never took an
extreme measure without finding an intellectual rationale for it.

Speaking at Chatham House in London in 1962, Lee endeavoured
to show the irrelevance of democracy in Asia. 'At a time when you
want harder work with less return and more capital investment,
one man one vote produces just the opposite,' he argued. 'This
system is not held in esteem anywhere in Asia.' Interestingly
enough, Lee seemed to have realized this only after he attained
power; until then he was a passionate advocate of the system. In
fact, even in countries where democracy did not function, the
people have held the system in esteem; it was the rulers who persistently pointed up its irrelevance – and that only after they came
to power.

Lee continued that the one-man-one-vote system leading up to
parliament, cabinet and prime minister had been 'superseded by
systems which give power effectively to one man or a group of
men for an indefinite period. Government to be effective must
at least give the impression of enduring, and a government which
is open to the vagaries of the ballot box when the people who put
their crosses in the ballot box are not illiterate but semi-literate,
which is worse, is a government which is already weakened before
it starts to govern. ... If I were in authority in Singapore indefinitely without having to ask those who are being governed
whether they like what is being done, then I have not the slightest
doubt that I could govern much more effectively in their own
interests. That is a fact which the educated understand but we are
all caught up in this system which the British export all over the
place hoping that somewhere it will take root.'

As an exposition on the transformation of a democrat, these remarks were revealing. They showed Lee's contempt for the ballot box, his inclination to see the complex greys of Asia in simplistic blacks and whites, his disregard for the existence of effective village democracies in several parts of Asia before Britain came on the scene and his firm belief that indefinite oligarchical authority was the best form of government. In the sedate atmosphere of Chatham House, it was a nice touch to refer to that need to ask the governed periodically whether they liked what was being done for them. In Singapore, even as Lee was speaking, the business of asking was rapidly becoming a mere formality – tolerated precisely for the purpose of impressing audiences in the Chatham Houses of the world.

Other speeches during these early years of prime ministership made the message still clearer. The running theme was that the checks and balances of democracy were relevant only when governments were headed by personally motivated men and when a country was fighting colonialism; the PAP government was a people's government and demonstrably selfless and wise, so that checks and balances were not only unnecessary but would prove impediments to progress.

Even the rule of law, accepted as the basis of civilized societies elsewhere, had to be edited to suit the Lee theory. This was a particularly delicate rationale for a British-trained barrister to develop. So Lee stretched a point here and laboured an argument there – until he discovered he did not really have to offer a justification at all.

In January 1962 he tried to explain to the University of Singapore's Law Society his variation on the rule of law. He said the 'sociological and economic milieu' of Singapore was different from that of the West which made it necessary to 'bridge the gulf' between the ideal and the practical. 'Forms and principles' were fine, but unless they were 'adapted and adjusted' to meet given circumstances, they would undo society. Singapore's young lawyers should 'bridge the gulf quickly' lest they spend years 'floundering in confusion'. The phrase 'law and order' was misleading for it implied that 'good law led to good order'. The phrase should be reversed, giving order precedence over law.

After this parade of phrases and ideas, it was easy to prop up the thesis that the British pattern of *habeas corpus* was unsuited to the 'sociological and political conditions' of Singapore. Only 'academic liberals' talk about 'individual liberty' and in this they were joined by a strange fellow-traveller, the 'communist revolutionary'. Lee could not have made his point clearer, and if the young lawyers still floundered in confusion it could only have been because they found it difficult to bridge the gulf between the discipline they had learned and the new-found philosophy of their prime minister.

A few years later the Singapore Advocates' and Solicitors' Society heard the prime minister go even further. This time Lee was questioning the relevance of the judiciary itself. He referred to criminal prisoners in Singapore and said some of them, though self-confessed murderers and kidnappers, had been acquitted on trial. The alert executive had continued to keep them in jail because 'to let them out would be to run the very grave risk of undermining the whole social fabric'. Lee propounded this amazing thesis and dwelt on the dangers of the judiciary apparently to prepare his listeners for what he had to say on political prisoners held without trial. 'We have over a hundred political detainees, men against whom we are unable to place even an iota of evidence.' But, Lee said with finality, their detention was necessary to maintain normal standards of society.

Now that he was on the other side of the fence, Lee had evidently forgotten his old speech about detentions on the basis of what X told Z who told Alpha who told Beta who told the Special Branch, and let the devil take the courts. It was a state of mind which made perfectly natural Lee's later abolition of the jury system, without so much as giving the Singapore Bar a hearing. The question of giving citizens a hearing did not arise.

Given this approach to detention and the rule of law, Lee never bothered to change – except to make it more repressive – the Internal Security Act which he inherited from the colonial administration he had fought. Indeed, the colonialists had administered the Act, then called the Preservation of Public Security Ordinance, with a degree of grace; detainees were released after a decent period of time and often brought to trial under the due processes of law. Under Lee, the grace disappeared. He consolidated the Act and made it the permanent base of political life in Singapore. If a Gandhi had arisen to lead a popular civil disobedience movement against the Lee government in Singapore, he would have found this Asian premier a harsher overlord than faraway Westminster, and he would simply have disappeared behind the high walls of Changhi Prison.

The Internal Security Act gave the government unlimited powers. Any citizen could be arrested arbitrarily on unspecified charges and held without trial initially for a period of two years. Then his case could be reviewed by an Advisory Board whose three members were nominees of the government and whose role was anyway strictly advisory. The revision completed, one could be detained indefinitely. The home affairs minister's decision was final and was not to be called into question in any court. The minister also made rules as to the manner in which representations might be made, and regulated the procedure for the Advisory Board. It was not necessary for him to disclose facts which he thought were against the national interest. In practice the government did not even say the Advisory Board had recommended the continuation of a prisoner's detention. It used the technique of juxtaposition and often announced its decisions subliminally: 'The case of Mr X was reviewed yesterday by the Advisory Board. The Government has decided to continue the detention.'

But rare were the occasions when the government took the trouble to announce an arrest. There were cases where the breadwinner of a family went to work in the morning and was never heard of again. The police would simply pick up a man and leave his family guessing about his fate.

The Act also empowered the government to 'provide for the discipline' of persons detained. It was up to the minister to decide how best to discipline a person – through solitary confinement, the dark-hole treatment, third-degree methods, even the use of drugs. A favourite method in the early days of the republic was to keep prisoners in separate cells and float rumours that one had squealed on the other. After a while they would be brought together and often, to the amusement of the police officers, fights broke out as the demoralized men accused one another of treachery.

Occasionally a detainee would be released. This happened, as one of them told the author, 'when you are found to have lost all potential to give the government any trouble'. Even then elaborate precautions were taken. 'They come and ask us to make a statement justifying our detention. This must be done not anyhow but along the lines the government has been putting out about us since our detention. I was asked to say I was working for the CUF. I did not even know what the CUF was and I guess I was still idealistic, so I said I couldn't. After eight years inside, I knew CUF was the Communist United Front and that it was the line I was expected to plead. By then I had lost all strength and I signed the statement.'

The man added that freed prisoners were asked to appear on television and otherwise give maximum publicity to their recantation. 'I was told to memorize replies for an interview. The idea is to destroy you in public.' The once great Lim Chin Siong had signalled his readiness to recant in 1967. But he begged that he be spared the humiliation of a public spectacle. Lee refused. It took two more years for Lim to crack.

The confessions followed a set pattern. Lim, after spending nine of his thirty-five years in prison, sent a pathetic handwritten letter to Lee saying: 'I have finally come to the conclusion to give up politics for good. It took me a long time to come to the above conclusion. First I thought I better commit suicide rather than taking an open stand, but after fierce struggles with myself I finally decided to face the fact.' The fact was the full formal confession, addressed to his party chairman, in which he said: 'I have completely lost confidence in the international communist movement' and 'communism is not as ideal as [we] think it is.'

A lesser-known detainee, Chong Chern Sern, said in his letter of recantation in June 1970: 'I no longer see any need for violent struggle and bloody revolution. I firmly believe that democratic socialism, not communism, is the road to happiness for the worker and the people of Singapore. Communist theories were formulated during the Industrial Revolution when workers were really oppressed by capitalists. Today all this has changed. There are even Industrial Arbitration Courts to see that both workers and employers get a fair deal.' Needless to say, Chong was an active trade union leader before he was arrested in 1969.

It was not as though a prisoner, by signing a confession, could buy freedom for the rest of his life. After release he was forced to live under very stringent conditions. The Act enabled the government to confine him to his residence, restrict him to a particular employment, prohibit him from going out of doors at specified times, direct him to notify his movements to the police, bar him from joining any organization and ban him from travelling abroad.

Sometimes his citizenship was withdrawn. The right to revoke citizenship was a weapon of terror the state used against critics. In jail a person at least remained a 'digit' in society. Rendered stateless, he became a non-person, one who lived but did not exist. He would find his employment subject to renewable work permits, the schooling of his children five times more expensive, travel impossible. He was a castaway.

Singapore, justly famous for its efficiency, was never more thorough than in the administration of the Internal Security Act. Rarely did one find a Singaporean willing to talk about such things as the life of a political detainee; it was a common saying that even the Roman Catholic Church's Legion of Mary had government informers in its ranks. For information on prisons and prisoners one was thus forced to rely on sources who, out of fear, were unwilling to let their identities be disclosed. A couple of letters by unnamed ex-detainees, and other documents, were circulated in 1971 by the left-wing Malaysians and Singaporeans for a Democratic Society (MSDS), an organization of students from the two countries living in Britain. Even after a margin was allowed for personal bitterness, the letters painted a picture which on the whole tallied with information given by other sources.

One ex-detainee said in part: 'Once detained a political detainee is treated worse than a criminal suspect; he is not given any legal safeguards and not charged in court and tried. Worse than criminal prisoners, they do not know when they will be free. One political prisoner was detained in 1957 during the time of British rule for militant trade union activities. He was imprisoned for twelve years without trial. . . .

'In detention political prisoners are subjected to periodic interrogations. During these periods they are put under solitary confinement in police lock-ups, not allowed visits from immediate families and relatives, and denied reading and writing material. Among the notorious lock-ups are those in Central Police Station, CID Headquarters and newly built prison in Queenstown. The Queenstown prison not only has quarters for interrogations, but is also fully equipped with close-circuit television to keep watch over political prisoners in their cells. When visits are allowed they are closely supervised and also covered by television.

'The treatment of political prisoners involves spiritual and political torture. The process of solitary confinement and interrogation, etc. continue until the prisoners are broken down or try to commit suicide. Lim Chin Siong was driven to attempt suicide. Those who cannot be broken are left to rot in prison. Many of over one hundred political and trade union workers detained since

1962 under the obnoxious Operation Cold Store are still in prison, not knowing when they will ever be released.'

Another detainee gave this account of prison conditions: 'The new political prison is called the Moon Crescent Centre. It has been specially constructed for political prisoners and is electronically equipped to monitor political prisoners around the clock. It has a staff specially trained in producing mental breakdown in political prisoners. Up to January 1971 no visits by solicitors have been approved. Dr Lim Hock Siew (Secretary-General of Barisan Sosialis, arrested in 1963 and now kept in Moon Crescent Centre) had been told that his request made four months ago to see a lawyer will not be approved unless he gives an undertaking not to mention anything about the treatment he is receiving. His conversation with his wife was terminated when he told this to her during a visit in January 1971.

'Seven political prisoners are known to be kept in a special cell in the Central Police Station at the present time. This place is notorious for beating up and torturing of political prisoners. . . .

'Excepting for biscuits, food from outside has been very severely curtailed at the Moon Crescent Centre. As the biscuits are taken out and exposed, they become soggy and fungus ridden in a short time. Writing material, fountain pens, articles of clothing and even calendars are not allowed in any more. Needless to say, the control of reading material is strictest of all.

'No doctors are allowed to see the political prisoners. Dr Lim Hock Siew had a duodenal ulcer and many others are sick, several needing psychiatric assistance, but no family physician has been allowed to see them. . . .'

One letter MSDS circulated was from a man still in prison. There was no mention of how the letter reached the outside world; perhaps MSDS itself had no clue. This letter told more or less the same tale as others:

'We have been in this new prison since May 1970. I do not know how many others are here but I think this place is meant to contain forty to fifty political prisoners. We are kept in groups of three and do not get even to see the others. Each of us is kept in a box-like cell without windows. The front of this box is closed by bars. We are kept in these cages all day except for meals and for five hours of forced labour. This forced labour, we have been told, is part of a compulsory "rehabilitation" programme.

'The door of our cage opens to a windowless corridor whose

walls reach up to the ceiling. There is no direct ventilation and the air is very hot and still. This is the worst place we have been in since our imprisonment without trial in February 1963. I have had several terms of solitary confinement for periods of three to six months each at the Special Branch headquarters where they used torture. Now this seems even worse – to live in a box for the rest of one's life! It seems to be that if they cannot break us politically then they intend to make us go mad in this place.

'Since coming here we have many times asked to see our lawyers but up to now we have not been allowed to do so. Visiting time is a very upsetting experience now. We are separated from our loved ones by soundproof glass and have to talk by telephone. A Special Branch officer listens in to the conversation and frequently intervenes. In truth he "conducts" the conversation. . . .

'Everything is strictly restricted so we are short of everything – writing paper, ballpoint pens, singlets and shorts, not to mention the very severely censored trickle of reading matter. . . . The food here is awful. It is cooked and served in a filthy mess. The only drink we are allowed is a nauseating concoction that is officially called tea. . . . There is virtually no incoming mail; even postcards from Amnesty have ceased arriving.'

Amnesty International naturally showed concern about the fate of political prisoners in Singapore – only to get condemned as a meddler and barred from the republic in early 1971. The previous year Amnesty's secretary-general had visited Singapore. In December the organization sent a part-time researcher, a British national named Estrella Carreras, to Singapore. She was unable to meet any senior government official. After meeting families of several detainees she went to Brunei for a two-day visit. When Miss Carreras returned from Brunei she was told at the airport that she was not allowed to re-enter Singapore. No reason was given. Later the Home Affairs Ministry issued a statement charging that Amnesty was giving respectability to illegal activities in Singapore and interfering in the affairs of political prisoners.

Like others trying to get information on Singapore's political prisoners, Amnesty also often ran into walls. One Singaporean contact wrote to an Amnesty group to say: 'I was afraid your letter would have caused the government authorities here to assume that I had some interest in the well-being of a detainee. You must be aware by now that though political detainees are being detained arbitrarily and without trial for year after year in this island, the government does not look with favour on anyone showing the least interest in the welfare or the rights of these detainees.'

Nevertheless Amnesty was successful in collecting a partial list of political prisoners. Some of the information contained in the secretary-general's draft report was set out in a letter written by Miss Carreras in September 1970 to an Asian newspaper editor who had inquired about journalist prisoners. She wrote:

'It would appear that the detainees are allowed one half-hour visit per week by a relative. Access is now through a glass wall and speaking is only possible through a telephone arrangement where the telephone call is monitored from a console; whenever the conversation drifts away from immediately personal matters the telephone line is cut and visits may be suspended.

'It would seem to be impossible to find out the names of detainees under the Internal Security Act. Even parents, husbands and other relatives are unable to find out whether in fact these people are in detention. It is possible, when someone is missing which may be by accident or that they have in fact gone underground, that in fact the missing person may be detained, but the government makes no acknowledgment of this fact. In the camps there may be one or two persons in a cell. They are not allowed to have a watch or clock or radio, but there are in a given period six books available which can be exchanged. They are allowed one letter each week and one newspaper. Some detainees are not allowed newspapers. They have to work, cleaning, scrubbing and other sundry chores. . . .

'Information was obtained concerning the following detainees. A man called Mr Tai Yuen, who was detained in Operation Cold Store. He was born in Hong Kong but had qualified for Singapore citizenship. This was then withdrawn and he was offered the opportunity to go to China which he refused. He is now not allowed to receive any writing or reading materials. He is locked out of his cell during the day, he has no work and nothing to do. He was a journalist on the *Sin Chew* daily paper. It seems that his father works on the *Sin Chew* as well. Two detainees, Mr Lee Tee Tong (an ex-Assembly man) and Mr Chua Kee Seng are both detained in Queenstown under a banishment order. With regards to Said Zahari, it is known in Singapore that he has been adopted by Amnesty International, as have in fact all the previous three, but it is thought that the group letters to him are censored.

'Apart from the usual conditions of release, renouncing communism in a written statement and on television broadcasts, the detainees are required to join the Ex-Detainees Assocation. Even if they refuse to comply with the last condition they are still detained. Although the detainees' cases can be reviewed every twelve months by the Review Board, the detainees have little confidence in the board and it is largely boycotted by them.'

Tai Yuen was released after eight years in prison and allowed to go to the University of Hong Kong.

The issue of prisoners received an unusual public airing in Singapore in January 1971 – and not only because of the banning of Estrella Carreras, which received wide publicity. The Barisan Sosialis chairman called a press conference to announce that about a hundred political prisoners had refused to eat since mid-December to protest against 'physical and mental persecutions and tortures'. He charged that prisoners were being held in solitary confinement in poorly ventilated cells for sixteen hours a day, were forced to do menial work though many were intellectuals, and received poor food and limited drinking water.

What was unusual was that the Singapore press was allowed to publish reports of the press conference. Besides, the Home Affairs Ministry broke precedent by commenting on the allegations. At first it was unclear why the government had permitted these departures from practice. Soon it became clear: it was the time of the Commonwealth Prime Ministers' Conference in Singapore and the government, ever mindful of its international standing, was keen on giving the impression that free debate was normal in Singapore.

The Home Affairs Ministry of course denied all charges of ill-treatment of prisoners. But it admitted that fifteen prisoners were on a limited hunger strike. It said that political detainees received vocational training and their own choice of books including works of Marx, Engels and Mao Tse-tung. This was stretching credulity a bit. If true, it meant that political detainees were in fact better off than journalists in Singapore who were barred from even subscribing to news releases of the New China News Agency, unless they obtained a licence to do so.

Another interesting titbit in the ministry's statement was its mention of the number of political detainees in Singapore. It put the figure at sixty-nine. A Hong Kong source with official connections with the Singapore police mentioned the figure of 700. Perhaps this included several who did not strictly qualify for the term political detainees. Amnesty International, meticulously steering clear of those detainees 'the circumstances of whose arrest would make them unlikely for consideration as prisoners of conscience because they may have been genuinely involved in terrorist activity, violent demonstration and such other activities', released in August 1970 the names of seventy-nine detainees. There have been some known arrests after that and perhaps several more unknown ones. Most knowledgeable sources put the number of political prisoners at around one hundred and eighty.

What made the fate of Lee's prisoners especially pathetic was that many of them were taken in for opposing Singapore's merger with Malaya, which only lasted two years. Writing in the *Far Eastern Economic Review* in August 1965, Chinese novelist Han Suyin recalled the 'MacCarthy type of hysteria' which had marked Lee's Malaysia campaign days and shed a tear 'for the unfortunates who, gifted with more foresight than the powers that be, protested in good faith against the ruinous arrangements for Malaysia and were branded anti-national, extremist or communist; some hauled off to jail, others losing their jobs, their families thrown out of their flats because guilt by association became a salient feature of proceedings during the episode of Malaysia.' Now that the episode was over, Han Suyin said, it was a good time for the prime minister to show 'wisdom and statesmanship' by remedying the prisoner situation. Lee has never been known to admit to a mistake. His critics remained in prison with no hint of a trial or release.

Subjugation of the trade union movement went hand in hand with destruction of political opposition. Unions had been the base of powerful left-wing leaders in the PAP; Lee could not eliminate them without also destroying their base. Besides, in his new Singapore he was determined to create a situation in which there could not possibly be a source of influence other than the government itself. Trade unions had been a potent force in Singapore's public life in the past, but now they had to yield to the sole fountain-head of all power. Above all, Lee proposed to orientate the economy along lines which would attract free enterprise capitalism – and one of the first steps had to be workers' discipline. Lee's efforts to break the back of the trade unions began almost as soon as he achieved power.

A few months after the PAP victory there was a strike over the dismissal of ten employees in an electrical plant. The government sent the riot police in. The labour minister told union leaders that, now that the PAP was the government, it was its duty to enforce the law. The union leaders argued that they had put the PAP in power and that therefore the government owed them a better deal.

The lines of battle were clear. Every time there was a serious labour situation, Lee hardened a little more towards unions. Overt as well as covert pressures became common, and threats to union activists frequent. Left-wing leaders frequently complained of police intimidation.

One case the government brought against a trade union leader won notoriety because in its anxiety to show its determination, it ordered the attorney-general to appear in proceedings before a magistrate. The union leader involved in this case happened to be Indian and the official propaganda machinery launched a campaign to show that he had deliberately used his union to inconvenience the public during the Chinese New Year season. Even racialist propaganda seemed in order when the government had a point to score.

Another union leader, now living in Malaysia, told the author how he was arrested by a police officer on a charge of intimidating workers during a strike. This leader had been hand-picked by Lee as one of 'Kuan Yew's men', to influence workers towards the government way of thinking. But he had shown a tendency to be independent and genuinely left-wing. After the arrest the government produced three witnesses, none of whom the leader had seen during the strike. On a hunch he called the police officer concerned as his witness. Apparently taken by surprise, the officer testified in favour of the leader. In spite of this, the union leader was convicted.

Lee's close associate, Finance Minister Goh Keng Swee, distributed a memorandum in 1960 to all trade unions setting forth the government's philosophy on trade unionism. The emphasis, the memorandum said, was to be on industrialization. The government wanted to attract capital by restraining unions through the establishment of wage norms. Workers should remember that capital went to Hong Kong and Malaya because of the uncertainty of wage norms and the danger of labour disputes in Singapore.

This rather frank clarification – from an avowedly socialist government – gave workers a clear idea of what they could expect. At first the Lee group in the PAP set up its own unions in various trades; these were completely overshadowed by the powerful unions led by Lim Chin Siong, Fong Swee Suan, Sandra Woodhull and other left-wing leaders. Then it tried to capture the leadership of the Singapore Trade Union Congress, a conglomerate which had been established to amalgamate numerous individual unions then in existence. This also failed because the leftists retained the majority in leadership elections.

Defeated in his attempts to gain supremacy through conventional channels, Lee moved on to somewhat unfamiliar ones. The government began using its executive authority to decide who should attend conferences between unions and the government and what kind of consultative authority should be enjoyed by whom. This had the effect of making the STUC practically de-recognized at the official level. After a while perhaps Lee himself got tired of the charade: the STUC was struck off the register.

In the meantime, Lee set up a rival organization called the National Trades Union Congress with his own lieutenants as leaders. At the start, this was not much help because it did not attract any significant labour support. Though the STUC had been killed, the leftist labour heroes were still at large and had established the Singapore Association of Trade Unions as their new vehicle. Eventually Lee plugged all loopholes by banning the SATU and ordering the mass arrests of left-wing union leaders. This was accomplished at the time of Operation Cold Store in 1963, which made the final break-up of independent trade unions a reality. From then on workers were sheep and the NTUC the shepherd.

Subsequent mopping-up was easy. The Industrial Relations Ordinance and the Employment Act, enforced in 1968, made arbitration compulsory. Lee's new (post-power) thesis was that opportunities for worker militancy could be removed by moving disputes to the arena of legal argument; worker-unity was no longer to be a criterion, nor collective bargaining a norm. Left-wing leaders pointed out that the language used in courts was English – which rendered impotent the most powerful of the unions leaders, who were Chinese-educated.

The 1968 laws, which were endorsed by the NTUC in the name of 'responsible unionism', also curtailed unions' right to strike, gave managements sole jurisdiction in hiring and firing, increased working hours, and reduced overtime, retirement benefits, maternity leave and sick leave.

Encouraged, employers did not hesitate to dictate terms to

workers. Dutifully taking their cue from the government, industrial arbitration courts took the side of managements, arguing that
the imposition of additional liabilities on employers for the benefit of workers would be tantamount to giving sectional interests
precedence over the interests of the national economy. The
government succeeded in its basic objective of giving foreign
capital the climate for profit which it could not get elsewhere.

In terms of free-enterprise economy, Lee Kuan Yew could fully
justify his anti-labour policy. The surprise was that he continued
to pose as a socialist, and that august organizations like the
Socialist International continued to accept him as such. Besides,
Lee was sowing the seeds of long-term conflict in Singapore. The
NTUC cover under which the anti-labour policies were carried out
was too transparent. The NTUC was seen as an arm of the government dependent on the government for the bulk of its finances and
lacking significant worker-support; in contrast to the 1950s, only
twenty per cent of the work force in Singapore was now unionized
and out of this only forty per cent was fee-paying.

While the NTUC remained unrepresentative on the one hand, on
the other, workers had reasons to feel that Singapore's prosperity
was being achieved at their cost. During the 1960s the cost of living rose by eleven to twelve per cent, but there was no comparable
rise in the wages of unskilled workers who constituted seventy-
five per cent of the labour force. Denied their share of the cake,
denied also their customary rights to organization and bargaining
independently of the government, Singapore workers tended to
be a demoralized lot. The lifting of the wage freeze and the
announcement of a limited bonus system in 1972 probably
indicated the government's awareness of the dangers inherent in
such a situation. But opinion persisted among close students of
Singapore that worker dissatisfaction could erupt into revolt at an
opportune time in the future.

In the short run the elimination of political opponents and independent trade unions seemed to secure Lee Kuan Yew's position
and the stability of his government. It also seemed to fit Singapore
into what had emerged as an Asian governmental pattern.
Although the level of efficiency brought to it was typically Lee's,
the suppression of critics was not a new idea devised in Singapore.
In many parts of Asia the end of white colonialism only marked
the beginning of a new Brown Sahib colonialism which carried on
the same political bureaucratic machinery left behind by the

European masters. Most first-generation leaders in newly independent Asian countries were nationalists who secretly relished the practices of the imperialism they had helped to throw out.

The more insecure among them tightened security laws and police powers instead of relaxing them – the shortest cut to survival. Singapore fell into this category. In the event, what happened to the living standards of some people in Lee Kuan Yew's Singapore was a well-known story of triumph; what happened to their minds was an untold tragedy.

The tragedy was the more poignant because every act in it was performed from a moralistic angle. The cabinet's resident philosopher, Foreign Minister Rajaratnam, once told a group of newspapermen about the need to differentiate between 'dynamic nationalism' and the old type of anti-colonial nationalism. 'The old nationalism had to create an ungovernable society because that was the only way of eroding the will of the imperialist government to govern. Anti-colonial nationalism was dedicated to creating a discontented, ungovernable society. But now that we are independent the political spirit and habits bred by the old nationalism have become dangerous anachronisms. So one of the immediate concerns of the new nationalism should be to reorientate people's attitudes towards governments and authority.'

People whose governments straightforwardly admitted to being communist or military at least knew where they stood. In Singapore, where professions were democratic while practices were dictatorial, the tragedy was compounded. Lee and his cabinet were men of extraordinary ability who could competently have governed a much larger country and tackled really complex problems. By choosing to be dictatorial in their small territory and achieving a degree of material progress in the process, they projected the dangerous thesis that an efficient Asian government could not also be democratic or humane.

If anything seemed to matter to Lee more than the never-ending increases in Singapore's official growth statistics, it was his image in the West as a democratic socialist. He attended meetings of the Socialist International, paid sabbatical visits to Harvard University, addressed any group of academics or intellectuals that cared to invite him and generally held forth as a convinced liberal cast in the English mould. The West accepted him as such. He was not only impressively articulate in English, he had been intellectually shaped by the West so that his success was flattering to the West.

He also had achieved visible progress for his country – success which demanded recognition. Besides, throughout the post-war period Lee was telling the West what it wished to hear: that Asia was not ready for democracy and that communism was the big danger which dwarfed everything else. Lee was at once the West's gift to Asia and Asia's tribute to the West.

Only by the 1970s did some faint cracks begin to appear in this carefully preserved façade. Lee's sledgehammer blows on the defenceless press in Singapore sent reverberations round the globe. His expulsion of the Amnesty International representative received widespread attention. Headlines were also made by the government's irrational excesses against long hair in Singapore. These were straws which suddenly floated in the wind, indicating that Singapore might not after all be what it appeared to the outside world.

Appropriately the voice of criticism came loudest from London, where previously the media and the government had together done much to glorify the Lee profile. In November 1971, when Lee was in London, the *Sunday Times* published an editorial under the telling title 'Doctor of laws and master of injustice'. It said:

' "He is himself essentially a democratic socialist . . . a passionate multi-racialist . . . bestrides his narrow world like a Colossus . . . not a demagogic operator but a master of reasoned argument . . . sees his country as both a Switzerland and an Israel of the East." For this moral giant of our time an honorary degree seems indeed the least reward. It is not the Public Orator's fault that he must put the candidate in the most flattering light. But in presenting Prime Minister Lee Kuan Yew of Singapore for the degree of Doctor of Laws last week, the Public Orator at Sheffield University omitted some especially relevant details.

'Mr Lee is certainly a multi-racialist, and he may call himself a democratic socialist, but his interest in reasoned argument is a narrow one – confined, in fact, to argument which he agrees with. Singapore has a one-party Parliament, which should enable a Prime Minister to liberate responsible dissent outside. Not at all. Free speech has been virtually extinguished by the well-known social democratic device of imprisonment without trial. The Singapore press is in chains. Newspapers can only be published on Government licence and Chinese as well as English-language papers have closed. Editors and journalists are now in prison, untried, because the passionate, reasoned and altogether Colossus-like Mr Lee objected to what they wrote.

'When outside critics, like the International Press Institute or the Press Foundation of Asia or the Commonwealth Press Union, demur at this, Mr Lee unleashes two further talents which the Public Orator at

Sheffield – and earlier at Liverpool University – overlooked. One is melodrama. The critics discover that it is not free speech they are defending, after all, but some sinister commercial interest associated at different times with the CIA, Lord Thomson, the Chase Manhattan Bank and Mao. The second talent is more subtle. Mr Lee brings his massive dialectical powers to the defence of the proposition that free speech is a danger because his people are incapable of resisting subversion and corruption by the media. It is an argument, but its affinity with democratic socialism is fully comprehended only at the universities of Sheffield and Liverpool.

'There is yet another achievement which they overlooked in their new Doctor of Laws. He abolished the jury system, which had been operative in Singapore since its foundation. From mid-April to December, 1969, when the law was changed, he silenced the attempt to debate it in Singapore. On his instructions the newspapers were forbidden to publish, when it mattered, the critical resolution of the special meeting of the Bar, and its memorandum.

'A good many English liberals, somehow overlooking this appalling record, have been captivated by Mr Lee's fluency, his intelligence, his manifest stature as an international statesman. He has ably led Singapore through many perils. But for two great British universities to honour him as a Doctor of Laws devalues the degree and dishonours the first principle of university life – that ideas shall be freely exchanged.'

A few weeks earlier the *Statesman* of India had similarly marked Lee's visit to that country with a blistering editorial attack. It attributed Singapore's agitation for a British military presence east of Suez to Lee's personal anglophilia and said:

'He does enjoy appearing on British television, saying rude things in an impeccable accent and receiving the plaudits with which the British are so free on such occasions. At home in Singapore however he does not cut so amiable a figure, and it is only by some violence to the word that he can be described as a democrat. In nine years of near-autocratic rule he has created a society of soulless conformists. The constitution is supposedly democratic but no party other than the ruling PAP can contest elections without inviting some sort of pressure and intimidation; a 'democracy' which succeeds in ensuring that all the 58 sitting members belong to the ruling party is too perfect to be true. A Singapore merchant indiscreet enough to stand against Lee Kuan Yew in 1968 found two of his closest associates arrested for reasons that have still to be revealed. A submissive press and the lack of an opposition have enabled Mr Lee to strut about his inconsequential stage and see himself as a Southeast Asian leader.'

Power did not make Lee Kuan Yew an autocrat. Instinct did. A child who invariably got what he wanted; a schoolboy who was idolized by his family into believing he was someone apart from the crowd; an undergraduate who impressed his mates as self-centred and domineering; a qualified barrister whose ability fostered an overwhelming contempt for others; a Hakka naturally prone to be aggressive; a Chinese with instinctive faith in élitism and the theory that some are born to rule while others are born to be ruled; a man alienated by his upbringing, driven by a need to make a place for himself – Lee Kuan Yew was a natural authoritarian. The caginess developed during the early years of life-and-death struggle with militant trade unionists in the PAP merely consolidated what instinct and environment had earlier laid out. Power only gave it scope, a chance to justify itself.

And he used power shrewdly. While Singapore took on the characteristics of a police state, Lee left just enough open ends to make it possible for him to argue that it in fact was a beacon of democratic socialism. Parliament was not dispensed with – though there was not one opposition member in it. Elections were not abolished – though all meaning went out of the exercise by 1963. The opposition Barisan Sosialis was not banned – though every leader showing any potential was either jailed or exiled. The press was not nationalized – though it was left a boneless wonder. With such hollow ornaments diligently preserved, Lee could periodically tell the West that Singapore was a democratic paradise where, if people did not like what he was doing, they could vote him out at the next opportunity.

In fact no such thing was possible. The policy of selective arrests and banishments had reduced opposition groups to political jokes unattractive to voters. Those who extended meaningful assistance to opposition parties were made to pay heavily for their indiscretions. Tan Lark Sye, one of Singapore's legendary millionaire pioneers who founded the Nanyang University with Lin Yutang as its first vice-chancellor, was foolish enough to help finance some Barisan candidates in 1963. Tan Lark Sye had his citizenship revoked.

CHAPTER EIGHT

The Mould of Conformism

The worth of a state in the long run is the worth of the individuals composing it. . . . A state which dwarfs its men, in order that they may be more docile instruments in its hands even for beneficial purposes, will find that with small men no great thing can really be accomplished.

JOHN STUART MILL

It is a measure of Lee's effectiveness that over the years he seems to have produced a new kind of young Singaporean who shares his conviction that democracy is a dispensable virtue in a society which 'must put survival above everything else'. The highest priority in his domestic policy has always been education and he has said that in fifteen or twenty years it is possible to turn out a generation thinking as the leaders want them to think. His favourite word when referring to Singaporeans is, characteristically, 'digits'.

Digits are mass-produced in the universities where, among the innocents, Lee is such a pop idol that often there is a craving to imitate his signature style, the way he writes L, the way he walks. Professor D.J. Enright wrote in *The Times* in 1969: 'The Prime Minister's interest in the younger generation is naturally rather flattering. Some of them are gratified to gather that their task is that of nation building – which strikes them as both grander and easier than the task of satisfying their teachers and building up their own minds. One brand new student, all rosy from Mr Lee's pep talk, informed me that the first year would attend in force a gramophone recital of *Macbeth* but not of *Lear* because the former was on the syllabus and the latter not, and "we Singaporeans are a pragmatic people". This is the drawback to the exhortatory method of nation building: the simple-minded, the second-rate and the merely self-committed come to the top while the intelligent and idealistic feel there is no place for them in a world which is new but not very brave.'

There are many digits in Singapore who readily jump to the defence of their prime minister, even on issues which relate to the denial of individual liberty to digits. It is the old argument all over again – that when communist conspiracies abound, when unfriendly neighbours cast covetous eyes on you and when economic progress is a pre-condition for survival, you must not unrealistically clamour for civil rights. That he has a section of Singapore's educated youth buying this line has no doubt strengthened Lee's conviction about the righteousness of his strong-man rule.

No boy or girl can enter a university in Singapore without written political clearance from the government, appropriately called a Suitability Certificate. A student-applicant's educational qualifications and academic record have no bearing on his 'suitability', which is determined on the basis of his and his family's political background. Decisions on the issuance of the certificate are taken not by educational authorities but by the department dealing with internal security; the department's guideline is that communists should be kept out of higher institutions of learning and potential centres of talent scouting and recruitment. The number of students denied Suitability Certificates is never announced.

Han Suyin called it 'the extraordinary law by which adolescents at the age of fourteen to seventeen are found guilty of "political left leanings" '. At first educationists as well as students protested against the pernicious system. That only hardened Lee Kuan Yew. Incensed by criticism from University of Singapore students, he made a speech pouring contempt on them: 'I often wonder whether you understand, whether you have a grasp of the realities of the society in which you are living. I have the feeling very often that because the administration is so effective, you are living – like fishes in aquariums.'

Protests soon vanished. Today Singaporeans accept the Suitability Certificate as a 'dead issue' with which they must live. It is one of the subjects which can never be publicly discussed in the island.

Lee Kuan Yew was apparently not satisfied with mere executive power; he wanted the ideological allegiance of his people. Great emphasis has therefore been placed on directing people's minds along approved lines, keeping harmful ideas out of Singapore's air and, above all, moulding the young.

It is not widely known that Singapore, like China, has its

Little Red Book: the *Code of Conduct for the Vigilante Corps Members* which sets out guidelines for Lee Kuan Yew's ideal citizen. Some excerpts:

The Concept. Human beings have basic needs. Human beings have basic obligations.
Basic Human Needs. Food, water and clothes. Housing. Medical care. Education. Security.
The State provides our basic needs. The Republic of Singapore is our society. We elected our Government and the Government is responsible for the organization of our society. It is through the efforts made by the Government, on our behalf, that we are able to obtain our basic needs.
Security is a basic need. A full-scale part-time National Service is our guarantee for deterring any threat from within or outside. If every young able-bodied individual is always available for the service of our Nation then the State will be constantly alert. The People's Defence Force, the Special Constabulary and the Vigilante Corps constitute a full-time National Service.
To conduct ourselves as good individuals, neighbours, citizens and National Servicemen, we must live up to our motto – From Each His Best.
As an individual: Rule One, Work Hard. Rule Two, Be Fit. Rule Three, Be Clean.
Work is an obligation. Nobody owes us our living.
Man must have sufficient natural food (non-fattening). Fasting occasionally is good.
Bathing in hot water is good for bodily cleanliness. Regular moving of the bowels ensures internal cleanliness.
As a neighbour: Rule Four, Be Tolerant. Rule Five, Be Just. Rule Six, Be Civic-Minded.
As a citizen: Rule Seven, Know Your Country. Rule Eight, Know Your People. Rule Nine, Observe the Law.
As a National Serviceman. Rule Ten, Be Loyal. Rule Eleven, Be Dedicated to Duty. Rule Twelve, Be Exemplary.

These precepts – which, incidentally, reflect a faithful image of Lee's personality – are, of course, to be commended. Undoubtedly citizens do benefit by keeping their bowels open, while industry and loyalty are fine qualities. What is disturbing are the policies considered necessary in order to make this wholesome and tidy way of life a reality.

One of the first steps the government took as it came to power was to establish the Political Study Centre which, donning academic garb, supervised an intensive re-education programme for government employees and others whom the government wanted to bring immediately under the umbrella of 'Singapore ideology'.

One of the men in charge of the Centre once went out of his way to tell the author that he was an official brainwasher. The style, as later inquiries revealed, was to shock the listener with what looked like frankness and then argue that the government had nothing to hide and that everything was being done in the best traditions of academic freedom.

The Political Study Centre conducted seminars and study courses conceived to explain Singapore to Singaporeans. After a while its work was taken over directly by the Ministry of Home Affairs which appointed staff tutors to carry on the programme. One year's schedule of activity gave an idea of the scope and targets of the scheme. Cyclostiled and stamped 'Confidential', it envisaged Police Academy courses, Special Police courses, armed forces research projects, courses for civil servants, courses and individual talks for schools and institutions of higher learning, and courses for trade unions. 'Singapore in the Modern World' was the subject of a twenty-seven-lecture course for Police Academy junior officers. It was reduced to a twenty-four-lecture course for senior officers and selected groups studying for qualifying examinations. This was complemented by a special six-lecture course for in-service CID officers.

Subjects covered for the armed forces included 'Communism in Singapore', 'Southeast Asia in the 1970s' and 'USA and USSR in Southeast Asia'. The theme of a twelve-lecture course for civil servants was 'Dynamics of Nation Building'. The lectures invariably propagated the notion of Singapore as Lee Kuan Yew envisaged it, condemned all other notions as unpatriotic and explained why it was the duty of government servants to identify themselves with the political leadership and help establish its ideology.

The message was carried to schools as well. Ten-lecture courses were given to pre-university students in several schools on 'Singapore and the Modern World.' The scope was enlarged in the programme of individual talks to take in such topics as 'Youth Revolt', 'Graduates and National Service', 'Democratic Socialism in the Singapore Context', 'Political Situation in Southeast Asia', 'Student Revolt and Responsible Participation in National Development'. These lectures were given not only to educational institutions but to a wide assortment of local institutions, from the Rotary Club and the Red Cross to the YWCA and the Sri Narayana Mission.

Trade unions received special attention from the organizers of the re-education programme. 'Modernisation of the Labour Movement in Singapore' was the commonest theme of the courses designed for workers. Seminars and workshops were held for the National Trades Union Congress, in addition to thirty-lecture courses. The lectures were often repeated to individual trade unions and smaller groups. The running thread in these courses was that agitation for workers' rights was unpatriotic in a free country and that the workers' primary objective was to help the government to achieve progress.

Recasting the education system itself was the most important item in the programme of thought-control. Lee never underestimated the significance of catching them young. He acknowledged the power of schools and universities to turn out desired types within the space of a generation.

Clear in his own mind about the types he wanted in Singapore, he began shaping the government's education policies with special care. Soon secondary schools were tamed and the universities became citadels of conformism.

A revealing insight to Lee's propensity for regimented education was the introduction of a daily patriotism drill. Lee is known as an Anglophile who holds Americans in contempt, but in his search for an educational system 'which will produce not softies but a rugged society', he hit on the American habit of schoolchildren being assembled before the national flag every morning to recite a pledge of allegiance. Singapore children were told to swear: 'We the citizens of Singapore pledge ourselves as one united people, regardless of race, language or religion, to build a democratic society, based on justice and equality, so as to achieve happiness, prosperity and progress for our nation.'

After that it was a short step to the system of compulsory military service for all students – a sensitive subject on which public discussion is discouraged. Lee seemed to believe that it was possible to achieve through drill and government fiat the lofty ideals he set for his education policy: 'Build in reflexes of group thinking, reshuffle the emphasis on various values, produce qualities of leadership at the top and qualities of cohesion on the ground.'

By enforcing changes in the management of schools, by revising the syllabus, by introducing PAP men into teachers' unions and above all by reorganizing and de-emphasizing Chinese education, Lee brought the network of schools under effective state control. The necessity to obtain Suitability Certificates before students could enrol themselves for higher education helped keep them in line, as did the practice of the Special Branch maintaining an individual dossier on students which was consulted at the time of their employment.

With the Security Department guarding admissions to the universities, it might have seemed possible to expect that the universities themselves would be left free to carry on their work undisturbed. But like trade unions, universities were of special interest to Lee because he had seen how influential they could be in shaping events in Singapore. He set out to bring the two universities under direct government- and party-control.

The offensive was two-pronged. On the one side he successfully introduced a heavy dose of politics into campus organizations, playing one against the other. On the other he used the prerogative of the government to argue that as state funds were being allocated to support the university, the government must have a say in its running.

At the University of Singapore the vice-chancellor resigned in protest. Thereafter the goverment's and PAP's role in the university steadily increased. Lee put his men into the university syndicate, the faculty and the student organizations. He also took men from the faculty into the government, giving the impression that those who 'showed promise' could look forward to proper rewards from the state. New 'politicians' in the faculty played the Local Staff Associations against the Expatriate Staff Association, making the locals envious of the privileges the expatriates enjoyed. Soon the government took the official position that expatriates should keep out of local issues – and local issues could include everything from Singapore art to traffic congestion.

In 1968 Lee executed his *coup de grâce* on the University of Singapore: abandoning all make-believe he appointed Deputy Prime Minister and PAP Chairman Dr Toh Chin Chye as vice-chancellor. For Dr Toh it was necessarily a part-time job, for he continued as a senior member of the Cabinet. But the arrangement brought the university finally and firmly under the thumb of the government and that was what mattered to Lee.

Rougher tactics were used to subjugate the Nanyang University, perhaps because of the traditional influence leftists enjoyed there. The government-supervised programme of 'reorganisation' was carried out specifically to rid the university of communist influence. Scores of students were arrested, scores more expelled and it was announced that the founder's citizenship was cancelled because 'out of extreme racialist sentiment he knowingly allowed himself to be used by his associates to advocate the communist cause in Malaya'. This punishment had the desired effect of instilling fear into the minds of the Nanyang people.

The fact that Nanyang was identified with the Chinese stream in Singapore gave Lee the opportunity to justify his crackdown on the university on the principle of racial liberalism. He said it was dangerous to make Nanyang a symbol of Chinese superiority. Throughout Southeast Asia, he told students, fifteen million Chinese were being discriminated against because they remained apart from local communities. 'Our geographical and ethnological positions are realities which we must face.'

That was in October 1959, months after Lee took office when friendship with and solicitude for Malaya was part of his creed. In fact geographical realities seemed hardly relevant to what he was doing to Nanyang, for he did the same thing to the University of Singapore, by no means a symbol of Chinese superiority. The real motivation appeared to be that the government did not want universities in Singapore to breed analytical minds.

This narrow approach to education became abundantly clear when Lee launched a campaign against 'think subjects' such as politics and philosophy. Apparently these were seen as fields where the seeds of intellectual independence were most easily sown. Some of the more independent-minded students and lecturers in the University of Singapore had been in the departments of political science and sociology and this seems to have made Lee abhor the humanities and liberal arts in general. At the university orientation meeting for freshers in 1970 Lee asked students to shun political science, philosophy and sociology and go for more useful subjects. In 1970-1 the Public Service Commission stopped all bursaries to students taking these subjects. Some of the 'reforms' Toh Chin Chye introduced as vice-chancellor had the effect of keeping 'think subjects' bottled up. He merged the political science department with the history department, which was headed by another cabinet minister. The number of political science lecturers was reduced from twelve to five at one stage. The ubiquitous secret police, the Special Branch, constantly kept universities under surveillance. Not only were the extra-curricular activities of teachers and students closely watched, but lectures in some departments were recorded.

At the student level, activities were plentiful, but none crossed the limits. Controlled outlets were provided for undergraduate idealism: elaborately organized elections for student unions, a student publication which would publish now an article on dissent, now a sarcastic speech on Singapore democracy by David Marshall. Such outlets served the essential purpose of giving some of the more active students the feeling that they were keeping themselves in the mainstream of life. But the government's watchful eye never left them. A network of official associations kept students under observation as well as busy.

The most ambitious of these associations were the 'Pyramids' established in the late 1960s. The Senior Pyramid was meant to be a recreational club with a programme of discussions, seminars and lectures. Membership was only by invitation and was extended to university staff and civil servants. The Junior Pyramid concentrated on attracting students with leadership potential. Members were offered overseas trips, recognition by the country's political leadership and the chance to get key positions in the PAP. Ministers met and addressed club members frequently. The Pyramids were essentially an extension of the government's programme of influencing students; they were housed at the Political Study Centre for a while. One student leader remarked: 'These days when a boy goes into the University, he is anti-PAP. When he goes out, he joins the PAP.'

If the Pyramids were a positive step in the government's bid to tame students, the subversion and eventual de-recognition of the University Socialist Club was a negative move, and perhaps more telling in its impact. The Socialist Club had a proud niche in Singapore's anti-colonial history. Founded in 1952 'to promote the cause of socialism in Singapore and Malaya', it became the colourful stamping ground of a succession of brilliant young undergraduates. Many of its leading lights later became prominent in government, the civil service and the professions. Lee Kuan Yew himself had used it as his first conduit to the campus. The Socialist Club had backed the PAP until 1961.

Its star began to set following its failure to abandon socialism when Lee and the PAP did so. As Lee's campaign to reorganize education gathered momentum, the Socialist Club became a prime target of attention.

The wheel of history took a most ironic turn in 1963 when Lee Kuan Yew banned the Socialist Club's famous journal *Fajar* (Dawn). He claimed that he had 'intercepted letters' to show that politicians were manipulating the student magazine. A decade earlier, when *Fajar* had attracted punitive action from the colonial government, it had been allowed to go to court and Lee as a defending counsel had helped free the magazine and its young editors on the strength of their democratic rights. In 'free' Singapore the question of legal remedy did not arise. No one dared even mention the irony of Lee Kuan Yew killing the very publication he had prevented the imperialists from killing. And the *Fajar* that Lee killed was a pale shadow of the vibrant *Fajar* he had defended.

In 1964 a rival organization called the Democratic Socialist Club suddenly appeared in the campus. It received well-publicized patronage from cabinet ministers and quickly became known as the proper club to which to belong. Simultaneously rumours spread that Socialist Club members who became too active ran the risk of losing their scholarships and winning a place on the government's blacklist.

In October 1970 Lee ordered the final act. The Assistant Registrar of Societies served notice on the Socialist Club to furnish proof of its existence within three months. A club representative said the number and names of members could not be revealed 'for obvious reasons'. One not-so-obvious reason may have been that membership had by then become so thin that the club did not want to publicize its weakness. In May the Socialist Club was quietly struck off the Register of Societies. Twenty years of historical bangs ended in an unheard whimper. Lee had cleansed the university.

Thanks to these effective tactics, most students developed appropriately grateful attitudes towards the government. They saw the appointments of ministers to the university staff as necessary because pure academicians were unable to produce what was required 'in the Singapore context'. They accepted the values given to them by ministers and said their first responsibility was to get a good degree, after which they were to help the government.

Occasionally one came across a student who seemed to have a different understanding of the situation. One such said the government had been over-successful in reshaping student attitudes so that 'there is intellectual sterility in the university'. Above all, there was widespread fear of infiltrators and informers;

no one knew for sure who was an active PAP cadre and who was not. Consequently the general feeling was that it was best not to get involved. 'If you are caught you will be blacklisted; there will be no jobs in government, no firm will employ you and parents will object to you. So why stick your neck out?'

Lee personally saw to it that students were left in no doubt that they were sticking their necks out if they took interest in what did not directly concern them. Whenever he addressed a student meeting his tone was intimidating. If a question rose from the floor, he would first insist on knowing the student's name, citizenship and subject of study. If a questioner said he was a Malaysian, Lee would say he had no right to ask questions. If the questioner said he was studying chemistry, Lee would chastise him for asking questions on politics. It did not take students long to realize that silence was golden. They became generally uninterested in public affairs and markedly docile in comparison not only with previous generations of Singapore students but with their contemporaries in neighbouring Malaysia and Indonesia. It was the consummation devoutly desired by Lee Kuan Yew.

Docility also became the dominant note among university teachers. Expatriates – such as C. Northcote Parkinson – had done much in the past to liven up the University of Singapore as a seat of learning. Under Lee, 'expatriate' became a dirty word, a symbol of degeneracy and anarchy. To one who looked upon the humanities as dangerous subjects of education, expatriates were guilty of a major Singapore sin: the inquiring mind.

Many expatriate teachers left the university, most of them unobtrusively, a few in a blaze of publicity, all with bitter experiences of government interference in education. An American professor of philosophy, Dr Ronald Pucetti, quit even though he was pointedly left out of Lee's list of evil men. According to a report distributed by the *New York Times*, Lee made a speech before the faculty in 1970 denouncing the foreign teaching staff and warning that he would not tolerate criticism of his government's policies from 'birds of passage'; he also threatened to close down the departments of political science, philosophy and history unless their syllabuses became what he described as more relevant to Singapore's national needs. Dr Pucetti was excluded from this attack, yet he resigned when his contract still had three years to run. In a farewell report he deplored the lack of contact between the administration and the staff and between the staff and students.

Many locals also quit in similar circumstances, including the chairman of the political science department, the dean of the law faculty and the dean of the science faculty. They told their associates before resigning that they were unhappy with unwarranted political interference in university affairs. One of them had reached retirement age, but even he did not leave without making his disaffection known to his colleagues.

The most celebrated 'defector' was D.J. Enright, chairman of the English department when Lee was settling down to power. The 'Enright Affair' was scintillatingly recorded by the professor-poet himself in his witty book *Memoirs of a Mendicant Professor*. The lecture which brought down the government's wrath on him, an innocuously titled piece on 'Robert Graves and the Decline of Modernism', was so brilliant that the temptation to quote it extensively is strong – but must be resisted because of lack of space. The gist of it was that it was important for new countries to remain culturally open, as art does not begin in a test tube. 'A society which has been thoroughly swept clean and garnished, brought to a high degree of spiritual hygiene, will not produce any art. Remove all "dirt" from a human being, and you will be left with an invertebrate. The boundary between "cleaning up" and "brain washing" is very uncertain. For that reason, and although I am not addicted to juke-boxes, I deplore their banning from Singapore. Singapore, we hope and believe, is a real place inhabited by real people. We do not wish to see life here decline into an interminable Sunday-school meeting.'

Unsuspectingly the poet had touched a nerve. The next day he was summoned to the Ministry of Labour. The treatment meted out to him subsequently was at once rude and dishonest. The rudeness was revealed first in the language used by the acting minister in his oral condemnation of the professor and then in the official note handed to him. The note said: ' . . . you have arrogated to yourself functions and duties which are reserved only for citizens of this country and not visitors, including mendicant professors. On two occasions you have used facilities afforded you as professor of English to involve yourself in political affairs which are the concern of local people. The Government has made clear before and after the elections that it will not tolerate any alien like you who misuses our hospitality by entering the political arena. We have no time for asinine sneers by passing aliens . . . particularly when it comes from beatnik professors.'

The repeated references in this diatribe to the functions and duties of the local people seemed particularly cynical. As Enright pointed out later, the argument would have been more cogent were it not that local citizens, unlike 'birds of passage', had been loth to disagree with the government precisely because they did not have anywhere to go to except prison.

The government's deception appeared in the formula of reconciliation which was eventually worked out between it and Enright. This was for Enright to write a letter of clarification which would be approved by the government, for the government to write a reply which in turn would be approved by Enright and then for both letters to be simultaneously published in the press. Enright's part of the agreement was observed. The government's was broken; it sent its chastising reply directly to the press, unseen by the professor.

A subtle undercurrent of this episode, so revealing of life in Singapore, was described by Professor Enright in his book. He referred to a photograph of his which often accompanied press reports of the controversy and said: 'Much later I bumped into the wife of a cabinet minister at a university party and she told me that what had set her against me at the time was not what I had said or the government had said (she did not take any of that very seriously) but my brutal sneering face as featured day after day in the *Straits Times*. Mind you, I had been let off lightly, as I realized during the period of 'Confrontation' when the *Straits Times* regularly printed a photograph of Sukarno which gave him an insane wolf-like visage with long needle-sharp fangs. In such small but telling ways can a newspaper aptly demonstrate its loyalty.'

Measures to ensure total media loyalty to the government were of course among Lee Kuan Yew's early priorities. Education and mass communications were two sides of the same coin. Indeed, elaborate arrangements to control universities were useless if the minds so carefully prepared were in the end exposed to the tender mercies of a free press. Always aware of the importance of mass communications, Lee had used them effectively when he was trying to catch national attention. The awareness continued after the attainment of power, and control of the mass media became one of his principal creeds.

The radio was no problem, for it was already a government monopoly. Lee made it an unapologetic channel of goverment propaganda. Such things as discussions on current affairs, news analysis or independent commentaries were unknown to Radio Singapura. Rather like the radio in communist countries, its news bulletins were packed with lengthy quotations from official speeches and statements. The only relieving feature was the time set apart for educational programmes.

Television was no problem either, for it was fathered by the government and conceived as another state monopoly. Television was introduced in 1963 and an official publicist called it 'the world's most remarkable television service'. This could not have been a reference to the originality of the programmes because they were no more original than those on the radio, or to their dullness because Cambodian or Thai television were not easy to beat on that count. In all probability the publicist was referring to the courage with which Singapore television cocked a snook at the Tower of Babel: it offered programmes not only in the four official languages – Malay, Chinese, Tamil and English – but in Cantonese, Hokkien and Hindustani. Language was to be no bar to Singaporeans' understanding of their government's thoughts.

Unlike radio and television, the press might have been a problem – not because the executive lacked the power to control it or the will to use that power, but because press control would be seen as such by the outside world. But Lee did not baulk at the prospect. He must have had enough confidence in his ability to justify a controlled press to a world which he expected to dazzle with economic achievements. And for a long time Lee's stifling of the press in Singapore was indeed seen as a negligible price to pay for growth.

Suppression of political opposition was disguised as tackling the communist danger, but the muffling of the press could not be fitted into that crusade. The first victim of Lee's intolerance was, for example, the *Straits Times*, which could not by any stretch of imagination be called communist. The fact that he turned against this newspaper and did not rest until it had become completely subservient to him showed that his aim was simply the elimination of all forms of disagreement; if this could not be done under the pretext of fighting communism, it would be done some other way. Arrests of political opponents, subjugation of trade unions, take-over of universities and smothering of newspapers were all part of the same relentless drive to achieve monolithic authority.

Probably the sin the *Straits Times* had committed was giving full publicity to all parties and politicians during the 1959 election campaign. Those were the days when the *Straits Times*, although leaning towards the colonial government, was a professional newspaper reporting politics in depth and in detail. It gave regular exposure during the campaign to politicians opposing the idea of merger with Malaya, as it did to Lee and other supporters of merger. It also expressed its own views – and one of them was to question Lee Kuan Yew's threats to the press. This, perhaps, was the unforgivable sin.

Lee was blunt about the vengefulness building up in him. As the *Straits Times* opposed him as a leader who threatened fundamental freedoms in Singapore, he accused the paper of subversion and, at one of the numerous lunch-time election rallies, warned: 'Any editor, leader-writer, sub-editor or reporter that strains relations between the Federation and Singapore will be taken in under the Preservation of Public Security Ordinance. We shall put him in and keep him in.'

The editor-in-chief of the *Straits Times* was the well-known Leslie Hoffman, a Singapore-born Eurasian. He understood the implications of Lee's threats and campaigned vigorously to get him to change his mind. He wrote editorials to point out that the question of subversion did not arise when a paper did its duty to report all sides of an election campaign. In a front-page editorial, under the heading 'Think Again Mr Lee', he said ominously: 'Not since the Japanese conquered this island has the press of Singapore faced such a grave threat as it does today.'

Hoffman's main argument, repeated many times, was that there were laws in Singapore under which a seditious person could be brought to trial and sent to jail. This in fact had been the practice during the colonial era, but now 'Mr Lee prefers to use the Preservation of Public Security Ordinance instead of the Sedition Ordinance – a strange choice for a man who on a previous occasion opposed the same PPSO in these words: "What he (the then Chief Minister) is seeking to do in the name of democracy is to curtail a fundamental liberty and the most fundamental of them all – freedom from arrest and punishment without having violated a specific provision of the law and being convicted of it." '

Hoffman did not yet realize that just as liberty had been fundamental to barrister Lee, its denial was fundamental to Prime Minister Lee. Hoffman carried on valiantly, took the fight to international assemblies and Commonwealth forums. Towards the end of the campaign he wrote that threats would never prevent the press from doing its job and that the *Straits Times* would continue to publish honest news whatever the consequences.

Lee knew better. As soon as the PAP won power, Hoffman escaped to Kuala Lumpur where he spent the rest of his working life. The *Straits Times*, deciding that discretion generated the best return on investment, bent like a bamboo to the wind from City Hall. Lee had made his first kill.

The noteworthy feature of the episode was not so much the triumph of the profit motive in the offices of the *Straits Times* as Lee's nonchalance. It was as though the roughing up of a newspaper was all in the day's work for a democratic socialist. With a thick skin he was telling university students in 1961, 'the heart of the problem in Singapore is getting people unafraid and prepared to make a stand'. In the Malaysian parliament he was roundly condemning the federal information minister's proposals to curb the press; he asked whether the minister's duties were 'to produce closed minds or open minds, because these instruments – the mass media, TV, radio – can produce either the open mind receptive to ideas and ideals, a democratic system of life, or closed and limited minds. I know the open debate is a painful process for closed minds. But let me make this one point – that five million adult minds in Malaysia cannot be closed, definitely not in the lifetime of the people in authority. It is not possible because, whatever the faults of the colonial system, it generated the open mind, the inquiring mind.'

The contradiction between the noble sentiments Lee aired in Kuala Lumpur where he was in the opposition, and the suppression he practised in Singapore where he was in power, did not seem to occur to him.

What started with the breaking of the *Straits Times*'s spine developed into a campaign which took in all journalism. Obviously the Singapore Union of Journalists did not get the message, for it persisted in trade unionism, questioned some of the methods of the government and criticized some aspects of the referendum on merger with Malaya. Its journal *Wartawan* (Newsman) spoke about government pressures on the press and 'the use of extraordinary laws which require no presentation of proven facts for depriving a journalist of his liberty.'

As the journalists saw it, they were being extremely fair-minded; in one issue of *Wartawan* they accepted the necessity to impose 'certain limitations on the freedom of expression' and said the union's only complaint was over 'the growing tendency to misuse these arguments as excuse to curb all criticisms and disclosures that question the wisdom of government policies and actions'.

But this was the kind of fair-mindedness the Lee government could do without: in its black-and-white world those who were not with it were against it. Arrests of journalists began within months of Lee's rise to power. He too was fair-minded, in his own way; if some journalists were arrested for being agents of communist China, others were taken in for ties with Kuomintang China. Soon half the executive-committee members of the Singapore Union of Journalists were in jail, while some were deported. At least one of them was deprived of his citizenship and left stateless in the island. Journalists as a community sank into the collective anonymity of Singapore. The message swamped the medium.

In 1959, the year of the PAP's victory, ex-journalist and Culture Minister S. Rajaratnam had told the annual meeting of the Singapore Union of Journalists: 'In the coming years newspapers should regard themselves not primarily as people who are selling news but also as valuable instruments in helping to reshape our political structure. The press should regard journalism first as a public service and only secondly as a money-spinner.'

In a few years Lee Kuan Yew was to amend this philosophy and adopt precisely the opposite position, namely that newspapers were welcome to run as profit-seeking business concerns but should keep off politics. Even Rajaratnam's early statement was less a call to conscientious public service than a friendly warning. The actions the government set in motion even as he was speaking made this abundantly clear. The press was to be a tool of the government, like trade unions and universities and everything else in Singapore, for the government alone knew what was good for the country and the government was infallible.

The Printing Presses Ordinance was enough in itself to ensure such a role for the press; the arrests and deportations were merely typical bullying embellishments. The ordinance left printers and publishers in a straitjacket. Any printing press in Singapore needed a licence which expired automatically at the end of each year – if it was not withdrawn by the government earlier. A newspaper publisher required a licence for his press and a separate licence for his newspaper which, too, was renewable each year. He also had to execute a bond, with or without sureties, to secure the payment of any penalties which the government might impose on the paper.

The Damocles' sword of annual licence-renewability was enough to keep publishers on their knees. Other provisions in the ordinance put still more pressure on them. Any justice of the peace could enter any newspaper office at any time and conduct a search. Appeals against a government decision could only be made to the governor in council, which meant to the same executive who had aggrieved the appellant in the first place; there was no provision enabling courts to intervene under any circumstances.

In fact the only relieving feature of the ordinance was that it contained one exemption clause. 'Printing of any visiting or business card, bill-head or letter heading' was left outside the purview of the ordinance.

If anyone did the impossible and slipped through this ordinance, there were other drag-nets waiting for him. The Essential Information (Control of Publications and Safeguarding of Information) Regulations gave the government powers to decide what was fit to print. Behind some government wall sat another incredible phenomenon – the Controller of Undesirable Publications. It was his sacred duty to scrutinize every printed word imported into Singapore and to decide whether it was safe enough to be passed on to Singaporeans.

Armed with such catch-all ordinances the government had no difficulty in keeping the press perennially on a leash. The prime minister's press secretary was in a position to telephone editors and tell them what to publish and what not to. Lee himself, while on a tour of Britain, reportedly sent a message to a newspaper boss back home to say that the journalist he had assigned to cover the tour was a nincompoop. The reason for the prime minister's ire was that when there were many photographs showing him sitting between Harold Wilson and his wife, the indiscreet Singapore journalist had chosen to send home for publication a picture in which Lee was sitting to the left of the Wilsons. He wanted the man recalled and the tour covered by someone who knew better.

While at home, Lee made a point of not cheapening himself by meeting the press. A couple of hand-picked reporters were occasionally called in when he had a special message to convey. For the rest, local reporters were not allowed even to report his public speeches. Transcripts of the speeches would be prepared in the prime minister's office, edited by the prime minister himself, and released to the press at his discretion, often several days after the event.

Foreign correspondents also were subjected to the process of careful selection: they had to be properly registered by the government before they could become residents. Lee was known to have his favourites among the resident foreign correspondents, the criteria for selection being the extent of the correspondent's acceptance of Lee policies and the status of his paper, in that order. The chosen few could expect to receive favoured treatment from the prime minister and the government. One persistent piece of gossip among the cognoscenti in the late 1960s was that the correspondent of a major Western newspaper had his house rent 'adjusted' by the government.

On the other hand, a well-known American correspondent working for the *New York Times* and the London *Economist* among others, was picked out for harsh treatment because, although most of his stories were flattering to Singapore, he was foolish enough to file one or two on the issue of political prisoners and the expulsion of the Amnesty International representative in 1971. The correspondent's house was bugged when he was away on tour, he was insulted and thrown out of a press conference by the prime minister's press secretary, and finally his residence permit was allowed to expire without renewal. By cultivating foreign correspondents who were amenable and by keeping out those who were not, Lee continued to assure himself a generally favourable press in the West.

But Singapore remained, in the words of a prominent local journalist now living in exile, 'a highly controlled situation. You can literally plug electroconvulsive waves to people's temples and get them to respond in a certain way by a few twists of the knobs. Every citizen is brought into a political address on an intellectual wheelchair. It's a pseudo James Bondish situation where you cannot get anybody to think.'

Such was the climate in which the meteoric *Singapore Herald* dared to appear. The explosion that followed was as inevitable as a Greek tragedy.

The men who started the *Herald* were veterans of the Singapore scene – Francis Wong, perhaps the most gifted English-language journalist in Singapore and former president of the Singapore Union of Journalists, who had met with Lee's disapproval and was working out of Kuala Lumpur; Jimmy Hahn who was technically a Korean but was married to a Singaporean and working in Singapore as the energetic general manager of Reuters; and a host of young Singapore journalists bored with the *Straits Times*. They started their bright new paper in July 1970 in the hope that advertisers as well as readers in Singapore would welcome a second newspaper for a change. They were right, but where they went wrong was in assuming that the government also would welcome another paper – an assumption based on explanatory sessions they had had with some ministers, and the approval these ministers had given the project.

Knowing 'the Singapore context' well enough, the *Herald* played it safe. Its survival depended on being different from the deeply entrenched *Straits Times*, so it occasionally went for items the over-cautious *Times* would not touch: now and then it published letters from readers which expressed disagreement with the government; it briefly reported the expulsion of an American woman journalist married to a Singapore teacher for participating in anti-American demonstrations in Manila; it published an edited photograph of a National Day military parade rehearsal. All fairly routine journalistic chores, but the *Herald* was stepping on the region's most sensitive toes. It so happened that the government did not want National Day photographs to be published beforehand – for what reason no one knew – and it certainly did not want any publicity for the expulsion of the American journalist.

Lee Kuan Yew watched the *Herald* with growing indignation. Apparently he could not tolerate the idea of an upstart little newspaper causing ripples in the glassy lake of Singapore journalism after all these years of deadly calm. In May 1971 he struck.

It would have been untypical of Lee if he had merely sent his police to close the *Herald* and jail its editors. He spun an intricate web of international intrigues, complicated financial conspiracies and mysterious political plots, worked himself into a position of taking the whole world on, brought a cross-section of Singapore papers into the arena and, by the time he was through, left two papers dead and the top men of a third in prison.

First to get the crack of the whip was the *Nanyang Siang Pau*, a leading Chinese-language newspaper with a circulation of 130,000. Detectives broke down the door at 3 a.m. on May 2 and took away Lee Mau Seng, former general manager and brother of the paper's publisher who had already sold his interest in the paper and was about to go to Canada. The editor-in-chief and a senior editorial writer were also taken in, and a fourth executive followed the next day. The government's charge was that the paper had been indulging in Chinese chauvinism and 'glamorising the communist way of life'. It offered to release the men if the paper agreed to change its editorial policy, but the paper refused, saying it was necessary to put up a fight for the principle of press freedom. Its circulation soared.

In fact, *Nanyang* was far from being a communal or communist paper. Being Chinese, it felt obliged to give news about the Chinese in Singapore, and being a newspaper, it found it necessary to publish news and photographs coming from China; these were mostly items distributed by established news agencies.

On May 8, with the *Nanyang* men already in jail, Lee made the first public reference to what he called 'black operations' in the Singapore press – meaning international conspiracies to subvert Singapore's security through the mass media. This very serious charge was made in the course of a speech at the anniversary celebrations of a small community centre. And the speech was released for publication only three days later. It was then that the public came to know that the government had a regular offensive going against the press.

Lee named no names in his speech, but what he said obviously fitted an inconsequential tabloid called the *Eastern Sun*; and government officials later confirmed that the *Sun* indeed was one of the papers Lee had in mind. The charge was that the *Sun*'s owners had taken large sums of money from Chinese communist sources in Hong Kong. The owners never said a word in reply, the senior staff interpreted this as acknowledgment of guilt and left in high dudgeon; the paper closed. The owners' silence and the ease with which the paper collapsed left people wondering what was behind it all. The best informed guess was that Lee might have caught the owners in some commercial misdeed and used that hold to conjure up the one insinuation which was not going to be denied. The extraordinary fact was that the *Nanyang Siang Pau* men, who denied the charges against them, were jailed without trial while the *Eastern Sun* owners, whose silence implied acceptance of the charges, were left free.

Then it was the *Herald*'s turn. It too had been tarred with the brush of Hong Kong-based 'black operations'. But Lee could not get a walkover in this case for at least two reasons. For one thing, the money the *Herald* received from Hong Kong was mostly commercial capital publicly invested by a professional newspaper publisher and the investment had been specifically cleared by senior ministers of the Singapore government. For another, the *Herald* did not remain silent.

Lee had made it clear by now that he had made up his mind to do certain things and nothing was going to stop him from doing them. He ordered the expulsion of three of the *Herald*'s foreign staff members. The battle was joined.

The *Herald* now became a crusading paper, crusading for its survival. Under the heading 'The Right to Live with Dignity', it gave a point by point reply to all government allegations against it and said that if it did not defend itself publicly 'we may be forced to disappear under a clinging morass of half truths, innuendos and downright inanity'.

Ignoring all arguments and world-wide protests which had by now started welling up, Lee moved in for the kill. He called a press conference and converted it into an inquisition. Before the assembled gathering, Lee directly cross-examined the manager of the Chase Manhattan Bank, which handled the *Herald* account, and left him in no doubt about what he wanted the bank to do. The manager announced his decision to foreclose on the *Herald*.

What followed was an anti-climax, except that popular reaction now rose to a crescendo. Chase Manhattan was flooded with calls from the public protesting against its move. Some fifty American families living in Singapore cabled David Rockefeller, chairman of Chase, asking him to intervene. The bank's manager called on the American embassy in Singapore to 'express concern about the public reaction'. Some British residents in Singapore cabled the National Union of Journalists in London to go to the aid of the *Herald*. Journalists in some countries including colonial Hong Kong collected funds for the *Herald*. Singapore citizens sent flowers, messages of support and pre-paid sympathy advertisements. Old women and college youths walked into the *Herald* offices daily and handed over small-denomination dollar bills as tokens of their admiration. The *Herald* staff volunteered to work without salaries. Restaurants sent free meals to the staff in the offices of the paper, filling-stations gave free petrol to staff vehicles. Motorists put up 'Save the *Herald*' stickers on their cars. Readers set up local committees to collect subscriptions, others undertook voluntary distribution of copies.

The *Herald*'s circulation tripled within a week.

Chase Manhattan Bank postponed its foreclosure and some local groups initiated moves to reorganize the *Herald*'s corporate set-up with a view to satisfying the government.

Lee Kuan Yew revoked the *Herald*'s printing licence without more ado. The ten-month-old *Singapore Herald* lay dead.

The fly-swat of the printing licence was a weapon Lee had held in his hand all along. Instead he had swung a sledge-hammer after building up a phantasmagoric stage setting. The general impression created was that Lee had mistaken a fly for an elephant. Perhaps he hadn't; perhaps he had deliberately used the sledge-hammer to let the world think that it was an elephant which had run amok in Singapore.

In the case of the *Herald*, at least, there was no mystery in Lee's desire to destroy. The paper was not as lifeless as the older ones Lee had disciplined, and it had caught the popular imagination: in Lee's scheme of things it had no place. The reasons for his actions against the *Nanyang Siang Pau* and the *Eastern Sun* were not so easily explained. One interpretation was that he did not want people to think that he was singling out the *Herald* for victimization. By bringing two very different sorts of papers into the picture, he hoped to make it appear as though a general policy was being implemented. The multiple offensive did succeed in confusing the people for a while and making any concentrated popular resistance impossible.

Another interpretation was that Lee was as usual killing two birds with the same stone. A lingering editorial tendency to show some degree of independence was one bird – an obvious one. The other was the powerful Chinese business establishment in Singapore. It was slowly becoming known in the island that local big business was growing disenchanted with some of the government's policies. The main reason for this was the apparently unlimited scope the government was willing to give foreign investment capital and trading houses while tending to look down upon local entrepreneurs. There were muffled whispers about the possibility of big Chinese business families joining forces with sections of the Chinese intelligentsia to promote new political platforms which could conceivably challenge the PAP at some stage, in some form.

The owners of the *Nanyang* and the *Sun* were among the business leaders of Singapore. By forcing one enterprise to close down under a cloud of scandal, and even more by summarily jailing Lee Mau Seng, leading light of one of the most powerful families in Singapore, Lee put the local business establishment on probation.

The most remarkable feature of the newspaper war was the level of public reaction; it was not only intense but spontaneous. By all accounts, Lee never expected anything of the sort. He tried to belittle the popular support the *Herald* received, and said the increase in the paper's circulation was not real because copies were being given away – but such attempts only made him look ludicrous in the eyes of Singaporeans who were witnessing every day the phenomenon of an unaccustomed ground-swell. There were reports that within Lee's cabinet itself there was strong resentment over an offensive which had attracted such adverse publicity. Lee budged not an inch, his whole posture revealing the political animal at bay.

Another noteworthy result of the crisis was that the inside story of Singapore was suddenly exposed to the world. Lee's approach to battle and style of fighting surprised a world which had tended to look upon him so far as a genuine democrat and socialist, albeit a no-nonsense administrator. The details which now came out told a story of such palpable repression that it could no longer be dismissed as the inevitable price of progress.

Lee's crackdown on the press had coincided with the annual assembly of the International Press Institute, and with customary brazenness he had gone to Helsinki to address the assembly. This made his actions at home front-page news round the world. For once Lee seemed unable to convince the world that he was presiding over Asia's model democracy. Singapore was seen, in the words of a Paris publisher, as 'a sort of martial law situation where for reasons of state elementary freedom of the press does not exist any more'.

Of course, what was involved was not the limited question of press freedom alone. If the newspaper crisis of 1971 served any purpose it was to point up a situation where the issue of human rights as a whole was at stake and, with it, notions of growth and government in Asia. Australia's national newspaper, the *Australian* stressed this succinctly when it said: 'Singapore is a one-party State that bears the injuries that all one-party States do to themselves. Those who see the power of the Singapore Government and the lengths to which Lee Kuan Yew is prepared to go to hang on to it are frightened by what is likely to be the result of it all. In Singapore the question is being asked more often these days: What is the point of being one of the best fed, best administered, best educated nations in Asia if that nation is also one of the least free?'

To ask that question was to recognize the essential emptiness of Lee Kuan Yew's concept of government. For the twin props of this concept were the infallibility of the government and the fallibility of the governed. Lee conjured up a patriotic halo round the denial of civil rights to an entire people. He would not only wipe out the slightest trace of independence on the part of editors, not only bully the working class into complete subjugation, but he would also meticulously regulate education, deciding who might not teach and who might not be taught. It was not merely a case of freedom being denied; it also was a case of minds being cast in a government-ordained mould. It was totalitarianism without the saving grace of honesty.

Can it really be argued that efficient government has to be inhuman? Is an orderly society above freedom of utterance? Are citizens by definition untrustworthy? The editor of a small-town newspaper in America, William Allen White, examined the question in the 1930s in words which seemed strangely applicable to Singapore in the 1970s. 'You can have no wise laws unless there is free expression of the wisdom of the people – and, alas, their folly with it. But if there is freedom, folly will die of its own poison, and the wisdom will survive. That is the history of the race. You may say that freedom of utterance is not for time of stress, and I reply with the sad truth that only in time of stress is freedom of utterance in danger. . . . Peace is good. But if you are interested in peace through force and without free discussion – that is to say, free utterance decently and in order – your interest in justice is slight. And peace without justice is tyranny, no matter how you sugarcoat it with expediency.'

Lee Kuan Yew brought peace to Singapore. He also brought progress. But his methods were tyrannical. The ultimate weakness of his government was that it got caught in a situation where continuous tyranny became imperative for the normal functioning of the state.

CHAPTER NINE

From Athens to Israel

He was a Rococo figure, complex, finely carved, all surface, like an intricately carved prism. His face was delicate but without depth, his conversation brilliant but without ultimate seriousness. Equally at home in the salon and in the Cabinet, he was the beau-ideal of aristocracy which justified itself not by its truth but by its existence. And if he never came to terms with the new age, it was not because he failed to understand its seriousness but because he disdained it.

HENRY KISSINGER on Metternich

Lee Kuan Yew certainly achieved discipline in Singapore, but even if that achievement justified his methods, the question remains: is that discipline durable? His own tendency to see Singapore and his government as perpetually threatened by crises suggests that, apart from his natural disposition of aggressiveness, he may have been conscious of the vulnerability of the system on which he built his state. For despite the social placidity and economic momentum he achieved, Singapore remained hostage to unpredictable forces both at home and abroad. Lee's policies have not only failed to eliminate these forces from a long-term point of view, but have endowed at least some of them with the capacity to erupt, at an opportune moment, with renewed vigour.

This reality about Singapore does not seem to have occurred to observers in the West. To most governments in the West what has mattered is Lee Kuan Yew's demonstrable success as an anti-communist leader, while to Western correspondents and sundry image-builders domiciled in or periodically visiting the island, Singapore's apparent glitter has been impressive enough.

The reading of Singapore's significance has been different in Asia. While most Asian governments have had their own reasons for keeping a wary eye on Singapore, non-governmental Asian observers have remained conscious of the power of historical forces at play beneath the placid surface of Singapore's political society. Their awareness of the Asian psyche makes them sceptical about the permanence of a tranquillity achieved through rigorous state pressure. This tranquillity seems particularly fragile in the case of Singapore because location and ethnic character have made the republic extremely sensitive to a host of geopolitical considerations. And Lee Kuan Yew's handling of Singapore's geopolitics, though imaginative in part, has been remarkably negative.

A distinguished political commentator, Juan T. Gatbonton of the Philippines, wrote in *Insight* magazine in July 1971 that the prosperity Singapore had achieved might prove to be 'highly unstable' because Lee had not properly appreciated certain forces within and around Singapore. Gatbonton said: 'Within Singapore, Mr Lee's best hope is obviously to expand the influence of the English-educated middle class that has proved most adept in taking up the industrial and secular virtues. But communalism – Malay as well as Chinese – has not disappeared. It has merely gone underground. Yet, even if Singapore became stabilized internally, it will still be very vulnerable to events in its neighbour-countries. It cannot hope to endure as an enclave of prosperity in a region of racial conflicts and economic despair. Protracted racial violence between Malays and Chinese in West Malaysia could spill over across the Johore Causeway. Another demagogue rising in Djakarta could focus Indonesian frustrations on Singapore. The resentment of Singapore as economic middleman already manifesting itself in the effort of both Djakarta and Kuala Lumpur to by-pass Singapore's entrepot facilities could escalate to subversion and terrorism, as during *konfrontasi*.'

Warnings such as Gatbonton's were clearly anticipated by Lee, for much of Singapore's foreign policy has presupposed unremitting hostility from its immediate neighbours; perhaps Lee also agreed with Arnold Toynbee's prediction that Asia's real danger point for the future was the Malay peninsula where the Malays and the Chinese could fall into a race war. But, just as clearly, he did not agree with the conclusion of Gatbonton's analysis: 'It is a truism by now to say that no nation is an island. But it is still meaningful to say that the ultimate fate of Singapore lies out of its hands. Perhaps this tragic realization is the reason for the morbid suspiciousness, the bravado, the irrascibility and the introverted intellectuality that make up the tightly wound personality of Lee Kuan Yew.'

It also explained why survival became a sacred word in Lee's lexicon, along with pragmatism and ruggedness. For all his accent on multiracialism, Singapore was a Chinese city-state surrounded by a Malay sea. Lee's unconcealed conviction that Malays were a lazy lot added to the dichotomy. For Singapore to survive on Lee's terms, an unchanging posture of aggressiveness became necessary. This set the tone of Lee's approach to geopolitics and of his foreign policy as a whole.

The need for Singapore to develop its own foreign policy arose only with separation from Malaysia in 1965. But well before this, Lee had become quite active in foreign affairs. As a Singapore official admiringly said on Radio Singapura: 'Our prime minister, like a moving pointer across the map of the world, has visited forty-five countries and every continent and in following the news of his journeys our knowledge of the geography and politics of the world has improved.'

Separation took place when Sukarno's confrontation policy was at its violent zenith. Lee's fears of Indonesia's potential for mischief made him cling to the British military installation as his best guarantee for survival. Prevarication punctuated bravado in Lee's pronouncements over the future of the British base at that time. In every newspaper or television interview he would assert Singapore's sovereignty over the base but, in fact, he was anxious that the base should remain indefinitely. Some 50,000 Singaporeans depended directly on the base for their livelihood – which was sufficient reason for Lee to want the continuation of the British presence. Even weightier was the sense of security that flowed from the presence of such a big base on Singapore soil. At the risk of appearing to be a willing tool of Britain's power politics, Lee used every stratagem to make Britain stay put.

But he did not lose sight of wider and idealistic foreign-policy goals. Beyond the immediate neighbourhood, he pursued policies which were imaginatively empirical. In the aftermath of separation from Malaysia, his primary interests were to identify Singapore with the Afro-Asian bloc and to establish nonaligned relations with the big powers. Both were indicative of a boldly independent approach, for not only was Singapore too tiny to be of any real significance in international diplomacy, but the prevailing trend in Southeast Asia was to take the short cut of seeking protection under one big-power umbrella or another. It would have been easy for Lee to find a willing patron and avoid the problems of an independent foreign policy with its attendant defence and security burdens. But he stayed true to form and decided to face the problems squarely. In the process a violent antipathy to America came to the surface.

Curiously enough, within a few years both his ardour for Afro-Asia and his hatred of America would be reversed. The shift would throw light not only on Lee's politics but on the external factors which had come to mean so much to Singapore's survival.

Lee's obvious eagerness to establish himself with the giants of Afro-Asia – Nehru, Nasser, Tito, Kenyatta – was manifested by his foreign tours of the early 1960s. He took delight and pride in conducting long discussions with these men and forging friendships with them. He had said he wanted India to be the first country to recognize independent Singapore; similarly he was, in Tunku Abdul Rahman's phrase, 'sticky' that he should get Afro-Asian sponsorship for Singapore's admission to the United Nations.

So anxious was Lee to get the approval of the Third World that he spent a great deal of time and energy in attempting to remove anticipated suspicions aroused by the presence in Singapore of a mighty British military base; and indeed, left-wing forces in Malaysia and Indonesia were already calling Singapore a neo-colonial stooge.

Lee, his deputy Toh Chin Chye and his Foreign Minister Rajaratnam toured African, Asian and East European countries to explain that Singapore was in fact no stooge, that it could give twenty-four hours' notice to Britain to quit, that it would never permit Britain to use the base for aggression. Lee argued that Cuba had an American military base on its soil but was still recognized as a non-stooge.

The British base – and Lee's desire to convince the Third World of his good faith – affected his early policy formulations towards the big powers. He went out of his way to placate the two communist giants. Just before independence the Malaysian Federal government had been moving to close down the Singapore branch of the powerful Bank of China, but Singapore said the bank could stay on. An appreciative bank manager, as always a top communist nominee, expressed the hope that trade between Singapore and China would greatly improve.

Lee's initiative on China was the more remarkable for his known opposition to the political and ethnic challenges China represented for Singapore. The breakaway from Malaysia had touched off talk about Singapore eventually developing into a Third China; such talk galled Lee. When official circles in the Philippines appeared to join the chorus, he said the gossip was intended to isolate Singapore in the international arena. 'That is why it is important to show to the world that Singapore is not a Chinese Singapore, nor a Malay Singapore, nor an Indian Singapore. It's a multiracial nation belonging to all Singaporeans.' This remained a fixed foreign-policy goal for Lee.

The Soviet Union, though communist and therefore suspect, was far away. The absence of ethnic pulls lent as much charm as did distance. A month after sovereignty, Lee sent Rajaratnam to Moscow. For good measure he called in a couple of Western correspondents and gave them a sensational warning: if Malaysia ever called in American forces to replace the British in that country, he said, 'I am telling the Tunku that I would consider offering Singapore as a base to the Russians – and I believe they should take it.' An enraged Tunku replied: 'Lee is talking through his hat. He has not got a head.' As for the Russians, in 1965 they showed no sign of being amused, but they must have remembered it as their post-Khrushchev activism in the Pacific–Indian Ocean region took shape and Singapore became one of the Soviet fleet's regular ports of call.

For a government leader who had spent more than a decade decimating communist forces in his state, the offer of a base to the Soviet Union was devastating. It indicated the intensity of Lee Kuan Yew's abhorrence of America at the time.

There has always been, of course, an element of anglophilia in Lee Kuan Yew because of his King's Chinese family background and Cambridge education. This contributed to his contempt for Americans who, in comparison with the British, struck him as an inferior people. The differentiation came out with stunning vehemence in the first days of independence. With the future of the British base the hottest topic of discussion, Lee repeatedly stated that if the British pulled out, he would go on with Australians and New Zealanders but would never let the Americans come near him.

The most revealing exposition of this stand appeared in the course of an interview Lee gave to a group of Commonwealth correspondents three weeks after independence. It was a full-throated tirade and seen as such by the men who interviewed him.

PRIME MINISTER: ... Now, I want to be quite frank with you here. If the British withdraw I am prepared to go on with the Australians and the New Zealanders. But, I am not prepared to go on with Americans.

QUESTIONER: Why not, Mr Prime Minister? Why do you think the Americans ...

PRIME MINISTER: Can I put it this way: I think they are a highly intelligent, often well-meaning, people, and some of their leaders like Mr Kennedy, the late president, had signs of growing greatness, depth. But, judgment or wisdom which comes out of an accumulation of knowledge of human beings and human situations over a long period of time: that is lacking, and it is not their fault. What have they got? Three, four hundred years of history, and they have become a nation just recently. I will tell you this. I have had three experiences, only three experiences, with the Americans. And they did not intend any harm in each one of them. But, the tragedy was, they did real harm. First – this is old stuff now – we caught an American CIA agent trying to subvert our Intelligence Special Branch Officer, bribe him, so that the Special Branch Officer will feed the CIA because the CIA wants to know what is happening. Subverting a Singapore officer! The man might have succeeded, but I am proud the officer, offered a large sum of money and continuing sums of money ... this was in 1960 ... refused and reported the matter to his chief who reported it to me.

QUESTIONER: Well, don't you think ...

PRIME MINISTER: No, no. Let me explain. The British have 400 years of Empire, and I will come to that. This is crucial to the whole of my thinking on this. Four hundred years of Empire, and they know this place, and they know human beings. If it had been the Americans in charge, I think today I would not be here, and you would not be interviewing me. Because, they lack what one calls wisdom, i.e. a computer fed with data, judgment which comes out of long experience. I will tell you this. Trying to do that! I told my officers, 'Lay a trap: microphones, everything.' The man was caught, arrested, enough evidence to send him to gaol for anything up to twelve years. We had got them by the throat. The American consul-general, shaking at his knees, knew nothing about it. And I really believe he knew nothing about it because this man flew in from Bangkok. And the ignominy of it! He was not really trying. The man was looking for a place of assignation to seek comfort. Do you get confidence in an outfit like that? That is how the Bay of Pigs takes place, that sort of an operation. The man was caught, locked up, and it was on a razor's edge whether we would charge him in open Court or not. Now, let me explain this. And, I told the American Government, 'We keep quiet, you take this man away, $100 million to the Singapore Government for economic development.'

QUESTIONER: Now ...

PRIME MINISTER: No, no. You listen to me. I never spoke to the Americans direct because they lack the finesse. They may say, 'Yes, give it to you. Why to the Singapore Government? Give it to *you*,' – to me,

6

which would have ruined me. But through an intermediary they
offered *me* and my party ten million dollars. The insult! I told them,
'You can keep it.' But I will say this for President Kennedy: that he
said no, his government would give me, if I wanted, publicly, but not
because I got him by the throat. No, no. I will say this for Kennedy –
I don't know if they have got other Kennedys coming; even Kennedy
didn't have the full maturity. In the end, I decided to release the man
because if I charged him, the damage it would have done with our
relations with Kuala Lumpur then – we wanted merger, Malaysia, we
fought for it – and Americans would have worked on Kuala Lumpur
and we would have been so antagonistic, merger and Malaysia would
have broken. They probably never knew why we released the man.
We just said 'OK, get out.' And the consul-general, who was a Rhodes
scholar, I have forgotten his name now – they sent a Rhodes scholar.
They thought a bit of the English polish on him, and he can get on.
Well, he resigned – or he left, anyway. They sent a new man. That is
when Mr Gilstrap came. That is experience number one.

Now, let me explain this to you. It is fundamental. If the British
bases go, there will be no American bases in Singapore. This is a matter
of the utmost importance for Britain, Australia, New Zealand, and
for America to understand that.

Second traumatic experience: you know, again they did not mean
harm, but they did a lot of harm. I should not go into the details. It
is unkind perhaps. Dr Goh and I were on our way to the United
Nations, and we got stuck in Hawaii. 1962. The plane broke down.
Delayed. So, our connection at Los Angeles was delayed. Mind you,
they were polite enough to have a minister of the Federal government
to meet us. VIP lounge and so on. And, I said, 'Look, I must get a
telegram through to the Malayan Embassy in Washington, and the
UN Mission. Otherwise, I won't make contact with them.' The chap says,
'No, no, no. Don't worry. We will look after it. We have got a special
network,' said he. Special network! We arrived. There was not a
soul. Not a soul. But when we went to the information desk, the chap
says, 'yes, sir.' And do you know what had happened? Hugh Foot,
formerly Sir Hugh Foot, now Lord Carrington . . . .?

QUESTIONER: Caradon . . .

PRIME MINISTER: Caradon . . . He need not have met me. But he did.
And, he left a message, at every desk – you know, Idlewild has twenty
or thirty reception desks, and every one had a message – the moment
the Singapore ministers arrived, Dr Goh and me, please contact him.
And, the British and the Malayans appeared. I was embarrassed; and,
mind you, they were so discreet. You know, this is purely a courtesy,
and so on, and so forth. But, your own network with this immense
apparatus and you can't get my message through, a change of aircraft.
What is this? And, I will give you my last experience very recently.
Somebody very dear to me – just a matter of days ago – was in need of
specialist treatment.* And, our local professor said, 'Well, I know

* The person concerned was Lee Kuan Yew's wife.

Professor so and so of such and such a university who is probably the best technician in this job for this operation.' And you know, I was a fool. I should never have done it. I had a word with an American representative – not a low representative, mind you – the ambassador from Kuala Lumpur came down to discuss important matters, and incidentally I said, 'Would it be possible for this person to come to help my professor to assess and then to decide?' He said, 'Yes, we will try and see what can be done.' Do you know what was the answer? The professor was busy. He recommends Professor xyz, but he does not know whether Professor xyz will come or not. Then, I get another phone call saying, 'The first professor is going to Geneva,' Professor A who was recommended. And, if the patient was prepared to fly to Geneva, the professor would look at him or her. You know, the impudence and the impertinence of it! But I was more sorry than angry, because I don't think that would have happened with a people with a background, a history, culture, cultured, civilised. . . .

. . . Let me say this to show you that I am not an anglophile. True, I know their culture, their history, their civilisation. I have read all about the daffodils and the bumble-bee and 'Heigh-ho, merry ho', and all the rest of it. It is part of my schooling. They pumped it. And, I hated what they did, and I joined up with the communists to get rid of them. But, you know, they had wisdom.

When I came back from London as a student on August 1, 1950, just over fifteen years ago – it was done so politely. The immigration officer whose name I remember to this day, Mr Fox, kept me waiting for one hour, and then looked at my passport, flicked through in a very civilised but cutting sort of way, in that way warning me that if I went on with what I was doing and saying in Britain, I was in for trouble. But I was prepared, not just for trouble, but for death if necessary, to get rid of British colonialism. And we joined in with the communists – Lim Chin Siong, Fong Swee Suan and the rest of them – and they knew that I was not a communist, they were communists, that if the British are defeated we have got to scrap it out among ourselves.

If it were the Americans, they would say, 'Ah! Commie! Fellow-traveller! Lock him up.' But not the British. You know, this is a personal tribute to a man on whose report perhaps I was spared: Sir William Goode, chief secretary in charge of the Special Branch, and later, last governor. And I was the spokesman for the first strike that started the series of strikes in the 1950s. 1952, early 52, February, the postmen went on strike about striped trousers and pay, and so on. And, we met across the table. And he's a 'toughie', you know. He's a boxer. Well, I don't look a toughie, because you know, only Englishmen can look that tough. The Chinese usually look gentle people. But he learned over the years that we were quite determined. And he watched every move, every speech, every statement. He was in the Assembly with us, watching me, the difference between me and Lim Chin Siong. And Lim Yew Hock wanted to scrub the lot of us out. And he said 'No.' I'm sure he must have said 'No,' because otherwise it was easier for Lim Yew Hock, Mr Lim Yew Hock, sorry, *Tun* Lim Yew Hock, for the PAP not to be there to contest the elections in 1959. But Bill Goode was calculating in terms of twenty, thirty, forty years of trying to get a group of people to emerge who can hold the situation. He knew that if we took power and the communists wanted that power, either we had to go along with the communists, in which case they would really have to do something, or we would have to fight the communists. It was a calculated risk. He released several senior officers who were close colleagues of mine – Dr Goh amongst them – from the civil service, to contest the 1959 elections. And we won. He stayed on for six months as Yang Di-Pertuan Negara. He did a good job for the British. He didn't do it for me. He did it for Britain. Let's be quite frank about this. It was in Britain's interests that Singapore should be outside communist influence. And he could not fight the communists – but the locals can. And I was one of the few that emerged. And around this group there is now the PAP.

Two years later Lee went into reverse. In October 1967 he paid an official visit to the United States accompanied by his wife. It looked as though the Americans had been waiting for just such an opportunity. President Johnson laid on an unusually lavish nineteen-gun welcome to the visitor which Lee himself said he found 'almost embarrassing'. Johnson was liberal with his encomiums. He said America was welcoming 'a patriot, a brilliant political leader and a statesman of the New Asia'. Singapore was praised as a bright example of what could be achieved wherever men worked for a life of freedom and dignity. The tempo was maintained at that pitch throughout the twelve days Lee spent in the US meeting the élite of the administration.

Perhaps the warmth of Johnson's praise impressed Lee. Perhaps pragmatism asserted itself: commentators noticed that the announcement of the visit was made close to a British statement foreshadowing the closure of their base in Singapore. It also was pointed out that the war had made Vietnam Singapore's customer, yielding US$100 million a year in direct exports and perhaps another $33 million in indirect exports. For whatever reason, Lee came home a changed man.

No longer was the US an object of contempt or the Vietnam war an unsavoury exercise of American power. His position now was that America was helping Asia by resisting communism in Vietnam, that Americans should consider Asia as important to them as Europe and that if America turned its back on Asia 'a grievous struggle' would engulf the small countries of the region.

In fact Lee vigorously condemned the idea of Asian solutions for Asian problems as a catchword meant only to enable the bigger Asian powers to provide solutions to the smaller Asian powers. Once he had spoken about the arrogance of power in America; now he said: 'I think there is as much arrogance in the Asian as in the American.' The men around the pres'dent were 'men with fine minds and sensitive souls'.

Once Lee had said: 'The communists are dangerous. So are American imperialists dangerous to me. They are crude people, so I say: Please stay out.' By 1970 large numbers of senior American military officers were regularly visiting Singapore. Factories in Singapore were making weapons for Vietnam. It was left to Washington to reject a Singapore request to train fairly large numbers of Singapore officers in the us; according to an American reporter, Anthony Polsky of the *Far Eastern Economic Review*, Washington was afraid that any such agreement, whatever Singapore's reasons for making the request, might interfere with the five-power defence arrangement for Singapore and Malaysia with Britain, Australia and New Zealand. Lockheed, the American aerospace giant, had a Singapore subsidiary company running an aircraft maintenance and repair base, and another American company, Grumman International, was setting up a similar facility. The us Navy maintained its own ship repair centre in Singapore. The commander of us military forces in the Pacific and the Far East was a frequent visitor to Singapore and in May 1971 he told a us congressional committee that 'we consider it essential that Singapore's military and commercial facilities be available to the free world in the event of hostilities in the region'. In April 1972 none other than J. Edgar Hoover announced that the American FBI was opening an office in Singapore to maintain close contact with investigative agencies in the region.

Lee's tacit withdrawal from Afro-Asia and his rapprochement with the us were two sides of the same coin. Some sections of the intelligentsia in Singapore made the point, during discussions with the author, that Singapore lost interest in Afro-Asia once it realized it did not have much to gain from the bloc by way of trade or other benefits. The same considerations, they said, made it turn gradually but steadily towards the Western developed nations. It was something of an obsession with Lee to pull Singapore's economy out of its early shop-window precariousness. He found that the Americans had the capital, the know-how and the interest to help Singapore achieve this end. For his part Lee had the practicality to appreciate the usefulness of these American attributes and to adjust his personal prejudices accordingly.

The shift in Lee's American policy was so sharp – and the contrast between early statements and subsequent actions so embarrassing – that the new stance was given no publicity at home; rarely did the visit of a school of American admirals to Singapore receive any notice in the local press. The sensitivity was understandable. But Lee could have afforded to be bolder, for the success of his new policy was indisputable. It gave him a second string as Britain was disengaging from Singapore and reducing itself to the status of an equal member of the five-power defence arrangement. The knowledge that America had developed a military stake in Singapore in turn made the island a specially attractive proposition for American capital.

Perhaps Lee also felt the compulsions of Singapore's history pressing down on him. Although the Lee government had been trying hard to play down the republic's entrepot status, Singapore remained essentially part of the colonial system left behind by Western imperialist powers. It still depended heavily on the import of primary products from the region for export to the West and of manufactured goods from the West for export to the region. It was still a clearing house for Western capital and know-how, a middle man through which the markets and resources of the region were exploited by the industrialized countries. The safety and continuity of its sea-lanes were still of paramount importance to the developed nations. Its politics, both internal and external, were still conditioned by the logic of colonialism. The only difference was that Britain had been replaced as imperial leader by the United States and Japan.

In his pioneering research work, *Singapore in Southeast Asia*, Iain Buchanan remarked: 'Singapore is both the child and the hostage of the system which is built upon socio-economic disparities, and which must sustain these to survive. Once the hub of British interests in Southeast Asia, Singapore is now regional headquarters for the imperialisms of Britain, Europe, the United States and Japan. This role can only last as long as the system which requires it.'

Singapore became, in Buchanan's words, 'an explicit part of the West's economic thrust into Southeast Asia and a tacit ally of its political and military penetration' as a direct result of America's 'conquest' of Indonesia within two years of Sukarno's fall and his country's consequent emergence as the most significant Western presence in the Malay world. This was a development Lee, with his passionate misgivings about the Malay peoples, could not lightly dismiss. He even worried about the possibility of the US supplying offensive weapons to the Indonesians for an attack on Singapore. He probably thought it best to decide: if you can't beat 'em, join 'em.

In immediate material terms, the shift towards America was productive for Lee. Third World idealism might have received a setback, but Singapore's economy received a forward thrust. It was a competent application of the principles of pragmatism, combining practicality with profitability.

While quietly welcoming the Americans, Lee kept the Soviet Union's goodwill constantly oiled – literally. In fact, the Russians could claim Singapore as their oldest friend in Southeast Asia. Russian ships were visiting Singapore for servicing, as well as American vessels. If the only way for small countries to participate in the power game is by playing all ends against the middle, Singapore could be described as playing it well. Lee had reason to feel gratified with his handling of the big powers.

The story was substantially different when it came to his Southeast Asian neighbours. Historical factors and personal predilections pulled Lee in opposite directions, making for policies at once contradictory and self-defeating.

Perhaps the failure of the Malaysia merger had left deep scars on his mind; perhaps the viciousness of Sukarno's confrontation tactics scared him more than he showed; perhaps the pace of Singapore's economic progress filled him with disdain for the neighbours who were unable to achieve anything of the kind. The intellectual gulf between him and leaders of neighbouring governments may have added to this disdain.

The result was that Lee became perceptibly arrogant towards his neighbours, publicly disparaging them. He seemed to derive some vicarious pleasure from holding other Asian leaders to ridicule before international audiences. He showed that he thought of Tunku Abdul Rahman as a rather dull and unintelligent man whose main objective was 'to preserve the orchid from wilting'. Malaysian Chinese Association President Tan Siew Sin was described as one whose statement on the PAP showed 'an imbalance of judgment of a magnitude to qualify its author for admission to an asylum for the politically insane'. Sukarno was called a histrionic character who remained in the ascendancy by mesmerizing people. Filipinos were described as 'America's protégés in Asia'. Asian governments in general were often ridiculed for their inefficiency and corruption.

The hostility generated by this attitude lent credibility to Lee's relentless efforts to build up Singapore's defences, but it also raised doubts about the wisdom of a policy which seemed to preclude the possibility of a truly friendly region. The premise on which Lee based his Southeast Asian policy appeared to be that Singapore could survive only if it acquired military strength. He did not seem to accept the possibility of an alternative course through identifying Singapore with the popular aspirations of its region.

Lee once said: 'My colleagues and I are by nature and by training calculators, not feelers; we like to make sure.' Perhaps the calculator in Lee had his reasons for erring on the side of caution. After all, Singapore was so tiny that a couple of unfriendly patrol boats could cause serious trouble. It was one of Lee's early preoccupations to drive home the point that no one should jump to conclusions because of Singapore's smallness. He would warn foreign countries that some shrimps were poisonous and the big fish which tried to swallow them could run into grave digestive problems; he would tell Singaporeans: 'Fortunately it is not size but quality which counts. Ancient Athens was a small state, but its vigorous and alert people gave birth to ideas and philosophies which are as alive today as they were 2,000 years ago.' On occasion he would abandon Athens in favour of Venice as an analogy for Singapore.

Another fact Lee had to live with was Singapore's Chineseness. However hard and sincerely he tried to fight racialism, no one was going to think of Singapore as anything other than a Chinese city. Lee himself, though outwardly above racial sentiments, often made references to his 4,000 years of history and his cultural heritage. He would also make snide remarks about how people around the equator tended to go to sleep in the afternoons and how Singapore was an exception to the rule.

The significance of Singapore's essentially Chinese character was that Lee had to take cognisance of the position of the Chinese in Southeast Asia and to note how Southeast Asian attitudes to the Chinese communities were likely to affect their approach to Singapore. He put it in his own way when he said the Chinese communities had been isolated and put on the shelf throughout Southeast Asia and, although Malaysia was a marginal case in this respect, Singapore was the only place where Chinese still held their heads high.

Singapore obviously could not escape the fact that it was only a part of a broad problem of racial coexistence in Southeast Asia. The communities of unassimilated Chinese migrants and their descendants were resented by the indigenous peoples because the commanding heights of national economies were in the grip of the Chinese. Such resentment was particularly strong among the Malays and the Indonesians. Lee was acutely aware that their grievances could some day focus on Singapore.

Lee's dilemma was that he could not counter this threat by allowing the Chineseness of his people to develop into Chinese chauvinism, for that would have meant not only clearing the deck for racial conflict but giving China an emotional stranglehold on Singapore. The concept of a 'Third China' in Singapore was totally unacceptable to him.

In effect this dilemma pointed to the overriding importance of developing a substitute nationalism in Singapore. From this realization flowed the multifarious efforts of the Lee government to inculcate in the island's population a separate Singaporean identity. As Lee saw it, a clearly distinguishable Singaporean national identity was fundamental as much to the survival of the society he was building as to the legitimization of his own cultural rootlessness.

Developing a new nationalism among people so deeply steeped in their own traditional national identities as the Chinese, the Malays and the Indians was easier said than achieved. At best there could be only a hothouse solidarity. Lee could not have failed to realize the nature of such an undertaking. Hence his resort to extraordinary powers – the regimentation of education, the imposition of tight control on mass media, the straitjacketing of opposition – in the hope that what was seemingly unnatural could still be achieved through executive compulsion.

Hence also, perhaps, his brinkmanship with neighbours, achieved through denigration of their leaders interspersed with warnings about the military threat they posed to Singapore. Constant harpings on the differences between Singapore and the countries around it was one way of instilling a sense of distinction into Singaporeans: others were stagnant while Singapore was progressing; others were torpid while Singapore worked hard. Nationality after all must begin from a sense of uniqueness, of being somehow apart from other people.

The ultimate dramatization of Singapore's separateness from the rest of Southeast Asia was the selection of Israel as Singapore's model. Efforts were subsequently made by some of Singapore's leaders to deny that Singapore planned to become Southeast Asia's Israel. In fact it did, and Lee had taken a considered policy decision to that effect. In October 1967 he publicly announced the decision. In Zurich for a meeting of the Socialist International, he said: 'We made a study of what smaller countries surrounded by large neighbours with big populations do for their own survival. The study eventually led us to compare three such tightly knit communities – Switzerland, Finland and Israel. In the end, Singapore opted for the Israeli pattern, for in our situation it appears necessary not only to train every boy but also every girl to be a disciplined and effective digit in the defence of their country.'

Ever since, Israeli advisers have been part of the Singapore scene – though a rather carelessly camouflaged part. Several Israeli officers were imported to help with military training in Singapore. The Singapore Armed Forces Training Institute was set up with their assistance. There is an unwritten agreement to play down the role of the Israelis in Singapore. Not a word about them appears in public. The first team of Israeli officers to arrive in Singapore were officially billed as 'Mexican agricultural advisers'. Even today Singaporeans refer to them as 'Mexicans', in a bid to avoid unnecessary embarrassment to anyone. Not without cause, for Singapore's decision to follow the Israeli pattern, however realistic in terms of defence preparations, was a political provocation of the first order as far as the island's neighbours were concerned. It suggested that the confrontation between the Chinese of Singapore and the non-Chinese of neighbouring countries was similar to that between the Jews and the Arabs. It implied the transference to Southeast Asia of the religious animosities of the Middle East. It was an emotional insult to Singapore's Muslim neighbours.

A spokesman of Malaysia's UMNO said Singapore was 'trying to create an Israeli state for the purpose of suppressing the Malays.

As has happened in Israel where Muslims were pressed down and suppressed by the Israelites, so are the tactics of the PAP government. In the long run the PAP government is trying to launch a war of nerves between the races.'

If Lee wanted nothing more than to ensure Singapore's survival, he could have chosen Lebanon as a model, or Hong Kong, with an attitude of 'live and let live'. But he appeared to be aiming at survival on his terms – as a rugged, militarized, superior state. Left-wing intellectuals attributed to Lee a more devious motivation. They said if he had chosen either Switzerland or Finland as the model, it would have had no dramatic impact or political dividend. By choosing Israel he had a chance to attract the subconscious sympathy of the powerful Jewish lobby around the world and, in particular, in the US. This could be expected to yield side benefits, especially on the economic front.

If the choice of Israel as a model struck neighbours as provocation, Singapore's armament strategy was seen as a direct threat. Singapore opted for tanks. Observers noticed at once that they were light enough to roll over the Johore causeway. Malaysia was not amused: during a joint five-power military exercise in May 1970, Malaysia refused to permit Singapore tanks to cross the causeway, saying that Singapore wanted to test the mobility of its tank units under the pretext of the exercise. Other major items on the priority hardware list were jet fighters and missile boats. This raised eyebrows in Indonesia. Singapore left no doubt about who it thought its enemies were, or might one day be.

It was natural in the circumstances that Singapore should have chosen to play a subdued role in the Association of Southeast Asian Nations (ASEAN), the organization which emerged as the most serious attempt at co-operation in the region. Founded in 1967 with Singapore, Malaysia, Indonesia, Thailand and the Philippines as members, ASEAN has achieved little besides a clutch of grand paper schemes. Yet its members, as well as other countries, realize that ASEAN has the potential of growing into a significant regional grouping. They have kept at it.

Singapore has remained out of the mainstream, with a highly equivocal attitude to regional power politics. In a television interview in 1967, Lee bluntly expressed his suspicions. He was agreeable to economic co-operation, but with serious reservations. 'If you are trying to fix me economically,' he asked, 'do you believe that I will believe that you are going to defend me? I mean, this is nonsense, isn't it? If Singapore is convinced that her neighbours mean us well, then we will really co-operate to mutual advantage. . . . Of course we like to make our neighbours strong, prosperous and powerful. But to what purpose? So that in twenty years' time they can eat me up?'

Predictably, Singapore persistently showed only lukewarm interest in the activities of ASEAN. Its position was that bilateral contacts were more useful than multilateral ones for economic co-operation. The perennial argument as to whether ASEAN should stick exclusively to economics (as originally envisaged) or should allow limited political co-operation found Singapore steadfastly arguing against any political content. Singapore's main interest in ASEAN appeared to be to get trade barriers removed – but this only aroused the suspicions of the other members who realized that Singapore would be the most substantial beneficiary in a barrier-less regional market.

Singapore's nonconformist position within ASEAN was highlighted in May 1970 when, following the American invasion of Cambodia, eleven Asian and Pacific countries gathered in Djakarta to seek an Indochina peace initiative. Indonesia had taken the lead in organizing the conference and it met under an ASEAN umbrella although several non-ASEAN countries participated. Singapore stood out as the only country which did not send its foreign minister to the meeting; it was represented by a lower-level delegation which made Singapore's disinterestedness clear.

Eventually the Djakarta conference achieved little, but Singapore's decision to stay on the sidelines was probably made for reasons other than the anticipation of failure. Five months after the conference, speaking at Harvard University, Lee Kuan Yew supported American military action in Cambodia as a move which 'hopefully will enable the South Vietnamese to strengthen themselves'. He added: 'I would hope very much the Vietnamization programme would succeed. So much has been put into it that it shouldn't be allowed to go down the drain.' Thailand was more deeply committed to American policies in Indochina, but it had agreed to go along with other countries and at least make an attempt to explore the possibilities of peace. Singapore was content to leave it to Washington, convinced beforehand that no Asian effort was worthwhile.

Twice, it looked as though ASEAN was about to collapse, and on both occasions Singapore was at the core of the controversy. The first crisis occurred in 1968 when Singapore executed two Indonesian marines, ignoring Asia-wide pleas for clemency. As coincidence would have it, the executions took place four days after Lee Kuan Yew left Singapore on an extended tour lasting nearly three months.

The two marines, Harun and Osman, were among the agents Sukarno despatched to Singapore during the days of *Konfrontasi*. A bomb they had planted in a building in Singapore's commercial district had killed three persons; the pair had been arrested in March 1965. For three years they remained in Changhi prison. During those years Indonesia was reborn. The government which had ordered the men to Singapore had fallen and Suharto had taken over the reins of power. Serious attempts were being made by both countries to improve their relations. It was a new era with pragmatism riding high on both sides of the Singapore Straits.

Suddenly Singapore announced that Harun and Osman were to be executed. The ghost of *Konfrontasi* was resurrected. Indonesians were embittered. In the wake of Suharto's rise they had felt remorseful about *Konfrontasi*. Now the case of the two marines became a matter of national pride. The government in Djakarta made it clear that it viewed the matter with the utmost concern. Suharto made a personal appeal for mercy and sent a special emissary to Singapore. When all his pleas were turned down, the emissary asked for a brief postponement of the executions for the purpose of making proper funeral arrangements. This request, too, was rejected. The Malaysian prime minister stepped in at the last moment with a clemency plea of his own. Various other diplomatic missions in Singapore were urged to make representations to the government. All was in vain. From Tokyo by telephone Lee Kuan Yew confirmed the execution orders. The two marines were hanged at dawn on November 18. The Indonesian embassy made detailed arrangements for a ceremony on the embassy premises, but Singapore would not permit the bodies to be taken to the city. The Indonesians had to take charge of the bodies at the Changhi airfield close to the prison and fly the dead marines home in a special Indonesian Air Force plane.

All hell broke loose in Indonesia when the bodies arrived. Vast crowds lined the streets. The two men were declared national heroes. Radio stations played solemn music and flags flew at half-mast. Students sacked the Singapore embassy in Djakarta and the residences of Singapore diplomats. In the East Java capital of

Surabaya an anti-Singapore rally turned into a riot against the Chinese, and the army had to issue a shoot-to-kill order to restore peace. The Indonesian Navy held exercises off Singapore to 'test naval alertness'. The commander of the marines said he would like personally to lead a task force of marines to invade Singapore. Calls for retaliation rose from all sections of Indonesians, including the legislature.

The explosion of emotions eventually died down because of Foreign Minister Adam Malik's insistence that popular anger against Singapore would serve no purpose. In due course state-to-state relations became normal. But the scars went deep. As the chairman of the Indonesian People's Congress said: 'The hearts of the entire Indonesian people have been sliced and their honour insulted.' Suharto was said to have felt personally offended. His government began a review of its relations with Singapore 'in all fields'; the episode was believed to have provided the main motivation for Suharto's plans to cut out Singapore's role as a middleman in Indonesian trade.

Although the government subsequently tried to forget the incident, publicly at least, a strong undercurrent of hostility towards Singapore persisted in many sections of Indonesian society. It was to surface occasionally in newspaper attacks. In January 1971 the *Sinar Harapan* published a series of articles accusing Singapore of a two-faced policy: pretending to carry out a good-neighbour line while practising policies which permitted illegal Indonesian traders to operate. This, said the paper, would eventually lead to an economic confrontation between the two countries. It also said Singapore immigration officials were 'stiff and arrogant' to visitors from Indonesia, including government ministers.

Singapore's insistence on the execution of the marines at a time when it could have won lasting Indonesian gratitude through a display of magnanimity remained a mystery. A long statement by the government emphasizing the need to uphold the rule of law failed to impress: executive pardon was accepted practice under rule of law and in any case the rule of law, as we have seen, has not been all that sacrosanct in Singapore. A widely accepted explanation was that Singapore was once again using an occasion to show its capacity for toughness, a demonstration of its size-induced inferiority complex. It underlined the toughness of its action by adopting a rather casual attitude after the event. From Tokyo, Lee

Kuan Yew's press spokesman said: 'We have no comment on the executions.' In Singapore Foreign Minister Rajaratnam said the whole thing would become a very small scar with the passage of time.

Exactly two years later it was time to show toughness towards the other neighbour. This time the incident was somewhat childish, but repercussions in Malaysia were no less serious.

In August 1970 three young Malay youths on a visit to Singapore were detained by the police, locked up, given a haircut and held for sixteen hours before they were released. Their 'offence' was that they had long hair and a hippie appearance – anathema to Lee's Singapore. Again Lee was casual and sarcastic about the affair. 'Things like this happen in the best of places,' he said. 'If any embarrassment has been caused, we can send them three wigs. We make wigs here.' But, he warned, Singapore's tough treatment of hippies would continue.

However, if Lee could dismiss the haircut incident as a 'small matter', Malaysia thought otherwise. The government in Kuala Lumpur said in a statement that the Malay youths were 'questioned and insulted with words against their person, race and leaders'. It was this part of the treatment which apparently aroused indignation in Malaysia. The government summoned the Singapore high commissioner and handed him a protest note expressing 'utmost concern'. University students demonstrated twice and demanded stern action against Singapore. The Malay press spewed venom at Singapore's leadership. Lee Kuan Yew cancelled, less than an hour before his scheduled departure, what was to have been his first official visit to Kuala Lumpur since separation. Relations between the two countries, instead of being normalized by the planned visit, sank to a new low.

The bad blood between Singapore and its neighbours was the result not so much of traditional racial hatreds or intractable political problems as of avoidable irritations provided usually by Singapore. This was particularly ironic because Lee could not have been unaware of the essential indivisibility of the politics of Singapore, Malaysia and Indonesia. A class-conscious ideology spelt equal danger to the ruling élites of all three countries so that common interest in suppressing such ideologies bound the three governments together. It was generally accepted that a communist party in Singapore could not ever hope to succeed without its counterpart in Malaysia registering simultaneous success. The emergence of a truly socialist régime in Singapore would likewise make an attack on it by either Malaysia or Indonesia or both a strong possibility, just as a socialist Malaysia or Indonesia would want to take care of a Singapore malingering in capitalist decadence. It was possible to visualize a viable socialist state comprising at least two of the three neighbours, Singapore and Malaysia; but for Singapore to become a solitary bastion of socialism in the region was unlikely in the extreme.

Rapidly growing American commercial interests in the region threw Lee even deeper into the company of his neighbours. Americans found fertile soil in Indonesia just when their influence was declining in South America, the Middle East and the Indian subcontinent. It was reasonable to assume that they would cling to Indonesia, with its enormous natural resources, market potential and political significance, even at the cost – if it came to the crunch – of down-grading their relations with a country like Singapore. Worse, they could try to keep Singapore in line through adroit use of the logic of conflict between the Chinese and the Malays. It was necesary for Lee to play along with American interests in the region and practise togetherness with America's allies in the Malay world.

The contradiction arose from the fact that both the continuing colonial role of Singapore and the personality of Lee demanded that the uniqueness of Singapore be fostered at the same time as its links with the region were emphasized. Effectively to perform the middleman role vis-à-vis the new imperialisms, it was not enough for Singapore to have a safely conservative, conveniently authoritarian régime. So long as the basic structure of Singapore's economy remained exploitatively colonial, its ethnic, political and intellectual separateness from its neighbourhood had to be maintained as in the days of direct colonial rule.

This was no problem, given Lee's personality and conviction that Singapore was intellectually as well as ethnically apart from the rest of the region. He did not want to be equated with other friends of old and new imperialisms in Asia. His belief in the superiority of the Mongoloid peoples over the Indo-Malay made it natural for him to resent the enforced political companionship of his immediate neighbours; 'innate ethnic qualities', he once said, combined with climate and diet to give East Asians such as the Chinese, the Japanese and the Koreans a cultural edge over the South and Southeast Asians.

The dangerous element in Lee's ethnic arrogance has been that it ignores the sensibilities of the Malay nationalism with which Singapore perforce has to live and which neither he nor his Western supporters can wish out of existence. The basic conflict between the separateness to which he is inclined and the togetherness forced upon him by Southeast Asia's geopolitics could in the long run bring about a serious upheaval. And the ethnic element Lee has worked into the conflict threatens to make such an upheaval catastrophically communal if it comes.

However, in the short run, the conflict has served to justify Lee's belligerence towards his neighbours and the repression at home. It has given sustenance to his concept of Singapore as a garrison state. The perpetual crisis mentality has become integral to his style of government. As Buchanan said: 'Neither the values which made Singapore, nor those which Lee presently upholds, are universally acceptable ones. By assuming that, in large measure, they are, Lee has trapped himself – and his country – in an ideological, communal and strategic cul-de-sac.'

It is significant that the 'forty-five countries and all the continents' visited by Lee did not, for a long time, include the countries in his own back-yard. Malaysia, despite Singapore's close social and economic ties with it, seemed a world away. Sukarno's successors in Indonesia were believed to have vowed for several years never to let 'that man' set foot on Indonesian soil. Prime Minister Lee has never visited the Philippines.

Towards the end of the 1960s Lee's attitude began showing some signs of change. His visit to Japan and the US in 1968 was said to have opened his eyes to the advantages of a subtle approach to supposedly hostile forces, and perhaps the hatred generated in Indonesia by his unnecessary provocation at that time made an impression on him. On his return home, selected foreign correspondents who interviewed him on television received the impression that he wished no longer to push the image of himself as an Asian thinker and statesman but to adopt a gentler approach, allowing for the sensibilities of his neighbours. 'The last thing we want to do is give advice,' said the man who had been a compulsive preacher until then. In early 1972 he at last paid an official visit to Kuala Lumpur and in 1973 to Bangkok and Djakarta.

Welcome as these contacts have been, it is not yet clear whether Lee for his part intends anything more than a tactical adjustment. The visit to Kuala Lumpur, characterized by heavy security arrangements, produced only an 'agreement' which in effect allowed the Malaysian government to sue the Singapore government over Singapore's appropriation of the letters 'MSA' without payment of goodwill; the two countries had fallen out on the operation of their joint flag-carrier, the Malaysia-Singapore Airlines, and Singapore had deftly named its new independent carrier Mercury Singapore Airlines to take advantage of the well-known MSA initials. Five months after the 'agreement' to go to court, Singapore suddenly agreed to settle the matter out of court; it gave up 'MSA' and renamed its new carrier Singapore Airlines, 'SIA'. It appeared that, summit contacts notwithstanding, Singapore was still inclined to follow as far as it could a policy of one-upmanship towards its neighbours.

Geopolitically, Lee's Singapore has served a definable purpose within the context of Western interests in Southeast Asia. His political style has fitted neatly into this pattern but, by the same token, it is valid only within the given context. The Syngman Rhees and the Ngo Dinh Diems whom Lee once contemptuously dismissed as irrelevant also served, in another era and another context, a specific purpose within the Western scheme of things for Asia. When the context changed, they disappeared.

The fundamental fact about Singapore under Lee Kuan Yew has been that its prosperity as well as its political viability have been built on artificial foundations which have only an artificial tenability. Were the West's need of Singapore in its present form to end, the *realpolitik* of Malay nationalism would still be there with all its potency. Even in its present form, Singapore could not hope to make itself more important to the West than its larger neighbours whose national politics hold longer-term historical relevance to Southeast Asia.

In sum, Lee's foreign politics have made Singapore a 'neo-colonial' beach-head in post-colonial Southeast Asia on the one hand and have completed its isolation on the other. Both have served his short-term purpose of militarizing and disciplining the people. But they have also exposed the long-term vulnerability of the establishment he has erected.

CHAPTER TEN

Under the Banyan Tree

Kissinger's arrogance lies in the belief that what he is getting is information so crucial that outsiders who contradict it can't be listened to. This is the spell of secret information – it makes them morons. Like Circe's spell, it turns them into swine.

DANIEL ELLSBURG on Henry Kissinger

Oxley Rise is not only impressively Anglo-Saxon in its name. It is a pleasantly shaded, almost quiet, corner in central Singapore. The prime minister has his residence there, one which he chose in preference to the majestically opulent mansion where British governors of the past had lived.

Naturally, Oxley Rise and the surrounding areas are heavily guarded. Lee Kuan Yew's personal publicists have recorded the emphasis placed on the prime minister's security arrangements – how armed security men merge with the trees in the golf course when he plays, how the radio jeep is never far from him, with police vehicles positioned in strategic places around whatever spot he happens to be in.

In June 1972 Singaporeans suddenly saw two convex mirrors installed in front of the prime minister's residence. Each measured three feet in diameter and they fixed passers-by like the weird eyes of some science fiction creature, giving a 180-degree view of each end of the road. They were set up so that the Gurkha guards could see what was happening up and down the road without leaving their sentry boxes.

The mirrors were a reminder that although Lee Kuan Yew refused to live in the old governor's house, his life has become rather like a colonial governor's. His house is surrounded by armed guards; citizens cannot approach without being carefully observed; to get to see the prime minister is a privilege. Lee regularly takes sabbatical leaves of absence, like a governor's furlough. Like a governor, he is the centre of power, has a cabinet which (like a governor's executive council) does what he says.

The trouble with being a governor used to be that all the power was attached to the office, not the man. Perhaps Lee's sense of insecurity rises not only from his personal alienation from Chinese cultural moorings, but also from the feeling that he is there less by popular will than because he is the cleverest man around, the one who can do the job and who has made the electoral process challenge-proof.

The men around Lee are also there because of their cleverness and loyalty to the leader. The non-political wing of the Lee team has never attracted public attention. It has consisted primarily of the leaders of the security apparatus and some key technocrats who deal directly with the prime minister. The extraordinarily efficient Special Branch, for example, has always had a chief hand-picked and personally instructed by Lee, invisible but omnipresent.

The political wing has consisted of the same nucleus with which Lee started his public career – Goh Keng Swee, Toh Chin Chye and Rajaratnam, close advisers and durable ministers. Rajaratnam is an electoral light-weight, perhaps because of his Ceylonese origin which makes him a minority among minorities, but as a theoretician and policy articulator, he enjoys a high reputation. He has a capacity to see problems on the basis of first principles, enabling him to put things across simply and cogently. He has done good work as a thinker and originator of ideas while his suave manner has made him a respected figure in international forums.

Toh Chin Chye has been the least noticed of the troika although he was billed as chairman of the PAP. He is basically a scientist, reputed to spend some time in the laboratory in white overalls every morning before going to his office. He dutifully carries out the tasks assigned to him by the prime minister, generally keeping himself in the background and proving his utility more through personal loyalty than by the originality of his contributions to the party and government. Toh is an honourable figure and, from Lee's point of view, is utterly reliable and harmless.

Of the three men, Goh Keng Swee has apparently been the most significant. He put his personal stamp on Singapore's twin corner-stones – its economic policy and its internal security system. Goh has never held up socialism as a glamorous goal, as Lee did initially. It took less than a year in power for Lee to come round to

Goh's pragmatic principle that 'Singapore is no place for normal socialist economic planning. You cannot take a great and complicated market and run it with civil servants. A socialist in Singapore has to plan for a just society without upsetting the delicate machinery of trade.' Much of the economic thrust Singapore subsequently displayed was attributed to Goh, so that the press nicknamed him 'Dr Goh-ahead'.

As for the Goh-ahead on security, Lee himself gave his lieutenant an unusual testimony as early as 1965. The month Singapore attained sovereignty, with internal security a major topic of discussion, Lee told foreign correspondents that police and other security arrangements were under the overall control of Goh 'who is not only an economist but also a corporal in the last war. You know Hitler was a corporal.' He hastened to add that he was not suggesting anything, but the point was made. Goh was credited with many of Singapore's regimentation ideas, including the Pyramid Clubs.

In political terms, the most important feature of the team at the top has been the gulf between Lee and the others: Lee has dominated the stage, the others have stayed in the wings. Goh Keng Swee has occasionally been known to 'talk back' at cabinet meetings, but it has never gone beyond the formality of an exercise. In all matters, it has been Lee's voice that prevailed.

This four-man inner council has never been penetrated by others climbing the leadership ladder. Most of them have been technocrats, used in particular portfolios for their particular expertise, who were content to remain in their corners. They have helped Lee carry on the business of government efficiency without interfering in any way with his politics.

Only one man of cabinet rank developed independent political muscle – Ong Pang Boon, the minister for education. A left-wing leader from the days of the PAP's early left-of-centre stance, Ong had strong roots in two influential areas, among the poor and among the Chinese-educated. He cultivated these two sections of the population shrewdly and diligently, yet without ever challenging Lee. Ong has worked as a team with his wife, Chan Choy Siong, a fire-brand champion of the underdog and a political leader in her own right. She was reputed to have profound influence in Singapore's Chinatown. At a meeting of PAP cadres in 1971 it became clear that Ong Pang Boon enjoyed more support than Lee Kuan Yew. This, it was generally believed, was why Ong and his wife were sent to the United States on a long sabbatical; earlier his wife had become one of the few PAP parliamentarians to be compulsorily retired to 'make way for new blood'.

What Lee and his men set out to achieve and the manner in which they went about it determined the quality of life in Singapore. The objectives were clear: economic progress and a distinct identity for Singapore. Both objectives were unexceptionable and this made it easy for the Lee team to carry the people with them. The assumptions which accompanied the basic objectives were not so easily sold, but the acceptability of the fundamental propositions combined with the implementational techniques of the government to keep the people in line. It was proclaimed that the prerequisites for both progress and national identity were political stability and security; and as a result political stability and security became the first objects of the patriotic man. If their price was the elimination of the checks and balances of democracy, it was argued that the ends were noble enough to justify this sacrifice.

The rationalization thus formulated provided the intellectual basis for the style in which the Lee government set about achieving its objectives. At the leadership level it demanded unified purposefulness; at the administrative level, efficiency; and at the popular level, obedience.

The methods the government used to achieve its objectives. affected everybody and everything. All life was organized by the government, all standards set by it. The organization amounted to a 'people pacification' programme which rested on at least four different pillars: suppression of conventional channels of popular debate, expansion of the police force, introduction of an elaborate network of area-control organizations and promotion of a theory of élitism. In turn the pacification programme sought to nourish a society based on three cardinal principles: a free-enterprise compradore economic system, a one-party political oligarchy and a militarized populace.

The conventional channels through which Singaporeans traditionally had expressed their views and participated in public affairs comprised the legislative opposition, trade unions, the press and the schools. These were among the first to receive pointed attention from the government; one after another they were subdued. Previous chapters have dealt with the efficiency and thoroughness of this eradication campaign and the abiding nature of its results.

The administration has seen to it that details of the police establishment in Singapore are among the most closely guarded of classified material. What is known, however, is significant: there are nine different divisions in the police department, each as well armed and intensively trained as military regiments in other countries. Their total strength has been officially given as 6,000 but is thought to be nearer 10,000 – one policeman for every 200 Singaporeans. They constitute a privileged order with vast powers.

The most glamorous of all the police units is the Special Branch, specialists in surveillance and infiltration, interrogation and re-education. Reputedly the most efficient in Asia, the Special Branch has contributed, no less than Lee Kuan Yew's political skill, to the systematic elimination of opposition parties and front organizations in Singapore. Britain laid the foundations of this tight-knit organization's efficiency. Faced with communist insurgency in Malaya, the British authorities needed a truly reliable security police and the Special Branch was raised as a professional team noted for the lack of corruption in its ranks. Lee Kuan Yew inherited this tradition and has improved upon it.

What consolidated the achievements of the police was the system of area control that Lee established through a network of civilian and paramilitary organizations. The backbone of these organizations was provided by the unseen but ubiquitous cadres of the PAP, perhaps numbering no more than 2,000. Recruited with great care, passed through several security sieves and forever sworn to keep their status secret, the PAP cadres have functioned in close coalition with the political leadership and the Special Branch. They have acted as the government's liaison men and community watchdogs, vigilantly keeping their eyes and ears open in every constituency of the republic, every trade union and student organization, clan association and religious group.

The various organizations set up to control and co-ordinate popular activities were always known to be manned by the cadres, sometimes openly, more often from behind the scenes. The availability of trained and trusted cadres has enabled the government to conduct these organizations without always appearing to do so. There has been no question of a popular organization taking shape without the official stamp of approval.

Residents of an area have not been permitted to form a cultural association, or youngsters a sports body, without first getting it registered by the authorities.

At the apex of the area-control organizations was the People's Association, established in 1960, a year after the PAP came to power. Lee had seen the useful and influential role played among his people by Chinese clan associations and apparently wanted to promote an official platform which would serve the purpose of the clan associations without the risk of independent initiatives to which the latter were prone. 'It is necessary', Lee said at the first People's Association leadership course, 'to keep in constant touch with the people . . . and inculcate in them social qualities which will be useful in the building up of our society.'

On the basis of Lee's proposal that the People's Association should mix mass organizations with elected political leadership, a cabinet minister almost invariably headed the association while a PAP stalwart functioned as executive director. It is the widest-based organization in Singapore and therefore perhaps the most significant instrument of social discipline. Every sort of activity has gone on under its omnibus umbrella, from mass rallies to kindergartens and infants' creches.

One of the association's major responsibilities has been running several community centres in each of the parliamentary constituencies of Singapore. These centres are the government's principal tools of local penetration. The local MP is always on the centre's management committee while local businessmen are pulled in on the grounds that they should participate in community service. With badminton courts, television rooms and a variety of recreational activities, the community centre has sought to attract local citizens; the prime minister has given it prestige by speaking at its meetings, often making major policy announcements in the course of such speeches. The centres are also the local distribution points for government forms and such items as tickets for National Day parades, so that citizens have to go to them for their requirements.

The principal weakness from which both the People's Association and the community centres have suffered is their obvious official patronage. This has prevented the People's Association from effectively replacing the clan organizations whose principal contribution was the facilitation of unofficial, if sectional, community contacts. The popularity that the traditional organizations enjoyed was beyond the scope of the People's Association which, along with the community centres, lack the virtue of spontaneity. The difference between the voluntary and the official has been emphasized as several traditional organizations were banned or otherwise subdued.

Another channel of area control has been the Citizen's Consultative Committee, organized as part of Lee Kuan Yew's plans 'to create and build up a whole series of grass-roots organizations in every village, in every street and in every community'. The committees were envisaged as bridges between the government and community leaders in various localities and Lee has constantly reminded the people that 'all those active in the interests of their fellow citizens can find rewarding work and recognition in the Citizens' Consultative Committees'.

The principle behind the committees is a constructive one: to enable the authorities to acquaint themselves with local grievances. But, like the community centres, the committees have suffered from over-identification with the government. Members have to be nominated by the local MP and approved by the Prime Minister's Office. In many cases, in fact, the key men in both the committee and the centre have been the same. Moreover the poor, who have the most grievances, are often the least effectively represented in the committees.

The civilian community associations are interlinked with and backed up by paramilitary organizations, the most important of which is the Vigilante Corps. Started initially as a voluntary home guard organization in the early 1960s, it was affiliated in 1967 to the police force and given wide powers. It does not usually carry arms, but is essentially a wing of the police establishment, more intimately meshed with the PAP apparatus and used in areas and situations where the regular police are best kept out of sight, such as community gatherings. Its strength has been estimated at 15,000, most of them national servicemen. Some are volunteers.

Superimposed on the 'grass roots organizations' which control life in Singapore is the policy of purposefully creating an élite top crust which hopefully will absorb the ideas and philosophies of the leadership which reared it and will perpetuate the system. Disciplining society and reorganizing education provided only the setting. Perpetuation of the values so imparted depends on the solidification of the class system.

Lee Kuan Yew has not concealed his faith in the class system and the destiny of the upper crust. Every society, he said in 1967, has some five per cent among its population 'who are more than ordinarily endowed physically and mentally and in whom we must expend our limited and slender resources in order that they will provide that yeast, that ferment, that catalyst in our society which alone will ensure that Singapore shall maintain its pre-eminent place in the societies that exist in South and Southeast Asia'.

This was the time when Lee's favourite project was the establishment of a boarding school patterned after Eton. Although the impression publicly given was that any bright student would be eligible for admission to this school, Lee's theory that brightness and intelligence were hereditary was not to be ignored. The Singapore Eton was to be the privileged sanctuary of the scions of a privileged socio-economic class. The discriminatory and retrograde character of the proposition forced some criticism to the surface. The proposal was modified, ostensibly at least. Eton yielded to what were called junior schools, the first of which was established in 1969. Based on the same élitist concept, these schools take in hand-picked children for an intensive two-year pre-university course, inculcating in them a feeling of superiority and distinctiveness, of their genetically determined duty to assume command of society and lead Singapore as effectively as the leadership which has picked them is leading it.

The pernicious effect of elevating the élitist concept to government policy has been even more clearly demonstrated in Singapore's family-planning programme. In most countries family planning is simply a means to prevent the gains of economic growth from being wiped out by population explosion. In Singapore it has a specific contribution to make to the class system; Lee sees it as a means to improving the quality of Singapore's population. When legislation was passed in December 1969 to legalize abortion, the objectives Lee set forth were based on the premise that unskilled workers, the poor and the ill-educated produce below-average children while professional and executive parents produce well-endowed children. 'Our problem', Lee said in his Assembly speech, 'is how to devise a system of dis-incentives so that the irresponsible, the social delinquents, do not believe that all they have to do is to produce their children and the government then owes them and their children sufficient food, medicine, housing, education and jobs. . . . We must encourage those who earn less than $200 per month and cannot afford to nurture and educate many children never to have more than two. We will regret the time lost if we do not now take the first tentative steps towards correcting a trend which can leave our society with a large number of the physically, intellectually and culturally anaemic.' If this concept is seen in association with Lee's complementary thesis that the Mongoloid race is more hard-working and self-reliant than the Indo-Malay, the possibilities assume disturbing dimensions.

Singapore's population-control programme has been the most successful in Asia. In 1970 the birth-rate was down to 2·8 per cent from the 1957 high of 4·4 per cent. There was no class-based breakdown of the national figure, but the official policy has been that low-income parents should limit the number of their children to two. The rich minority's prosperity has boosted Singapore's *per capita* income to a flattering level; the poor majority has brought the population growth down to an equally flattering rate. The role earmarked for the poor in both cases illustrates the success with which Singapore has the socialism cake and eats it too.

The Singapore society Lee has fostered with his carefully orchestrated pacification programme is a faithful reflection of his personality and outlook on life. A believer in the proven advantages of the free-enterprise system, he has built Singapore on the foundations of a capitalist economy; an authoritarian by instinct, he has shored up the economy with a political system where there is no scope for dissent; a stickler for discipline, he has promoted mass obedience by fitting people into a militarized routine of life.

If advancement was the end of all economic systems, Singapore would have done well under compradore-capitalism; Lee Kuan Yew could be proud of the trend towards progress which his country has registered under his leadership. But he insists on calling it a socialist system (unlike Goh Keng Swee who publicly stated in 1965 that the Singapore government's policy was 'the encouragement of private enterprise by all means possible'). That year Lee told the Asian Socialist Conference in Bombay that he was an unrepentant socialist. The next year he told the Socialist International in Uppsala: 'I believe in socialism because I believe it is one of the most effective ways of mobilizing human resources.'

If a governmental finger in every planning pie was the hallmark of socialism, then Singapore's would indeed be one of the most socialist economies in the world. But if the question 'planning for what?' is raised, the perspective changes radically. For planning in Singapore is not for the purpose of ensuring a co-operative society based on equitable distribution of wealth; rather, Singapore has planned to keep wages low, to prevent collective bargaining by workers and to maintain order and discipline at all levels so that foreign capital would be attracted and private enterprise would grow unhampered. These goals have been achieved, yet Lee has not had the courage to own up to the system he has used with advantage.

Often, however, he has made statements which underline his faith in capitalism and his lack of faith in socialism. His insistence on still calling himself a socialist may indicate an ideological schizophrenia. At Bombay he pointed out that private industry's profit-sharing practices and bonus schemes produce better results than do government services where both efficient and mediocre employees receive identical compensation. Returning from the Bombay conference, he complained that socialism is not realistic enough. 'Democratic socialism, basing its emphasis on human values, and democratic-socialist leaders, wanting to give immediate results in spreading the benefits of national production to workers too quickly, were unable to maintain the momentum required for progress.'

At Uppsala he analysed Burma, Ceylon, Indonesia and India as examples of stagnation under socialism. By contrast, he said, 'some very unsocialist governments in Southeast Asia – Thailand, Malaysia, Laos, the Philippines and Pakistan' – had made more economic progress. The lesson, he argued, was that democratic socialists should ascertain the various factors that make for growth and prosperity and then 'adapt it to our particular circumstances'. He did not elaborate how, when the adaptation had gone far enough to make the end product capitalism, it could still be called democratic socialism.

As early as 1960 he told a Rotary Club meeting in Singapore what the newly formed PAP government's policy was going to be. He said: 'Basically we are not reformists. . . . The interests of the whole community in our entrepot situation require the active participation of the managerial and professional élite. We understand how you came to be leaders of trade and commerce, or captains of industry, or distinguished yourselves in the professions. We also understand that the incentives were material ones. And since it is our desire to see that the system continue to operate effectively and efficiently, it must necessarily follow that we are prepared to allow the old incentives to continue.'

If the economic advantages of capitalism have drawn Lee to the right, the intellectual 'dangers' of socialism have set him against the left. He seems to believe that civil rights are synonymous with socialism and socialism synonymous with communism. Describing his negotiations with an underground communist leader in the early years, he said the talks ranged over 'more democratic rights, more cultural freedom, more free importation of books, more free immigration permits, all of which means, in short, more opportunities for communist activities'. Apparently, Lee's early political struggle against the communists affected him to the extent that he sees all cultural freedom, all books, as communist plots. That socialists do not see things his way is yet another ground for disillusionment. 'When communists come to power,' he told the Socialist International in 1964, 'they stay in. The democratic socialists lack understanding of the mechanics of power and, worse, lack expertise in the exercise of power.'

Such are the ideas and concepts which have provided the thrust to the policies the Lee government has followed. By the time Singapore attained sovereignty, the government had been in power for six years and had successfully overcome the fact that it owed its success to the backing of the workers and the promise of socialism. Rajaratnam found it necessary to explain that the PAP had not turned anti-labour. But he also clarified that the party had come to realize that workers constituted a class with a vested interest while the PAP had to work for the whole country rather than for one class. In the process, what the working class lost, the élite gained.

Having ridden to power as a socialist party, the PAP could hardly have made the nation accept free enterprise as a goal without bringing left-wing elements in particular and potential dissenters in general under effective control. This is why the fostering of a capitalist society went hand in hand with the entrenchment of a one-party oligarchy in Singapore.

Technically, of course, there are fifteen parties in the republic (all but four of them totally inactive) so that those meticulous about definition must avoid the term 'one-party system' and call Singapore a 'dominant party system' or a 'one-party situation', and Lee can speak to audiences in Europe and the United States about the proliferation of parties with which he has had to cope, and the unending battle for voter support. In fact Singapore came under a one-leader party as well as a one-party system of politics within three years of the PAP's rise to power. Given the real threat the Malayan communist movement posed to Singapore in the early years and the subsequent material progress his government brought to Singapore, Lee could have owned up to the system he practised and still found enough intelligent people to back him. But his path was different. He told the world press in Helsinki in 1971: 'I do not think there is any place in South and Southeast Asia where a social democratic group went into a united front with communists, then broke from them and fought them on radio and television for heart and mind and won that battle for heart and mind, won it in a referendum, won it in a subsequent by-election, before it put the leaders who lost that election away.'

A claim with more terminological inexactitudes would be difficult to imagine: we have seen how that battle for heart and mind was fought; how that famous referendum was won; how critical by-elections were lost; and most important, how opposition leaders were 'put away' *before* the 1963 general election. With that election, the PAP put its unbreakable seal on Singapore.

After that watershed, the government and the party became one. Thomas Bellows observed that periodic implementation of both government machinery and PAP party strategy was designed to incapacitate – though not totally to annihilate – political opposition. The impact of this technique was clearly visible in the electoral position. In 1963 the PAP won thirty-seven out of the fifty-one seats; by 1967 its strength rose to forty-nine, two seats being 'uncontestable' as they were technically occupied by Barisan candidates who had gone underground without formally resigning; in the 1968 election it won all fifty-eight seats, fifty-one of them unopposed.

The hundred per cent dominance won in 1968 was not the only tell-tale evidence of the status the PAP achieved. When the merger with Malaysia collapsed in 1965, there was not a murmur against the party leadership which had staked everything on merger and failed to make it work. In 1966 a party stalwart and member of the Central Executive Council, Tan Kia Gan, was expelled and again there was not a single voice raised in support of Tan even from his own party branch where he was known to be popular – a far cry from the days of Ong Eng Guan's expulsion. There was hardly any campaigning for the 1968 election, for none was thought really necessary. When Lee dropped nine MPs on the plea that he wanted younger elements to gain experience, there was still not a whisper of complaint from anyone. It was established by now that Lee's word was law, that a person's standing in the party depended not on his strength in a particular constituency but on his relationship with the party and on Lee's estimation of him.

Lee is admittedly tough towards critics and dissenters which has helped bring about a situation where his supremacy is equated with the national good. The toughness became a fixture of his political posture as a result of his personal encounter with communists. His appreciation of communist methods confirmed it. He has often seemed to begrudge communists their reputation for high-handedness. 'Our tragedy,' he said in 1965, 'is that we know that if our foe wins we will die, and die painfully, but then when we win our foe lives comfortably in prison with butter and eggs and meat according to special rations which the rules of the game lay down upon us.' That was a revealing statement which showed why Lee has never been impressed by charges of cruelty towards political prisoners in Singapore: according to his book, he was doing them a favour by letting them live.

The way Lee has conducted the government and the party as two arms of what he has projected as the same patriotic national movement has also contributed to the PAP's dominance. People came to look upon opposition parties as something anti-national and unpatriotic. The Special Branch and the party cadres did nothing to discourage the impression. In her history of the PAP Pang Cheng Lian was constrained to remark that one reason why the PAP remained unchallenged was 'the common fear that joining an opposition party may jeopardize one's future'. As a non-resident of Singapore, Thomas Bellows was more forthright. He said that because of the furtive quarrels and the conspiratorial posturing of the Lee group and leftists in the PAP during the 1950s, 'many PAP non-communists have tended to treat all opponents, regardless of political complexion, in a conspiratorial and manipulative style. This has retarded the evolution of internally democratic parties and externally competitive, bargaining and tolerant party system.'

Lee's own view of it was obviously different. He apparently saw parties and view-points other than his own as irrelevant, because his own party represented the national interests. Speaking in the Assembly in August 1960, he said: 'There are three possible situations in which the PAP can find itself. Firstly, where what is good for the people and the PAP may be bad for the communists. Secondly, where what is good for the people and the PAP may also be good for the communists. Thirdly, where what is bad for the people and the PAP may be good for the communists.'

The obvious fourth possibility never occurred to him: where what is good for the people may be bad for the PAP and the communists. 'People and the PAP' always went together in his mind.

With free enterprise and political hegemony firmly established, Lee could sit back and watch Singapore making the kind of material progress he valued. But given his all-or-nothing approach to power, his insistence on the total allegiance of the people and his love of discipline, he saw the economic and political organization of Singapore as only part of the job. The injection of an appropriate social policy was necessary to complete it, and it had to be a policy which would enable the government to retain supervisory control. Militarization filled the bill: it promised to instil in citizens all the virtues Lee held dear – discipline, ruggedness, self-reliance, security consciousness, physical fitness and, above all, a disposition to obey orders.

The process of militarization in Singapore started as an offshoot of the security problem which was high on the government's priority list from the very beginning. The concept of Singapore as a garrison state was developed with a view to ensuring its security in an unfriendly neighbourhood. But soon it seemed as though the Lee government was doing everything it could to keep the neighbours unfriendly, as if to strengthen the garrison state mentality. Within three years of separation from Malaysia, 'defence' began to figure as the most important item in the budget, and the cult of the uniform enveloped the republic.

In 1967 the allocation for defence was seven per cent of the national budget; in 1968 it was sixteen per cent; in 1970 it shot up to thirty-three per cent and in 1972 it rose to thirty-eight per cent. The provision for defence in the $1,449-million budget for 1972–1973 was $566.4 million which meant that the government was spending more than $280 *per capita* for 'defence and internal security'. In Malaysia in the same budget year the provision was for $620 million (out of a total budget of $3,350 million) or a *per capita* defence expenditure of $70, less than one-third of Singapore's.

Most of this money went into buying and developing sophisticated weapon systems. The strength of the armed forces also increased steadily. By 1971 the professional army was estimated to number 7,500 men. Together with the police divisions and national servicemen, a ready ground force of more than 36,000 armed men was available to the government in addition to air and naval units. Additionally, an equivalent of three battalions went into the reserves each year along with supporting arms.

There have been many who questioned the need to build up such a disproportionately large military machine in Singapore. Such criticism invariably made the government leaders bitter; they condemned the critics as innocents who did not understand the realities surrounding Singapore, or as mischief-makers who wished to see the republic's future jeopardized. The obvious explanation for the build-up was no doubt Lee Kuan Yew's suspicions about his neighbours' intentions: the theory of a communally inspired attack from one or another of the neighbours helped keep the people's survival consciousness at high pitch and justify the enormous expenditure of time and money on defence.

Lee was also attracted by the 'nation-building' potential of a militarized way of life. Only this could explain his objective of 'making every citizen a soldier' and of organizing uniformed brigades for small schoolchildren and women. Whichever way Singaporeans turn there is a uniformed organization waiting for them – military and police cadet corps, Singapore girl pipers, special women's police units, people's defence forces with a separate wing for women, vigilante corps, university contingents, uniformed sports troupes and an array of bands and drill units. Private institutions, including churches, have been encouraged to maintain their own uniformed organizations such as boys' brigades. Early-morning calisthenics have been promoted as a matter of state policy. Drills and parades have become an everyday feature of life. Together these organizations and activities reinforce the impression of a militant people dedicated to upholding high moralistic and nationalist values, reminiscent of Mussolini's Italy and Papadopaulos' Greece.

And Lee and his men never tire of emphasizing the advantages of drill and discipline. Almost every speech Lee has made before local audiences has contained some reference to the importance of training, of every citizen becoming a disciplined digit in the national scheme of things. He has sometimes used expressions and similes not complimentary to the listeners, but which made his

7

point in a particularly telling manner. Addressing a community-centre meeting in 1967 he explained how the present generation had a duty to see that the next one grew up robust and healthy. 'We will be to blame if youngsters ten years from now become hooligans, ruffians and sluts. They can be trained to be otherwise. Even dogs can be trained as proved by the Police Training School where dogs, at a whistle, jump through a hoop, sit down or attack those who need to be attacked.'

Humans have what must seem to Lee a tiresome tendency not to be dogs, but still the tone of life in Singapore has come pretty close to what must prevail in the Police Training School, and Singaporeans in general have accepted the life chalked out for them by the government. Perhaps they found they had no choice. Perhaps they found the life materially comfortable and therefore acceptable. Perhaps they even agreed with Lee's rationalization of a regimented life. They are an assortment of cultural entities, and no doubt each has had its reasons for deciding that conformism is the better part of valour.

The predominant Chinese community consists of an English stream and a Chinese stream: the former conformed as a matter of course, the latter as a result of pressures. The English-educated section, though it includes most of the liberals who were disillusioned by the government's strong-arm policies, has stood to benefit the most from the élitism of a modernizing Singapore. It constitutes the ruling class and has been clearly identifiable with the government. It is also the easiest to manage. Lee has described the English-educated Chinese as 'devitalized, almost emasculated, as a result of de-culturalization', but for all his contempt, they readily accepted his ideas and philosophies, being the natural partners with him in Singapore's prosperity.

The Chinese stream has remained suspicious of Lee. Its have-nots resent his efforts to de-emphasize Chinese culture, while its haves are additionally upset by his preference for foreign business interests. They have, however, been left with no alternative but to comply with the government's policies. Not only are critics, whether political leaders or business tycoons, quickly put down, but the Chineseness of the Chinese has been subjected to a steady process of anglicization. The principal of a Chinese school explained the shift by saying that it was difficult for Chinese-educated to get jobs in Singapore. Before the PAP came to power Lee strongly opposed any policy aimed at encouraging English in education, and dramatized his resistance to it by announcing that he was sending his own son to a Chinese school. Once he was in power, English rapidly became the language of education and of the state; and his son spent only a few years in a Chinese school before going on to Cambridge.

The Malays as a community have not counted for much except insofar as Singapore's ties with Malaysia gave them some political significance. Official spokesmen explained that the recognition of Malay as one of the national languages was 'an act of faith, not of political opportunism', but it was nevertheless a hang-over of the Malaysia merger. After separation, organized Malay activities were controlled by Malay leaders in the government who constantly urged their flock to demonstrate that they were Singaporeans. Now and then some incident occurs and tensions rise in the predominantly Malay areas; but generally, thanks to the dominance of the Chinese community and to the determination of the government to keep communal divisions under a tight lid, the Malays in Singapore lie low.

The Indians, Pakistanis and Ceylonese are a group so small that they had perforce to accept the government as it was – or face the consequences. They used to play a key leadership role in public affairs, especially in trade unionism. When the unions were disciplined, the message became clear to the leaders. The government's policy of multiracialism made Singapore a safe place for minorities, but the minorities' part of the bargain was to keep out of the government's way and remain satisfied with such prosperity as they could derive from their country of domicile.

Singapore, in short, has developed the personality Lee Kuan Yew wanted it to have. Its economy is tied to the industrialized West, its politics are firmly anchored to one party and one leadership, its society has accepted a conformist mould, its sights for the future are adjusted to the viewpoint of an élitist class. The result is a life style which has no parallel in Southeast Asia.

In Malaysia, too, the authorities are touchy on 'sensitive issues', but it has remained possible for opposition parties to function meaningfully, even to capture power in one state or another. In Indonesia, even under Sukarno, students could make a contribution to public life (as they demonstrated when he was ousted), and they have shown Suharto more than once that they retain their capacity for collective action. In Thailand, an established military dictatorship, newspapers were able to put up organized resistance to a draconian press bill drafted by the government in 1970 until it was withdrawn for reconsideration.

Civil servants in Singapore, for all their integrity and efficiency, have never been known to stand up to the cabinet; whereas in Malaysia they are reputed to act as a sobering influence on politicians. (Early 1967 it was said that Lee had complained at cabinet meetings that some of his senior officials were uncouth fellows who could not be taken out of their offices to discuss business matters informally; he asked the Political Study Centre to rectify this.)

The effects of the persuasion of force rather than the force of persuasion are visible everywhere. Numerous have been the cases where exemplary punishment was meted out to people who stepped out of the line. A youth was sentenced to three months' imprisonment and three strokes of the cane for throwing a cigarette butt into a road-side drain; another was given a year in jail and three strokes for damaging a telephone booth; a man in whose garden a rain-filled paint tin was found breeding mosquitoes was told he was 'liable to prosecution under Section 21 of this Act and on conviction to a fine not exceeding $1,000 or to imprisonment for a term not exceeding three months'. Another was sentenced for plucking flowers in a park.

Litterless streets, mosquitoless gardens and flower-filled parks impress visitors to Singapore. Nowhere else in Asia can they see such discipline. Even the young people in Singapore are unlike young people in other Asian countries, for although other Asian governments also frown on the hippie cult, the Singapore government has frowned more efficiently.

'We merely enable hippies to move on to their next destination,' said a government spokesman explaining the policy towards travelling flower-children. Policy towards indigenous ones shows no trace of humour. It is based on the theory that if effective measures are not taken here and now, in ten years Singapore will be swamped by 'street bums living off the State'. Official circulars have been issued to all government departments instructing them to serve long-haired people last, and to make it plain to them they are unwelcome. Private firms were told to do everything to discourage long hair among their employees. The culture minister once told university students that he would 'recommend' conscription of those boys who protested against the government's hair policy.

In early 1972 the policy was given fresh teeth. At the border with Malaysia, immigration authorities began restricting the entry of people whose hair reached their collars, whatever their immigration status. A notice was put up to say 'Passports should be marked long hair'. An Australian businessman complained that government officials accosted airline passengers making brief stop-overs in Singapore, ordering them into town for quick haircuts. Some foreign embassies asked the government for clarification on the hair policy. Private associations in Singapore began issuing elaborate instructions to their members on correct hair styles. The Teachers' Union said even girls should not wear their hair below their shoulders and should not have 'permanent waves'.

Singapore's crew-cut young men have developed an appropriately serious attitude to life. Buffeted by high-principled advice from the government and inhibited by the maze of social, educational and employment restrictions it imposes, they have become more interested in jobs, the future and security than in pop, fads and permissiveness. At least they appear so. Young people in the universities and elsewhere can be heard discussing the economy, the political chaos in neighbouring countries, the nature of foreign investment and the dangers of communism. Significantly, most of these discussions follow a set pattern made familiar by Lee Kuan Yew during more than a decade of speaking.

There is also pride in Singapore among the young people. They are pleased that their prime minister is idolized in the West, that their country has become known and respected around the world, that their material advancement is palpably more impressive than that of their neighbours. They are gratified, despite the price they have paid, that Singapore is clean and green and orderly. For them Singapore's success has been their success. Whatever its drawbacks, the Lee government made it all possible and they often seem grateful.

A young woman whose idealism had driven her to join the Singapore *Herald* went off to Hong Kong after the paper was shut down by the government. Although a victim of that government's intolerance and forced to live in an unfamiliar city, she still said: 'I am sure our prime minister would not have done what he did without very good reasons. He is wiser than all of us and some day maybe we will come to know why our paper had to be killed.' She became upset at any suggestion that individual liberty in

Singapore had been curtailed, and invariably drew attention to the dangers facing the republic internally as well as externally which made extraordinary security measures necessary.

And she was utterly homesick. She spoke of the chauvinistic mood of the Hong Kong Chinese in contrast to the cosmopolitanism of the Singapore Chinese. She nostalgically remembered the wholesome food-stalls of Singapore where delicacies were available so much cheaper than in Hong Kong's restaurants. She detested the congestion and filth of Hong Kong and longed for the green open spaces of her native city.

Confronted by Singaporeans who are not only prepared to accept the life their government has mapped out for them but who also appreciate it, critics who bemoan the demise of civil liberties in the republic sounded irrelevant, even tendentious. Evidently, Lee Kuan Yew is pretty close to rearing that responsive generation he always said he could rear, given the time and the organization.

Lee has clearly been aiming at a future in which the relative creature comforts he has provided will combine with the cumulative impact of education and social engineering to produce a citizenry ready to accept his system without any reservations. The élite class he has consciously been grooming will hopefully take up the command of such a society and carry on unhampered. It is a plausible proposition. But it assumes that man can live by bread alone. It calls for a rewriting of the history of the human spirit.

For every predictable conformist the visitor meets in Singapore, it is possible to meet another who, if convinced of the visitor's 'reliability', will be willing to talk of frustrations and suppressed emotions. On rare occasions – admittedly getting rarer as time passes – even the young will summon enough courage to betray their natural sentiments.

Lee Kuan Yew himself had a taste of this when he went to address the University of Singapore in mid-1969. The reception the university community gave him was far from friendly. A lecturer's long-winded question on the Abortion Bill so over-taxed the prime minister's patience that he pushed the chairman aside and grabbed the microphone to cut the questioner down. Jeers arose from the audience; this upset the prime minister a great deal.

Not to be cowed, Lee called a separate meeting of first-year students. There was no doubt that this was to be a command performance; notices put up by the university authorities demanded that the freshman students should turn up for the meeting with their matriculation cards so that an attendance register could be made. Vehement protests from the Students' Union persuaded the authorities to take the notices down.

Before addressing the first-year students, Lee met the executive council of the Students' Union and hinted that any student who stepped out of line would be called up for two years' full-time national service. In the address that followed, he warned freshmen to beware of senior students as well as of expatriate teachers who were less than responsible in airing their dissenting views. He said the government knew precisely what was going on inside and outside the classrooms. He did not welcome opposition for the sake of opposition, he explained, but was prepared to allow dissent on 'non-fundamental issues'. On fundamental issues he would come down really hard. These were national security, national service, multiracialism, economic survival and the democratic political system. It was left to the young listeners to figure out what was left out of this list.

At the end of the address it was made known that the government did not wish the speech to be reported. However, the Students' Union instructed the editors of the university paper, *Undergrad*, to go ahead and publish a report. An ugly confrontation seemed inevitable. Then the Prime Minister's Office quietly pointed out that the printing licence of the *Undergrad* had expired six months earlier in December 1968 and that if an illegal issue was brought out the printer and the editor would be liable to a fine of $4,000 and twelve months' imprisonment.

No *Undergrad* appeared – and no report of Lee's speech. The incident came to light only when the *Far Eastern Economic Review*'s Singapore correspondent, Bob Reece, reported it. Reece, who later became foreign editor of the Singapore *Herald*, was the first man to be thrown out of the country when that newspaper subsequently came under the axe.

CHAPTER ELEVEN

Alone against Tomorrow

Do you think there are no crocodiles because the water is calm?

MALAY PROVERB

By 1973 Lee Kuan Yew had been in uninterrupted power for four-teen years. He once spoke vaguely of another decade in office which, if realized, would put him in the same bracket with the all-time Asian record-holders of China.

During his long tenure Lee has given Singapore a name and a habitation. He has also made it a subject of controversy. To some Singapore means progress, to others exploitation; to some demo-cracy, to others tyranny; to some Asia's model state, to others a dangerous Asian precedent. In the final analysis history's balance sheet on Lee's Singapore is likely to be decided by the long-term political viability of the state and the objective validity of the values it symbolized. In Henry Kissinger's words, 'when the voice of controversy is stilled, what matters will be whether what was done made a difference, whether it marked an episode or an epoch'.

One of the main reasons why the Lee years might prove only an episode in Singapore's history is the preponderant role one man's personality has played in shaping events. Singapore in the 1970s mirrors not the collective aspirations of a people or a generation but the ideals, convictions and prejudices of Lee Kuan Yew. The country is the man – and the man has had to use extra-parliamentary force to make it so.

Singapore's contrived individualism derives logic but not legi-timacy from Lee Kuan Yew's cultural rootlessness. His inability to 'belong' was painfully emphasized when Malaysia rejected him. It then became all the more essential to create a Singapore which would lend him relevance and significance. Hence his tendency to see Singapore's survival as different from the survival of other countries. Hence also the evangelic fervour of his exhortations – his constant emphasis that 'in Singapore we are trying to solve problems which few bigger and more powerful countries are called upon to solve' and his insistence that every undertaking be treated as a matter of life and death: 'If you slacken [on the cleanliness drive] there will be flies, plague and pestilence,' he said.

Lee is so sure of the rightness of his path that he has no sympathy for other points of view. He is contemptuous of the public will when it intrudes on his own convictions. He has much to be arrogant about, but he has antagonized people and countries by displaying arrogance without grace. He lacks the Chinese gift of compromise. He is a clever man who seems to lack wisdom. This is particularly unfortunate in a region of ancient civilizations which traditionally see wisdom as capable of existing without cleverness. It has been pointed out that in Asian thinking, the wise man is cool but not necessarily calculating, shrewd but considerate, his wit not cutting, the precision of his mind not metallic; and his ambitions do not call for the subjugation of other people. The moral overtones which surround Lee's utterances do not hide from Asian peoples the fact that he is, as Tunku Abdul Rahman said, 'too clever by half'. He always sounds like the Chosen One who has just come down from the mountain after personally receiving the tablets from God. He gives the impression of feeling sinless.

This expresses itself most tellingly in his fixation that those who oppose him are necessarily anti-national. It emerges too in some strange personal postures. For example, it is generally recognized in Singapore that it is useful for a corporation to retain Lee and Lee as its legal consultants. A communication on the official letterhead of the law firm has impact. Although Lee and Lee is very ably led, it might have been thought appropriate, in a tightly knit and tightly managed society such as Singapore's, for the prime minister to recognize the delicacy of his wife's running a law firm. Its discontinuation would have been a small sacrifice to make for the sake of 'form' and the reputation of a leadership sensitive about personal and public morality; but the leadership is so convinced of its own morality that it has not been made.

On the other hand, a friend of the prime minister's father reported how the old man, with all the old-fashioned loyalty of the King's Chinese, was anxious to have a personal meeting with Queen Elizabeth when she visited Singapore in early 1972. But he was not invited to any of the functions and, when he summoned up enough courage to ask his son for the favour of an invitation, he was told to go to the public reception at the Istana, the presidential mansion.

Lee, it appears, is sinless only by his own definition of sin. It is his definitions and ideas which become policy in Singapore. To the extent that a policy stems from one man's notions of life and morality, its validity is restricted to the duration of that man's office. Lee's valiant efforts to raise his notions to the level of a lasting philosophy do not carry with them the promise of success because they depend so heavily on executive power and on a series of questionable premises about people's willingness to go on accepting the exercise of such power.

Singapore in the 1970s gives the impression of a people generally satisfied with their government. Lee can appreciate the wisdom of an ancient Chinese sage who advised a king that if he wanted his subjects to remain peaceful, he should keep their stomachs full and their heads empty. The majority of Singaporeans appear happy with the prosperity that has come their way. More and more young people are being turned out with no notion of broad democratic values and apparently quite content with the good life they are enjoying.

The question remains whether this is because they have no choice or whether in fact Lee Kuan Yew has succeeded in creating a New Man whose only concern in life is material gain. While the improvement in living standards acts as a major factor in keeping the population quiescent, it seems too optimistic to assume that that is all that matters. In fact, one of the dangers that Singaporeans face is the temptation to live soullessly in order to make money. The prospects of becoming a society which knows the price of everything and the value of nothing is among the points of criticism Lee's adversaries raise.

Lee himself is aware of the implications of a society becoming too toneless. He once said that if strong-arm measures were used beyond what was necessary, 'then you have a quiescent and dead population'. Therefore, he claimed his measures were calculated to 'give full play to youthful boisterousness, exuberance, vigour, vitality and idealism'. It is, however, exuberance as seen by a person who takes a dim view of music, films and literature. The deadly calm he has imposed on his population indicates, by his own yardstick, that strong-arm measures have been used beyond what is necessary. At the same time he seems to think that he has to go on using them, for, even after the end of the 1960s, he is in no mood to relax them. It is as though there is a gnawing fear deep inside him that he will lose his grip if Singapore loses its sense of crisis.

This is a familiar state of mind among politicians. As former US government officials Richard Barnet and Maurice Raskin said in their book *An American Manifesto*: 'Hitler recognized that the bigger the crisis, the bigger lies people could swallow, because their dependence on the leader grows in time of crisis. Leaders have always protected their power by hinting at mysteries which only they know and only they can control.... The effect of official secrecy is to make the citizen doubt his own judgment and his own best instincts. "If you only knew what I knew," his leaders continually tell him. The official pretence at knowing more than what a conscientious newspaper reader and television viewer would know disarms the citizen, makes him more dependent on the keepers of the secrets and permits the government to play on his hopes and fears.'

Lee's dependence on the crisis atmosphere and his I-know-things-that-you-don't posture are major factors behind his staying power. Other factors are the carefully engineered electoral process, the organization of the military system, control of the political machinery and the security network. These are so carefully meshed together that Lee can reasonably look forward to more years in power.

The people elected Lee in 1959 on a left-wing, democratic, anti-colonial, Malaysia platform. Today his government supports capital against labour, denies democratic rights to the people, facilitates the continuance of a colonial logic in Southeast Asian economics and is out of Malaysia. Having thus repudiated his mandate, Lee rules by sufferance.

It is not realistic to say that elections have taken place since 1959, renewing Lee's mandate every time. Post-1959 elections in Singapore have been largely empty exercises, as shown by the deceptive 'choices' given and the methods employed for the referendum in 1962, the mass arrests of opposition leaders prior to the general election in 1963 and the hundred per cent PAP control of parliament since.

Outwardly Lee has often tried to put up a dead-pan face over the absence of a single opposition member in parliament. The argument is that if the people want to elect only PAP candidates, is it democratic to deny them the right? The disingenuity of the argument must have been obvious to the PAP leadership for, when another general election became imminent in 1972, the talk at the top was on how to give away some seats to non-PAP candidates. Discussions were said to have led to the conclusion that seven to nine seats in the new sixty-five-seat parliament should be yielded, but not to any opposition party. Clearly, the PAP is anxious to end its all-too-revealing monopoly of parliament, but to do so only for the minimum purposes of appearance.

In this exercise it received unexpected assistance from the Barisan Sosialis which, after boycotting elections for a decade, announced its decision to enter the next fray. The Barisan's capable leaders have been in prison or exile for nine years and Lee deftly saw to it that the party remained in the hands of men who would make it an object of ridicule rather than of respect. The Barisan had no hope of making any dent on the PAP's parliamentary pre-eminence, but its participation in the election was guaranteed to give the process the credibility it had lost over the years. Whoever was to participate in the elections, no one imagined for a moment that Singapore's 'one-party situation' would undergo any significant change under the prevailing system. The electoral process is so heavily weighted in favour of the ruling party that unseating it through the ballot box is inconceivable.

At the other extreme, no such thing as a military *coup* is considered possible in Singapore. Here too Lee has been far-sighted, making full use of his capacity for innovation and organization. Speaking in the Malaysian parliament in December 1963, he said that in Southeast Asia armies when expanded had a tendency ultimately to take over and 'we should be extremely chary' about any such expansion plans. He for one was not only extremely chary but extremely clever. Even as he pushed a general line of militarization, he provided for built-in safety valves. Emphasis on national service leading up to volunteer reserves is the cornerstone of his policy; it eliminates the danger of a large standing army. At the same time, the officer class is kept away from publicity; offhand it is unlikely that an average Singaporean would know who is the top army officer or even what is the top army post. The top command of the standing army is pegged low. There are no generals in Singapore. The highest post is brigadier and the first incumbent was a headmaster seconded to the army. When he went back to teaching in 1971, a Singaporean of Indian origin who had started out as a civil servant and was formerly commissioner of lands was promoted brigadier.

Ethnic diffusion at the top as well as the absence of a really professional soldier class with any traditions make it virtually impossible to organize a military *coup*.

Within the PAP the three men who share the limelight with Lee come from outside Singapore – Goh Keng Swee and Toh Chin Chye from Malaya and Rajaratnam from Ceylon. Besides, Goh was a civil servant, Toh a scientist and Rajaratnam a journalist before they became political figures; they had, and have, no political base of their own. Education Minister Ong Pang Boon is the only politician with a standing of his own and the very fact that he is an exception enables Lee to keep a watchful eye on him.

Additionally, Lee has the Special Branch and the PAP cadre system protecting his flanks. With a highly secretive organizational set-up, these networks are personally controlled by Lee. They are his eyes and ears. No other leader is in a position to get a real hold on them and Lee is sure to keep it so for as long as he is in power.

Reassuring as these devices are, Lee cannot be unaware of the existence of factors which at least theoretically have the capacity to upset the carefully maintained balance should the wind shift. Economic disparities in general and labour frustration in particular are among them. By slightly lifting the long wage freeze in 1972 Lee gave workers the promise of a juster share in the republic's prosperity. As additional insurance, the government has been encouraging the lower-income groups to buy on easy instalments the government flats in which they live, on the theory that the accumulation of property will give the poorer sections of society a vested interest in the *status quo*. Such measures are effective in buying time for the government, but insofar as the basic attitudes of the establishment continue to be in favour of an exploitative economic and social system, the potential of the working class becoming a possible source of challenge to the authorities cannot be entirely ruled out.

To this should be added the so-far unexpressed resentment of important Chinese *taipans* who, for cultural as well as business reasons, have been becoming disenchanted with the government. Enormously wealthy and steeped in the Chinese style of organization through family and clan connections, they are not the sort of people the Lee government can afford to ignore indefinitely or to suppress through arrests and intimidation. Reports persist that influential sections of the Chinese business establishment are constantly exploring ways of promoting opposition to the PAP. Hedged in as they are by the government's many-headed security apparatus, they are not in a position to mount an open campaign, but they remain an influence which can turn against the government if a new set of circumstances develop.

One reason adduced by Western intellectuals for Lee's staying-power is the traditional Chinese reverence for authority. The Chinese, it is said, are accustomed to being governed; they look upon government as something to be obeyed or at worst bought. After all, is it not traditional for the Chinese to weather a storm by bending to it?

If this were strictly so, Chinese history would not be so replete with civil wars culminating in the communist revolution. In any case, Lee Kuan Yew does not seem to accept this innocent interpretation of the Chinese temperament for, if he did, he would have found it possible to relax among his people. On the contrary, Lee might well be aware that if and when he is challenged, it is more likely to be by the Chinese than by any other group.

Lee's public posturings until the mid-1960s ironically contributed to this possibility by feeding the very fires of Chinese emotionalism which he wanted to put out. In his fight against leftists and even more during the all-out bid to get a slice of the Malaysia cake, he found it useful to employ Chinese chauvinism as a weapon. By pointing up the inefficiency of other races, by underlining the special virtues of immigrant peoples and by constantly harping on the superiority of Singapore, he reinforced the sense of separateness of the Chinese. Having nourished such sentiments when it was politically expedient, Lee may have given them a rebellious edge by subsequently turning against them.

In any case, Lee Kuan Yew's chances of success in his attempts to unmake the Chinese in Singapore must be seriously doubted. As C. P. Fitzgerald argues in his *Southern Expansion of the Chinese People*, dissolution of Chineseness and rapidity of assimilation become more difficult as Chinese *hua ch'iao* communities gain in literacy and wealth. Some of the English-educated Chinese in Singapore may find the going good under Lee, but the majority may well be waiting for an opportunity to escape from the prospect of becoming deculturalized by an anglicized ruling class. The Chinese who bent with the Lee Kuan Yew wind could be the first to stand up again when they find it possible to do so.

Lee is justified in assuming that the Chinese pose a security problem to him. But, thanks to the peculiarities of the Chinese family structure, it does not lend itself to time-worn Western-type solutions. There are top Singapore businessmen, for example, with blood brothers who are communists active in the business. Wealthy Chinese businessmen elsewhere who act as agents for Peking's trade have family outlets in Singapore. The Chinese all over Southeast Asia operate on a basis of vertical integration achieved through relatives in various countries. This integration includes the civil service in the countries concerned. Lee had a choice of tackling this situation the Chinese way, at the family level, with pragmatism and an easy-going attitude such as the colonial administration in Hong Kong had developed to a fine art. He chose instead the Special Branch way. It has very effectively cleared the branches, but has almost certainly left the roots intact.

While internal challenges might be nipped in the bud for many years to come, challenges from outside do not lend themselves to control through any of the methods Lee is prone to use. He has no control over the physical reality of Singapore, over the compulsions of Southeast Asian regional politics and over the sense of independent destiny harboured by the Malaysians and the Indonesians.

However hard Lee tries to project Singapore as the linch-pin of Southeast Asia, the fact remains that only politically is it a country. In every other sense it is a mere city. Neighbouring countries have truly national economies and urban–rural complexities to cope with, whereas Singapore is a place where every citizen can be reached through one television announcement; if it is past show time, the saying goes, a messenger can be sent out on a bicycle to reach any citizen within thirty minutes. To compare the progress of Singapore with that of a full-blown country is somewhat unrealistic. Singapore's natural comparison is with Hong Kong. It may even be compared with Petaling Jaya, but not with Malaysia; with Makati, not with the Philippines. When it comes to the crunch, Singapore counts for very little in world trade or in Southeast Asian economy, except as an entrepôt. Its tiny population has minimal influence on other countries, even on the overseas Chinese as a community. And Lee Kuan Yew is an isolated leader on the Asian scene.

For such a land and such a leader, it is short-sighted to attempt a life without relevance to the region of which it is a part. It cannot do without the region any more than post-imperial Britain can do without Europe. Yet Singapore has voluntarily chosen the 'Little Israel' image as if to emphasize its alienation from its neighbourhood. Like Israel, Singapore is ever ready for war, and will perhaps prove good at it – but why should it be unable to strike up peace and mutual trust with its neighbours? Israel has neighbours who were hostile from the beginning; Singapore has no such historical conditioning to belligerence. Israel has the backing of a mighty international lobby bound to its support by immutably religious and ethnic bonds; Singapore has no such backers.

Above all, the Jews in Israel are people who have regained a homeland after centuries of diaspora and who are therefore committed to it heart and soul. The Chinese settlers of Singapore still feel the emotional pull of China very strongly. The new Singaporean nationalism which Lee assiduously tries to develop can at best be a political device, not a deeply felt social and cultural ethos.

Lee has ignored these realities and put his faith in the capacity of an authoritarian state to change human nature. He has chosen to stand defiantly alone. The logic of Southeast Asian politics and of Southeast Asian communalism suggests that such a policy must put long-term survival in jeopardy, and that merging with the surrounding landscape, arousing no neighbourly enmity and envy, would have been wiser. Singapore could have emulated Switzerland rather than Israel; Switzerland too is well armed and has an unpopular national service system, but it does not array itself in prickly nationalism and hurl the gauntlet at its neighbours at every opportunity.

What will happen to Singapore will almost certainly depend, in the long run, on developments in Indonesia and Malaysia, and on the attitudes of other powers to these developments. Indonesia is steadily regaining confidence and energy and is staking claims for a say in the region's affairs, while Malaysia likewise is developing new attitudes based on its resources, its size and its ethnic character. The two countries have been getting together in a way previously thought impossible, and the further this development goes, the more precarious will be Singapore's position as shrimp in the middle.

If, on the other hand, these two vast neighbours suffer setbacks, then Singapore's position might become even more difficult. An Indonesia which failed to improve its people's lot might conceivably pass into the hands of a militantly Islam-bound leadership, and such a leadership might well build up Singapore as a bogy in order to provide a focus for Indonesian frustrations. While a Malaysia in which the present moderate leadership had been succeeded by one emotionally pledged to Malayanization would almost certainly bring disaster to Singapore. Already, in 1969, when communal riots caused an emergency in Malaysia, the passions aroused came near overflowing the causeway, and Singapore would be extraordinarily lucky if it escaped a second time. It could, indeed, become a specific target if Malay nationalism took an ugly turn.

The goodwill of Indonesia and Malaysia is likely to become increasingly important to the outside powers. Britain, with its special interest in Singapore, was pretty well out of the picture by 1972, and the two new giants, the USA and Japan, while they have large stakes in Singapore, have even larger ones in Indonesia. Australia is going out of its way to strengthen its Indonesian ties – indeed both Australia and New Zealand, now that they are moving to the left after long periods of conservative government, are likely to look on Singapore's one-man government with less favour than heretofore. If this shift of interest on the part of the Western powers becomes established, will Lee Kuan Yew revert to his idea of offering Singapore as a base to the Russians? Will he try to fend off threats by encouraging China's presence in the republic? It would not be in the interests of Singapore to push outside powers to the point of taking sides, but under the present leadership, the republic's ability to control events of this nature appears to be limited.

If Singapore were plunged into a crisis, either by the united thrust of a resurgent Indonesia and Malaysia, or by the putsch of ultra-nationalism on the part of either, latent dissent within the republic – that of the low-income groups, the students and the Chinese – would be given the chance to rally round a political platform calling for a policy more in keeping with the geopolitics of Southeast Asia and the region's popular aspirations. In other words, a grave threat to the long-term viability of the Singapore created by Lee stems from his own policy of keeping it apart – and provocatively so – from the rest of the region.

By early 1973 Lee Kuan Yew was hurriedly re-examining his position. The prospects of peace in Vietnam seemed to scare him. He continued to cultivate the Russians and to send tentative feelers to the Chinese in the form of trade delegations and tourists from Singapore. But it was to the Americans and his long neglected ASEAN partners that he turned with zeal. Breaking his own tradition he paid a seven-day visit to Thailand and canvassed support for his thesis that Thailand should be built up as a buffer against expansionist communism. He began publicly advocating continued American military presence in the region and pleaded with President Nixon not to abandon his allies in Asia. It was a strange turnabout for a government leader who had begun his independent career by vehemently attacking American culture as well as American policies in Asia. It was as though it took the threat of peace to make Lee conscious of his vulnerability.

But a strident return to evangelical anti-communism not only seemed singularly ill-timed in an era of pingpong diplomacy but overlooked the potential sources of more significant problems for Singapore. Lee was taking a fresh look at his neighbours but the neighbours were apparently in no hurry to forget his record or set aside their suspicions of him. The Thais arranged for him a programme geared more for a holiday than for serious political discussions. And powerful voices were raised questioning the visitor's motives in projecting Thailand as a convenient shield for Singapore.

The validity of the ideals Lee's Singapore symbolizes is even more fragile. Like its politics, Singapore's values have also tended to run against the grain of popular sentiment in Southeast Asia.

The philosophy encompassed in Singapore's Little Red Book quoted in Chapter 8 sounds disquietingly familiar. Mussolini's Black Shirts were fit and clean, loyal and dedicated. Mussolini himself was a man of action and achievement who made the trains run on time, drained the Pontine marshes, built roads and schools by the hundreds. But there was something grievously amiss in the fundamental assumptions guiding him, and when he went under, his values went with him.

If Lee Kuan Yew's aims and methods have not worried the world too much, it is partly because Singapore is too small for the world to worry about and also because 'the world' tends to mean 'the West'. By and large Asia is suspicious of Lee, but the West tends not to be. Apart from the fact that Lee is a Western-educated, anti-communist leader who has become a useful cog in the machinery of Western strategy for Asia, the general post-war attitude of the West contributes to this. As colonialism receded, the West developed a half-complacent, half-patronizing view of Asia which replaced old preconceptions with a new disposition to 'understand'. This view finds frequent expression in such statements as: 'Singapore's critics tend to judge it by Western standards'; 'By Western standards, the laws [curbing trade unions] are fairly draconian'; 'Lee Kuan Yew was preoccupied with the initially grim business of laying the foundations for broader development'.

It may be that after a couple of centuries of colonial exploitation, a guilt-ridden West is anxious to bend over backwards and 'apply Asian standards to Asia'. Or it may be the opposite: a habit-bound West subconsciously judging Asia by its old colonial interests. Autocrats who believe in free enterprise and Western military pacts are accepted calmly; it is autocrats who do not believe in them who are deemed fit to be taught the lessons of democracy. Sukarno's army rule was reprehensible, Suharto's is all right. Burma's dictatorship is ugly, Thailand's is beautiful. For all of two decades Pakistan was under military dictatorship while India, with all its failings, nourished a self-respecting democracy, yet Nixon's America spurned India and found Pakistan as noble a pillar of the Free World as Greece and Spain. Lee Kuan Yew's strong-man rule is admirable because it has produced dramatic prosperity; Kim Il Sung's strong-man rule has produced equally dramatic economic progress in North Korea but that is unacceptable.

What is forgotten in this exercise of convenience is that some standards are not classifiable as Western or Asian. Dictatorship stifles people whether it is communist or anti-communist. To keep a critical newspaper editor in prison indefinitely without trial is not merely 'initially grim' but perennially so. To deny university admission to a bright boy because his uncle or father was a leftist is indefensible by any standard. The spirit of justice is universally desirable in all societies. To recognize this is to apply not 'Western standards' but human standards.

True enough, different peoples have different traditions, and procedures which are part of the tradition in one society may be completely alien in another. But while this may mean that the sophistication of Westminster democracy is unworkable in Asia, it does not apply to the essence of democracy itself. Shorn of the trimmings which vary from place to place, democracy simply means a government respecting the governed and being accountable to them. It is a political means to fulfil the human potential.

It is not 'understanding' to argue that because feudalism has prevailed in large parts of Asia for centuries, it must continue to be accepted; that, because suppressed peoples have made a virtue of their submission for generations, they expect to be suppressed for all time. Resistance to feudalism and suppression also has a long history in Asia. It continues as part of the social evolution which provided the setting for Europe's own emergence from medievalism. It is coarse to suggest that civil rights are of little consequence to Asian societies which have not had the benefit of an industrial revolution. Significantly, Lee himself has argued against civil rights only in relation to Singapore; in Malaysia, for example, he sang a very different tune.

Lee Kuan Yew's Singapore must be seen in the perspective not of the West's or of his own laboured justifications, but of fundamental human values and of Southeast Asian realities.

In these terms, Lee Kuan Yew's record leaves much to be desired. Almost every publicized achievement of Singapore has a little-known negative side carefully kept under wraps by the authorities. For example, the housing estates, spectacular as they are, have a suicide rate hardly ever publicized but mentioned with concern by Singapore social workers who visit other cities. It would be helpful to see figures backing this charge, but these are inaccessible. One only has the word of social workers to go by. According to them, the suicides follow from frustrations and tensions generated by the dislocation of erstwhile slum life. For all their squalid appearance, city slums are settled communities which have had to evolve a degree of harmony and mutual help for survival, and slum-dwellers have a choice over where to live and how. Transported to new high-rise government blocks where even the lighting is controlled by government edict, people lose all rights of choice and are forced to live with strangers. If they disagree with their neighbours, there is nothing they can do except resort to drastic remedies. They also have to pay more for their accommodation. Life in government estates often proves too tense for many people.

Purely business achievements have a dark side. The development of Singapore as a financial centre is a case in point. Before Singapore emerged as the Asiadollar centre, Hong Kong was wooed to accept the business and it is revealing to examine why the British colony turned down the proposal. A condition put forward by the initiators of the move was that the legal domicile of the funds be some point outside Hong Kong. The reason for this suggestion was said to be the circumvention of the fifteen per cent interest tax levied by Hong Kong, but this could hardly have been so when a constant and embarrassingly large flow of foreign funds into Hong Kong banks has been maintained despite the interest tax and the Asiadollar market in Singapore. As Hong Kong saw it, manœuvring was afoot to keep Asiadollar funds outside the purview of the Hong Kong government's control and regulations. The colony was not agreeable to this.

It was after Hong Kong made this considered decision that bankers went to Singapore where they found an enthusiastic welcome. Singapore waived withholding tax for Asiadollar deposits and effectively subsidized interests paid on these deposits in an attempt to make them an adjunct to the Eurodollar. No doubt Singapore gained a well publicized position as a financial centre, but apparently it had to agree to conditions which Hong Kong found unacceptable.

Even Singapore's famous graftlessness has an unseen face. Petty bribery is, of course, unknown and no minister or government official grows fat on illegal takings – a unique virtue in Southeast Asia. But this does not preclude the existence of a form of political corruption. Falling in with the government's line of thinking is recognized as a way of getting official favours such as the allotment of choice apartments; a proportion of housing estates' accommodation is set apart as a reward for political support. Government pressure through red tape is brought to bear on industrialists and traders to make them do what official planning demands. If, however, the businessmen concerned are personally close to the top political hierarchy, they are spared the pressures. There are tycoons who, hating golf, take to the game as a means of cultivating leading politicians, which points to corruption by social acquaintance.

From the government's point of view, all this is acceptable: the government is the embodiment of all good, so anything which keeps it so is just what Singapore needs. There are no exceptions to this assumption, not even the judiciary. In mid-1972 the Chinese newspaper *Nanyang Siang Pau* was prosecuted for publishing a letter on national service which, the government charged, was written by a national serviceman without authorization. The district judge who heard the case dismissed it for want of evidence. Within the week he was demoted.

At about the same time Singaporeans seemed to be passing through a phase of self-doubt. Lee Kuan Yew made a strange admission on Australian television that he had been exporting communist students to Australia for ideological rehabilitation, which indicated that Singapore was still producing communist students despite more than a decade of crusading by the government. With another election due, there were whispers that Lee's standing among PAP activists was no longer what it used to be. There were rumours that Singaporeans were buying land in Malaysia. On the Singapore Stock Exchange almost all increases were confined to Malaysian shares while Singapore shares either remained stagnant or dipped. It was as though there was a loss of the familiar sense of direction and the element of uncertainty had crept into the minds of those in the know.

Perhaps it was no more than a passing mood. Even the PAP was considering the wisdom of letting opposition parties make a showing in the coming election, and changes in big power diplomatic postures in Asia had inspired Indonesia and Malaysia to try new regional initiatives, all of which may have inspired an uneasiness that was no more than transient. Nevertheless, it showed how moods can change and calculations go off at a tangent at short notice.

Few Singaporeans – only those who have suffered in various ways under Lee's régime – are heard to question whether their government's methods of achieving order and prosperity are necessarily the only ones, or the best, but plenty of Asian observers ask this question. Even those who are convinced that the communist threat between 1959 and 1965 was such that only a leader of Lee's type could have tackled it, have to acknowledge that the situation has changed substantially since then. By refusing to recognize this change, Lee has limited his country's achievement in terms of values. The prosperity he has brought about has been accompanied by deterioration in the quality of life.

Singapore is led by a man whose subjective reactions are so forceful that he can turn a difference of opinion between nations which ought to be perfectly manageable into a potential war situation; who stifles the free exchange of ideas and the experimentation through which alone a society can improve its standing in the modern world; who casts a pall of conformity and caution over the lives of the people he controls. He seems to assume that a sense of national identity can be created from television sets, apartments and jobs, disregarding the citizen's right to respect and equality: that basic right which enables each 'digit' in a social whole to stand up and express his views. In the absence of respect and tolerance, order has to be achieved by enforced obedience, not by enduring loyalty, and it is forced obedience that Lee commands.

It is easily conceivable that an urbanized, business-experienced city-state such as Singapore, which did not lack technocrats or a professional class, could have achieved economic progress if it had been directed in a democratic way by other minds. The negative side of the picture, on the other hand, is the inevitable result of one strong man's getting his own way. The latter was not essential to the former. To make it seem as though it were – to make the one strong man's contribution appear indispensable – Singapore has to be constantly threatened by bogies, there must always be an enemy round the corner. It amounts to a kind of institutional conspiracy against a technocratic society. Ironically, by changing his society without changing himself, by leading Singapore to its present impressive degree of development while himself remaining fixed in his pre-1965 posture, Lee Kuan Yew has made himself unnecessary to Singapore's continued progress.

He has given his country a great deal. His successes have been impressive. But these successes are mostly municipal rather than of a kind to claim a considerable place in history, while his failures are on a grander scale. History is what Lee has had his eyes on, and the growth in Singapore's gross national product may mean less to history than the collapse of his larger dreams.

Those dreams were noble: union with Malaysia, a grand regional alliance for economic co-operation, a truly multiracial society which had overcome communal tensions, Singapore a force for good in world affairs. Lee has failed to turn them into reality, but they have not lost their validity. There are, indeed, indications that they will be revived and, let us hope, realized at some future time when co-operation between Singapore and its neighbours has again become possible. It is tragic that Lee, a man of such extraordinary abilities, should also have faults so extraordinary that the observer is forced to hope that his departure from the scene he commands will not be long delayed.

Bibliography

Two dissertations on Singapore's ruling party, the PAP, are essential reading for those who want to collect information on, and get an insight into, the complex politics of Singapore:

The People's Action Party of Singapore; Emergence of a Dominant Party System, by Thomas J. Bellows. Yale University Southeast Asian Studies, 1970.

Singapore's People's Action Party: its History, Organisation and Leadership, by Pang Cheng Lian. Oxford University Press, 1971.

Current journalism supplements these volumes, Singapore-Malaysia being an area frequently examined by periodicals covering the region. Two publications are of especial interest:

American Universities Field Staff Reports, Southeast Asia Series (Specialist on Singapore: Willard A. Hannah).

Far Eastern Economic Review, Hong Kong (editor: Derek Davies).

There is a long list of titles providing general background on Singapore-Malaysia and on Chinese communities in Southeast Asia. Many of them are specialist studies on particular periods and issues. Among the more useful general volumes are:

Malaysia in Focus, by Ronald Mckie. Angus & Robertson, 1963.

Southern Expansion of the Chinese People, by C. P. Fitzgerald. Barrie & Jenkins, 1972.

Singapore in Southeast Asia: an Economic and Political Appraisal, by Iain Buchanan. G. Bell & Sons, 1972.

The Chinese in Malaysia, by Victor Purcell. Oxford University Press, 1967.

A Law Unto Themselves, by C. Northcote Parkinson. John Murray, 1966.

A History of Southeast Asia, by D. G. E. Hall. Macmillan, third edition, 1968.

Memoirs of a Mendicant Professor, by D. J. Enright. Chatto and Windus, 1969.

Malaysia and Singapore in International Diplomacy: Documents and Commentaries, by Peter Boyce. Sydney University Press, 1968.

Ownership and Control in the Malayan Economy, by J. J. Puthucheary. Eastern Universities Press, Singapore, 1960.

Lee Kuan Yew's own speeches provide not only an invaluable source of information on the events and trends of the period examined in this book, but a unique insight into the working of his mind. Fortunately, he has spoken at great length, repeatedly and on almost every subject.

Edited versions of these speeches are available in Singapore government publications such as:

Towards a Malaysian Malaysia
The Battle for a Malaysian Malaysia
Socialism and Reconstruction in Asia

and in

Lee Kuan Yew, by Alex Josey. Donald Moore Press, Singapore, 1968.

Index

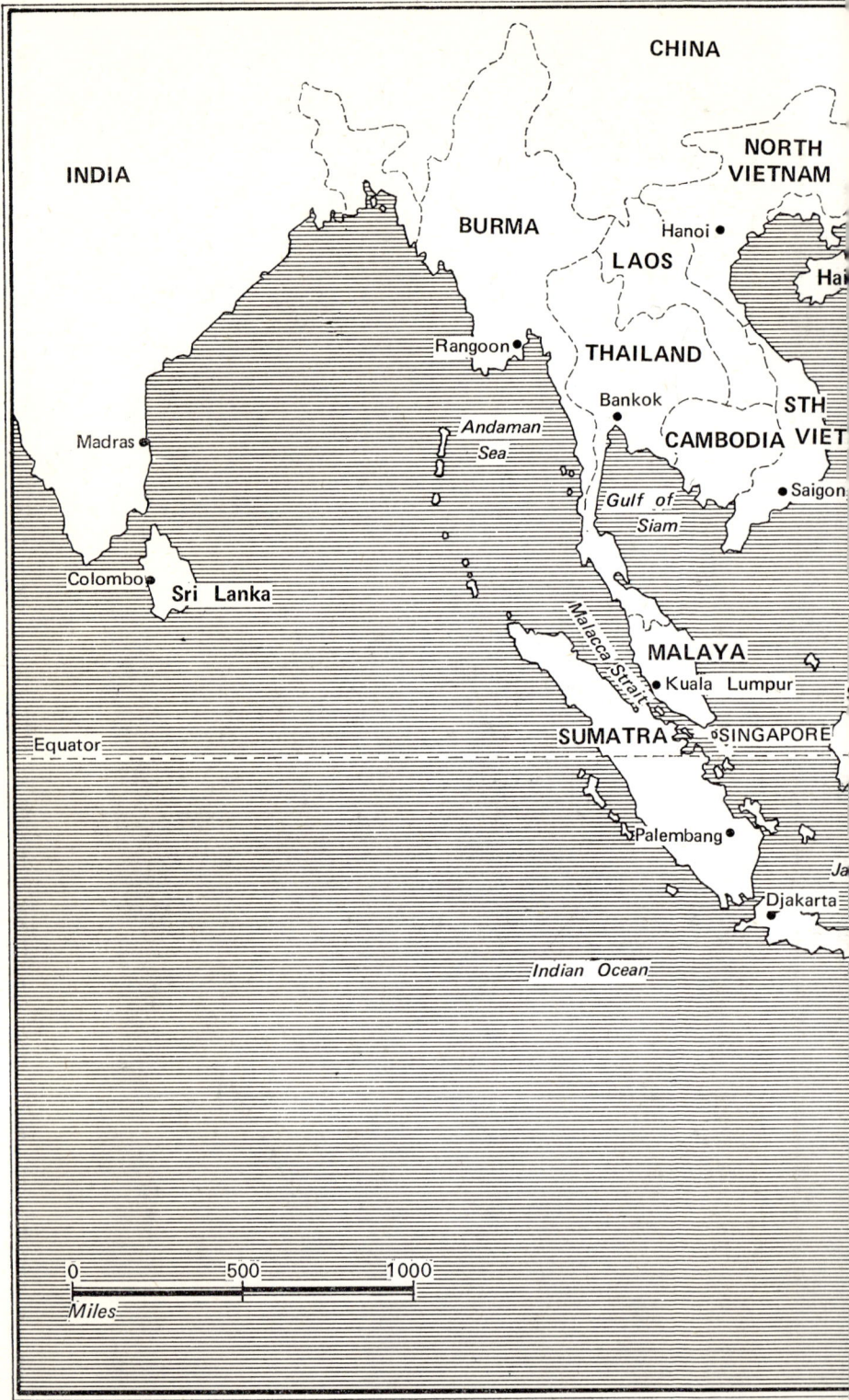

CHINA

INDIA

BURMA

NORTH
VIETNAM

Hanoi •

LAOS

Hai

Rangoon •

THAILAND

Bankok •

Andaman
Sea

Madras •

Gulf of
Siam

CAMBODIA

STH
VIET

Saigon •

Colombo •

Sri Lanka

Malacca Straits

MALAYA

Kuala Lumpur •

Equator

SUMATRA

SINGAPORE

Palembang •

Ja

Djakarta •

Indian Ocean

0   500   1000

Miles